Landmark Essays

Landmark Essays

on
Writing Centers

Edited by Christina Murphy and Joe Law

Hermagoras Press
1995

Landmark Essays Volume Nine

Copyright © 1995 Hermagoras Press

Published 1995 by Hermagoras Press,
P.O. Box 1555, Davis, CA 95617

Cover design by Kathi Zamminer

Typesetting and camera-ready production
by Graphic Gold, Davis, California
Manufactured in the United States of America
by Braun-Brumfield, Inc., Ann Arbor, Michigan

ISBN 1-880393-22-0

2 3 4 5 6 7 8 9 0

Acknowledgments

We gratefully acknowledge James J. Murphy, for his belief in this project and his kind support during its completion.

Eric Hobson, Director of Writing Programs at the St. Louis College of Pharmacy, and Byron Stay, Chair of the Department of Rhetoric and Writing at Mount St. Mary's College, the best of colleagues and friends, have encouraged our efforts from the very beginning.

Our colleagues in the William L. Adams Writing Center at Texas Christian University—Mary Nell Kivikko, Mary Lane, Margaret-Rose Marek, and Steve Sherwood—made our work possible through their generous gifts of time and guidance.

Our friends and family—Frida Blumenberg, Amy Whitten, and Curtis and Adnie Law—believed in us and our work. Their kindness, affection, and willingness to listen are appreciated.

About the Editors

Christina Murphy is the Director of the William L. Adams Writing Center and the Co-director of the University Writing Program at Texas Christian University in Fort Worth, Texas. She received her B.A. from Temple University and her M.A. and Ph.D. from the University of Connecticut. She is the First Vice-President of the National Writing Centers Association and will assume the Presidency of the NWCA in 1996. Her research interests include writing centers, rhetorical theory, and psychoanalytic theory. Her essays on these subjects have appeared in a range of composition and psychoanalytic journals. She is the Editor of *Composition Studies, Studies in Psychoanalytic Theory*, and *English in Texas* and serves on the editorial boards of *The Writing Center Journal* and *Dialogue: A Journal for Writing Specialists*. With Steve Sherwood, she is the author of *The St. Martin's Sourcebook for Writing Tutors*.

Joe Law is the Assistant Director of the William L. Adams Writing Center at Texas Christian University and a member of the English Department there. He received his B.A. from Southwestern Oklahoma State University and his M.A. and Ph.D. from the University of Missouri. In addition to writing centers, his research interests include Victorian studies and connections among the arts. He has published essays on writing instruction, literature, aned music in such journals as *Review of English Studies, Composition Studies, Yearbook of Interdisciplinary Studies in the Fine Arts, The Opera Quarterly,* and *Twentieth Century Literature*. He is the South Central Writing Centers Association representative on the Executive Board of the National Writing Centers Association. The Associate Editor of *English in Texas* and *Composition Studies*, he is also an editorial reviewer for the *English Journal*.

Table of Contents

Part Three: Writing Center Praxis

Introduction

Landmark Essays on Writing Centers
by Christina Murphy and Joe Law

This collection of landmark essays introduces the reader to the ideas that have shaped writing center theory and practice. These essays have been selected not only for the insight they offer into issues but also for their contributions to writing center scholarship. They provide both a history and an examination of the philosophies, praxis, and politics that have defined writing centers as an emerging field. This volume demonstrates the ways a clearer profile of the discipline has emerged from the research and reflection of writers like those represented here. Ultimately, these essays help to chart the legitimation of writing centers. As former National Writing Centers Association President Jeanne Simpson has stated, "The evidence indicates that we have achieved a kind of legitimacy: writing centers have become academically respectable programs."

Historical Perspectives

One of the misperceptions the essays correct is the belief, common among academicians, that writing centers sprang up within the past two decades. In actuality, writing centers have been part of American higher education since the 1930s and have undergone numerous redefinitions in responding to (and shaping) the dominant paradigms of writing instruction in the twentieth century—as Muriel Harris' overview indicates. Lou Kelly's account of her experiences in one of these early writing centers outlines some of these transformations in a specific context. As her essay reveals, writing centers emerged while the conservative model for education was at its high point. In writing instruction, this model focused on the text as a "product" that could be modified to be brought into accord with the accepted standards and conventions of edited prose. Robert H. Moore's essay typifies this conservative attitude, which views the writing center exclusively as a site for diagnosing and removing language deficiencies. As a result, writing centers very quickly became identified as "the grammar and drill center, the fix-it shop, the first aid station" (North).

This identification with "fix-it-shops" created several problems, as Peter Carino points out in his study of the metaphors with which writing centers have been defined. First, the work of the writing center was separated from the work of the classroom. Classrooms instructed; writing centers remediated. Second, the focus on remediation tended to push writing centers to the margins of the academy as supplemental—essentially peripheral and expendable—instruction. Thus, the first stage of writing center history was characterized both by this marginalization and by efforts to attain legitimacy within the academy. The essays of Gary A. Olson and Evelyn Ashton-Jones, Judith Summerfield, and Jeanne Simpson represent efforts to obtain a higher status for writing centers and writing center professionals within the academy.

Theoretical Foundations

The second stage of writing center history was marked by a paradigm shift from a conservative model of writing instruction to a liberal or expressivist one. The expressivist model dominated writing instruction (and therefore writing centers) from the 1970s through the 1980s. Here the emphasis moved from the text to the writer—specifically, to the writer's intellectual and creative processes involved in generating texts. Stephen M. North's essay is considered both a manifesto of expressivism and the herald of a new understanding of the writing center. In North's view of writing center practice, " . . . the object is to make sure that writers, and not necessarily their texts, are what get changed by instruction. In axiom form, it goes like this: Our job is to produce better writers, not better writing."

Within the expressivist paradigm, writers worked as individuals and pursued solitary aims. Little attention was paid to the way society and culture influenced them. With the emergence of social constructionism in the late 1980s, the romantic vision of the individual writer was replaced by one in which knowledge emerged from consensus within discourse communities. Meaning was no longer an absolute truth discovered in solitude but a construct negotiated by like-minded peers. A new pedagogy emerged, one that emphasized collaborative learning and writing and was highly attuned to sociocultural influences—particularly the social dimensions of language, knowledge, and writing. Social constructionists advocate the extensive use of peer group critiquing to reflect the workings of discourse communities and to minimize the role of the tutor as an authority figure. Collaboration and collaborative learning play a central role in social constructionist pedagogy, as individuals learn to negotiate meanings and construct knowledge.

This progression in writing center ideology from conservative, to liberal, to liberatory philosophies is traced in the essay by Christina Murphy. Lisa Ede and Andrea Lunsford develop the liberatory aspects of writing center pedagogy by focusing on the social and historical mechanisms by which knowledge is created and meaning is communicated by writers. Marilyn Cooper emphasizes a liberatory pedagogy of empowerment, arguing that writing centers have "the essential function of critiquing institutions and creating knowledge about writing."

As writing centers defined their standing within the academy, one of the most significant issues they faced was establishing a theoretical basis for tutoring—particularly peer tutoring. Throughout most of the modern era, peer tutoring has been central to writing center pedagogy. As Kenneth A. Bruffee states, "peer tutoring was a type of collaborative learning. It did not seem to change what people learned but, rather, the social context in which they learned it." Even though peer tutoring redefined the context and process of students' learning experiences, the principles and effects of peer tutoring went unexamined by scholars for decades. As Bruffee notes, "peer tutoring harnessed the educative force of peer influence that had been—and largely still is—ignored and hence wasted by traditional forms of education."

Alice M. Gillam presents a way of approaching the conflicting goals often set for writing center tutors—"normalizing" the writing of students to fit with institutional expectations and encouraging free self-expression. Drawing upon the theories of Mikhail Bakhtin, she argues that these conflicting views of writing are symptomatic of two opposing forces inherent in language: centripetal forces that "centralize, unify, and stabilize language" and centrifugal forces that "perpetually destabilize language through multiple meanings, variable contexts, and the free play of dialects." To deal with these situations, Gillam recommends that tutors adopt Bakhtin's concepts of *addressivity* and *answerability*, concepts that raise productively complex issues of audience and ethics.

Defining Praxis

Whereas the essays in the previous section present theoretical perspectives, those in this section explore ways such assumptions are played out in the day-to-day activities of writing centers—administration, assessment, professionalization, self-definition, and pedagogy. The essayists here recognize the impossibility of providing a single framework for understanding the writing center's purpose, function, and significance. Since institutional demands and settings differ, so do administrative philosophies and designs. Jeanne Simpson, Steve Braye, and Beth Boquet examine how perceptions of the writing center's marginality affect the fulfillment of its mission. They raise a question central to writing center administration: "How do we walk that tightrope between our own goals, often contrary to the institution, and the goals of our schools, which we must serve in some way in order to have any effectiveness or power?" They argue that change often can be made more readily from a position outside traditional boundaries and question how much of this flexibility will be retained if writing centers seek institutional status.

Muriel Harris applies concepts of collaborative learning to writing center administration, stressing the need for flexibility by examining several scenarios from different perspectives. Dave Healy explores still another relationship—that between the writing center and classroom. Rather than arguing that both sites of writing instruction are essentially the same, Healy contends that distinctions between them are necessary and valuable. While upholding the merit of classroom instruction, Healy maintains that "...tutors and writing centers provide an alternative to the authority of teachers and classrooms"; in addition, "that alternative is important as a catalyst to students' developing sense of independence and their own authority." Similarly, Ray Wallace and Richard Leahy investigate the writing center's relationship to classroom instruction in writing-across-the-curriculum and writing-to-learn programs.

While all these essayists debate the institutional standing of writing centers and writing center practice, their discussions demonstrate ways in which writing centers provide a practical arena for testing theoretical assumptions about education. In addition, the range of these debates indicates the varied and changing philosophies that inform writing center praxis. One practice that has come under particular scrutiny is peer tutoring. Harvey Kail and John Trimbur describe several models for peer tutoring, delineating ways these models fit into institutional structures. In a multicultural narrative, Anne DiPardo contextualizes the political implications of peer tutoring. DiPardo's analysis leads her to conclude that all individuals "negotiate among multiple identities, moving between public and private selves, living in a present shadowed by the past, encountering periods in which time and circumstance converge to realign or even restructure our images of who we are." Consequently, "as increasing numbers of non-Anglo students pass through the doors of our writing centers, such knowledge of our own shape-shifting can help us begin—if only begin—to understand the social and linguistic challenges which inform their struggles with writing." Meg Woolbright, too, advocates a reconceptualization of the tutor's role. Approaching writing center tutorials from a feminist perspective, Woolbright contrasts the collaborative learning of writing center tutorials with traditional classroom pedagogy, emphasizing the connections of the former to feminist thought: "Both feminist and writing center commentators advocate teaching methods that are non-hierarchical, cooperative, interactive ventures between students and tutors talking about issues grounded in the students' own experience. They are, above all, conversations between equals in which knowledge is constructed, not transmitted." Woolbright's analysis of an individual tutorial, though, demonstrates how tenuous a feminist/collaborative approach must remain in the patriarchal context of the modern educational system.

The Idea of a Writing Center: Future Directions

The essays in this volume chart the emergence of writing centers and the growing recognition of their contributions, roles, and importance. As a nascent discipline, writing centers reflect the concerns with marginality and with finding a respected place in the academy that characterize any new field of academic inquiry, practice, and research. Concomitantly, professionals in these fields seek standing within the academy and a way of defining and validating their contributions to the educational process. Reflecting upon these goals in terms of writing center history reveals the development of an alternative pedagogy—one that might seem radical but that has its roots in the philosophies of Socrates and Aristotle. The "radical" dimensions of writing center pedagogy legitimately shift the focus of the instructional process back to the individual learner. That learner's text, creative processes, and socio-historical background are addressed and responded to in writing center tutorials. While the focus of attention might shift from text, to writer, to social context, writing center pedagogy continues to be committed to the goal of assisting writers as individuals who bring particular talents, histories, and imperatives to the tutorial.

As writing centers—and the scholarship that defines their efforts—move into the next century, the concerns of the original writing center movement are not lost, only modified by changing actualities. Writing center professionals still seek to explain and validate their work; they still battle to avoid marginalization and the misapplication of writing center resources to noncompelling ends; they still respond to and challenge paradigms of writing instruction and interpretations of educational objectives and aims.

The emphases have changed, though, from narratives of a fledgling discipline to rigorous, scholarly investigations of that discipline's contributions to the knowledge structures of the academy. As writing centers advance toward the next century, their scholarship and practice will continue to respond to the ways in which knowledge is created, assessed, and implemented within a culture. Certainly, too, scholarship and practice will critique and determine the ways writing centers can contribute to this process. Consequently, both enterprises will emphasize the writing center's role within society rather than solely its place within the academy. As recent writing center scholarship indicates, the focus of inquiry is already shifting from practitioner lore to a broader understanding of the social influences upon knowledge production within a culture. Contemporary writing center theorists look to interdisciplinary and multidisciplinary investigations to interpret the work they do and to clarify their aims to the academy at large. Their work employs a variety of philosophical perspectives, ranging from sociolinguistics to psychoanalytic theory, to show the complex nature and potential of writing center interactions. The idea of a writing center has now become the multidimensional realities of the writing center within the academy and within society as a whole. What the writing center's role will be in future redefinitions of the educational process, how that role will be negotiated and evaluated, and how writing center professionals will shape educational values will constitute the future landmark directions and essays on writing center theory and practice.

Original Citations for Essays in This Collection

Bruffee, Kenneth A. "Peer Tutoring and the 'Conversation of Mankind'" *Writing Centers: Theory and Administration.* Ed. Gary A. Olson. Urbana: NCTE, 1984. 3-15.

Carino, Peter. "What Do We Talk About When We Talk About Our Metaphors: A Cultural Critique of Clinic, Lab, and Center." *The Writing Center Journal* 13.1 (1992): 31-42.

Cooper, Marilyn. "Really Useful Knowledge: A Cultural Studies Agenda for Writing Centers." *The Writing Center Journal* 14.2 (1994): 97-111.

DiPardo, Anne. "'Whispers of Coming and Going': Lessons from Fannie." *The Writing Center Journal* 12.2 (1992): 125-44.

Ede, Lisa. "Writing as a Social Process: A Theoretical Foundation for Writing Centers?" *The Writing Center Journal* 9.2 (1989): 3-13.

Gillàm, Alice M. "Writing Center Ecology: A Bakhtinian Perspective." *The Writing Center Journal* 11.2 (1991): 3-12.

Harris, Muriel. "What's Up and What's In: Trends and Traditions in Writing Centers." *The Writing Center Journal* 11.1 (1990): 15-25.

Healy, Dave. "A Defense of Dualism: The Writing Center and the Classroom." *The Writing Center Journal* 14.1 (1993): 16-29.

Kail, Harvey, and John Trimbur. "The Politics of Peer Tutoring." *WPA: Writing Program Administration* 11 (1987): 5-12.

Kelly, Lou. "One-on-One, Iowa City Style: Fifty Years of Individualized Instruction in Writing." *The Writing Center Journal* 1.1 (1980): 4-19.

Leahy, Richard. "Writing Centers and Writing-for-Learning." *The Writing Center Journal* 10.1 (1983): 29-34.

Lunsford, Andrea. "Collaboration, Control, and the Idea of a Writing Center." *The Writing Center Journal* 12.1 (1991): 3-10. Rpt. *Writing Center Newsletter* 16.4-5 (1991-92): 1-6.

Moore, Robert H. "The Writing Clinic and the Writing Laboratory." *College English* 11 (1950): 388-93.

Murphy, Christina. "Writing Centers in Context: Responding to Current Educational Theory." *The Writing Center: New Directions.* Ed. Ray Wallace and Jeanne Simpson. New York: Garland, 1991. 276-88.

North, Stephen M. "The Idea of a Writing Center." *College English* 46 (1984): 433-46.

Olson, Gary, and Evelyn Ashton-Jones. "Writing Center Directors: The Search for Professional Status." *WPA: Writing Program Administration* 12.1-2 (1988): 19-28.

Simpson, Jeanne. "What Lies Ahead for Writing Centers: Position Statement on Professional Concerns." *The Writing Center Journal* 5.2/6.1 (1985): 35-39.

Simpson, Jeanne, Steve Braye, and Beth Boquet. "War, Peace, and Writing Center Administration." *Composition Studies/Freshman English News* 22.1 (1994): 65-95.

Summerfield, Judith. "Writing Centers: A Long View." *The Writing Journal* 8.2 (1988): 3-9.

Wallace, Ray. "The Writing Center's Role in the Writing Across the Curriculum Program: Theory and Practice." *The Writing Center Journal* 8.2 (1988): 43-48.

Woolbright, Meg. "The Politics of Tutoring: Feminism Within the Patriarchy." *The Writing Center Journal* 13.1 (1992): 16-30.

Part 1:
Historical Perspectives

The Writing Clinic and the Writing Laboratory

by Robert H. Moore

Writing clinics and writing laboratories are becoming increasingly popular among American universities and colleges as remedial agencies for removing students' deficiencies in composition. A recent survey of one hundred and twenty leading universities and colleges throughout the country was made at the time that a clinic was established at the University of Illinois, to determine the incidence, methods, and effectiveness of such agencies. It procured fifty-five replies, forty-nine of them indicating in some detail the nature of the remedial measures being pursued. Of these forty-nine institutions, twenty-four now make use of writing clinics or laboratories of one sort or another, and eleven others are contemplating their establishment. In other words, 70 per cent of the colleges indicating the nature of their remedial work either now use or are considering using the clinic or laboratory in the solving of students' writing difficulties. And, even if it be assumed that none of the other seventy-five institutions are interested in the device, there remain at least 20 per cent of the colleges selected for the survey which are using the method, and an additional 10 per cent considering its adoption.

The survey was primarily concerned with the clinic and the laboratory rather than with remedial measures in general, so that it is not always possible to determine from the data assembled how much of the remedial burden in a given college is shared with such other devices as the precollege-level course, the segregating of poorly prepared freshmen into special sections of the regular elementary composition course, the upper-class remedial course, the specialized course in technical writing, the graduation proficiency examination, or individual tutoring.[1] The University of Illinois, for example, uses the clinic to supplement all the above devices except the segregation of freshmen into special sections of the regular course. Yet it can be said that the two devices are sufficiently successful to enable thirteen universities to depend on the clinic or the laboratory for all remedial work; and at least one, the University of Miami, uses the laboratory method exclusively in its elementary composition program.

Reprinted from *College English* 11 (1950): 388-93. Originally published in 1950 by the National Council of Teachers of English.
[1] Remedial reading, a related problem, is most often handled by a separate agency, frequently under the guidance of trained psychologists rather than of English teachers.

The techniques of the clinic and of the laboratory are, of course, far more widespread than are formally established agencies. The clinic is primarily concerned with the diagnosis of the individual student's writing difficulties and the suggestion of remedial measures that might profitably be pursued. Such diagnosis and prescription are an early concern, as well, of the class instructor in conference, the counselor in a university tutoring bureau, the individually procured tutor, and the instructor in the laboratory. The laboratory, in turn, is primarily concerned with the direct and continuing supervision of the remedial efforts of the individual student, and such supervision, in greater or less degree, must also be given by the class instructor, the tutor, and the clinician. The advantages of the formally established agency, then, lie less in its possession of esoteric methods than in its ready accessibility, its concentration on the removal of specific deficiencies, and its development of instructors particularly skilled in remedial procedures.

As the methods of the clinic and the laboratory overlap, so does the terminology. As the names imply, the clinic is chiefly concerned with suggesting measures for self-help, the laboratory with work done directly under the guidance of an instructor; but in practice the terms are almost interchangeable, "laboratory" being the more common and the laboratory approach being more often used, particularly in those schools depending on such agencies for the bulk of their remedial efforts. For convenience in discussing operating procedures, however, I shall draw theoretical distinctions between the two, with the final reminder that only the initial emphasis on one approach or the other serves, in the last analysis, to distinguish the relationship between the individual student and the clinic or the laboratory to which he turns for help.

The writing clinic customarily supplements other remedial devices, such as the compulsory upper-class remedial course for students whose writing proficiency is deemed inadequate to meet standards prescribed for graduation. Consultation with the clinic, consequently, is likely to be voluntary and to spring from a student's own realization—often reinforced by a dean's or an instructor's comments—that his writing skill is less satisfactory than it should be and is handicapping him in the writing of examinations, term papers, and reports. Occasionally, compulsion is involved, most frequently through the device of withholding credit for a course in which writing deficiencies have been noted; but usually the clinic is an agency to which the student himself as an individual applies for help in removing a deficiency of which he is personally aware.

As a result, the problem of diagnosis is often not difficult. A preliminary interview may in itself disclose the basic weakness, particularly with upperclassmen or graduate students who have had a good deal of experience with college writing problems. If the problem is one of spelling or punctuation, for example, the student himself can easily identify it. More frequent, however, and more baffling to the student are weaknesses in the organization and development of papers or examination answers or the tendency to write vague, telescoped, or garbled sentences rather than concise and specific ones.

The student with such deficiencies usually knows only that his writing somehow does not say what he thinks it does. But, even with these more complex problems, the experience of the clinician can often enable him to uncover the basic difficulty through an interview alone.

If the preliminary interview does not expose the difficulty, various other means may be employed. If the student has suddenly been impelled to seek assistance because a returned examination or term paper was less successful than he had anticipated, he is likely to have brought the paper with him, particularly if his impulse has been reinforced by tart comments from his instructor. If he has not brought it with him at first, he usually has it at home, perhaps with several others like it, and can produce it for analysis. The most successful diagnosis, probably, is that which results from an analysis, with the student, of specimens of the writing that he has actually done in his classes. And, incidentally, the student can be made aware of the direct connection between writing deficiency and unsatisfactory grades and so takes the first remedial step in the midst of the process of diagnosis itself.

If specimens of his classroom writing are not available—if his consultation, for example, has sprung from a recommendation by a dean concerned with his general academic record—at least two other diagnostic measures may be used, neither wholly satisfactory. One is the analysis of a paper written for the purpose, the other is the interpretation of a diagnostic test or tests. The disadvantages of the first are threefold: it is difficult to find subjects not too remote from the classroom subjects, it is impossible to reproduce the classroom conditions and (a point to which I shall return) it is impossible for the student to write *as he usually writes when he is not thinking primarily of the quality of his English;* the writing which he produces to order for analysis, consequently, is not his normal writing, whether for better or for worse. The disadvantage of the diagnostic test lies in its basic artificiality: no test of which I am aware is more than indicative of probable deficiencies, so that reasonably certain diagnosis must still await analysis of actual writing, preferably that produced for a classroom situation.

Diagnosis having been made, by one or several of these means, the remedial measures to be followed must be outlined. The more intelligent and eager the student, of course, the easier it is to discover the difficulty in the first place and to determine means to enable him to remove it. The clinic is not, as a rule, concerned with the direct supervision of remedial efforts, with providing extensive tutoring; it is therefore most satisfactory as a supplement to a wider remedial program, since only the intelligent and eager student can be wholly successful in applying even the best self-help measures. Here, as elsewhere, the more resourceful the clinician is in suggesting new approaches to old problems, the more quickly does self-help become effective help. A student who is deficient in many ways may be urged, and in some institutions required, to enroll in remedial classes or to seek private tutoring. Where the clinic is a supplementary agency in a balanced remedial program, the students with numerous and glaring deficiencies will usually have been caught elsewhere in the remedial net. The students who consult the clinic are, as a result, troubled by specific and limited weaknesses, and remedial efforts can be concentrated on those.

Students exhibiting weaknesses in the handling of purely mechanical problems can be referred to specialized study groups, if they are provided, or can be urged to secure private tutoring directed toward removing the specific deficiencies involved, or can be made aware of the existence of numerous specialized remedial texts dealing particularly with their problems. In the last connection it might be remarked that a single publisher provides a convenient, inexpensive, and, on the whole, admirable series of remedial pamphlets, of whose existence most students are completely unaware. In the handling of spelling problems, for example, the appropriate pamphlet in that series offers the best presentation with which I am familiar of the very complex procedures necessary for the removal of spelling difficulty. Spelling classes following the same procedures, however, are superior, since it requires intense ambition on the part of the student to persist in the work on his own. Frequently, of course, the clinician can himself supplement these formal aids with teaching devices suggested by his own experience and the circumstances arising during specific interviews and, wherever possible, will do so. Conscientious work by the student with such materials and periodic visits to the clinic for assistance and for checks on progress will usually result in the removal of the mechanical difficulty. It depends on how willing the student is to make the effort.

Problems in the organization and development of material are more complex but, with intelligent students, are more quickly removed. Frequently, little more is necessary than a demonstration of the technique of phrasing a thesis and constructing a scratch outline which permits winnowing and re-arranging ideas. Practice at such preliminary planning of subject matter, with clinical analysis of the resulting writing (writing, preferably, which is directly related to his college courses) can do wonders for the student who some-how—usually because of youthful indifference—never realized that the same techniques, when they were presented in his elementary composition courses, would someday be of personal use to him.

Similar writing practice, with emphasis on specific diction, concise phrasing and the necessity for revisional rereading of *what was actually written,* not what was merely intended, can be of nearly equal assistance to the student who, in the haste of writing examinations or belated papers, produces vague, telescoped, or garbled sentences. It must, however, be pointed out that such writing often accompanies garbled information or habitually confused thinking. Psychological clinics can sometimes be called on for assistance in the latter event. The same psychological clinics are frequently equipped to assist in removing writing difficulties which stem from reading deficiencies[2] or from complex personality disorders. They lie, properly, outside the province of the writing clinic.

The writing clinic works with the individual student. The writing labora-

---

[2] Only a few English clinics deal to any great extent with remedial reading problems.

tory on the other hand, is far more likely to work with the individual as a member of a group, usually a group with varying problems. It is more economical than the clinic, in that one instructor in a given hour can work with ten or twenty students where the clinician can scarcely work with more than four at most. Further, the laboratory can more successfully be used as the sole remedial agency, if the institution is willing to provide only one. It is less likely, however, to uncover individual difficulties as rapidly as the clinic does or to avoid wasting the student's time on material that he does not need. And it adds the actual tutoring of students to the costs of the remedial program. Only by considering the remedial needs of a particular student body can a final choice be made between the two types of agency on grounds of economy.

Customarily, many or all of the students coming to the writing laboratory attend—often willingly, of course—under compulsion, as the result of failure in proficiency examinations or of faculty referral, the latter being frequently accompanied by the withholding of course credit pending the removal of deficiencies. Most laboratories, however, are also open to students voluntarily seeking assistance. With the laboratory, as with the clinic and all other remedial devices, satisfactory results are most readily secured when the student, whatever the means of his coming, is personally convinced of the desirability of improving his writing skill.

Initial diagnosis in the laboratory is more likely than in the clinic to depend upon available tests or on the student's own analysis of his weaknesses. However, some laboratories do also use analysis by the instructor of specimens of the student's writing—of term papers, examinations, or "themes" produced for the purpose. The most successful laboratories, like the clinics, attempt to individualize the work throughout, which, of course, increases the cost and the complexity of the program as it increases its effectiveness.

The remedial treatment used in the laboratory varies widely. Frequently, an entire group is put through the same review course, with roving instructors constantly available to answer questions, advise on organizational problems, and check on progress. Less often, particularly in laboratories to which students may come at any time and leave at will, personal files are kept to record the difficulties and progress of each student, and the instructor turns from each problem to the next as it arises. Least often of all, students with similar problems are segregated in small groups, or students may even be handled individually, particularly in the early stages. Both the last two types of treatment can readily concentrate instruction on specifically defined needs.

Following diagnosis of the student's needs—and those needs are usually fairly clear cut and limited in kind—remedial measures are prescribed. Workbooks or handbooks are often used for preliminary review,[3] the work

---

[3] Those who use workbooks, it might be remarked, are at least balanced by those who object to them violently.

with them being done in the laboratory, with the instructor available for consultation or, if the entire group is struggling with the same problem, for group explanation and discussion. As soon as the student convinces the instructor that the basic principles are clear, he is put to practicing the kind of writing with which he has trouble, whether he writes "themes" to assigned or self-suggested topics, expositions of subject matter drawn from his other courses, sample answers to examination questions, or the actual papers assigned in his other courses. During all this work the laboratory instructor and the laboratory dictionaries, handbooks, and other reference books are there for the student to consult when his own resources are unable to carry him further. As problems arise, the instructor makes use of all the teaching devices at his command to clarify the basic principles involved and to stimulate the student to apply them in his own practice. The laboratory is a highly successful remedial device for those students who are willing to make intelligent use of the assistance provided.

Most institutions employing the laboratory method send at least some of the students to it under compulsion. The machinery for releasing them from that compulsion is usually of one of two kinds: either a formal proficiency examination, set by the laboratory instructors in the laboratory or by a separate testing agency, must be passed, or the instructors must certify from the work the student has done that he has demonstrated that he has become capable of writing satisfactorily. (Only rarely, it might be remarked parenthetically, is the examination, if there is one, purely of the objective type.) Students who come to the laboratory voluntarily are, as a rule, allowed to stop coming whenever they themselves feel that they have attained a satisfactory degree of skill.

Except for students working in the laboratory as a regular, assigned part of their composition courses, credit is customarily not given for either laboratory or clinical work.

A very few universities charge the students fees—ranging from five dollars for two quarters to two dollars and a half an hour—for the service. Most of them offer the service without charge, accepting the handling of remedial composition problems as a necessary, if deplorable, part of the task of American colleges and universities. The expense of the agency is usually borne by the English department, perhaps on the ground that it will be blamed anyway—surely unjustly—for all student lapses in English in other courses throughout the university and that it might better protect itself by being able to point to the remedial agencies which it provides. Occasionally the expense is borne by the university itself, as an administrative rather than a teaching expense.

Clinic and laboratory staffs are likely to be self-made. Customarily they are experienced members of the English department who are particularly interested in remedial composition, though much of the direct tutoring in the laboratories is provided by graduate assistants, who are, of course, often themselves experienced instructors. Only rarely do members of the staff devote full time to the work, though the equivalent of several full-time instructors is provided for the larger laboratories.

As with all remedial measures, much of the enduring success of the work of the clinic or the laboratory depends on members of faculties outside the English department. The complaint is nationwide that members of other departments carp bitterly to their colleagues in English about the quality of student writing but can only with difficulty be persuaded to point out to the students themselves that clear and effective writing is important. Three universities report having tried the clinic or the laboratory and then having abandoned it because too few students came or were sent to it.[4] The students' indifference to the quality of their writing springs inevitably from faculty indifference to it, even though that faculty indifference may be more apparent than real. In his writing, as in much else, the student will do no more than he has to. I remarked earlier on the difference that often exists between the quality of the writing which a student can produce when he is aware that his writing skill is to be considered and that of his habitual writing. If instructors in non-English courses would insist on the best writing of which the student is capable, they would find—amid much student grumbling—that the English departments have builded better than is often supposed.

---

[4] A fourth institution abandoned its clinic when the director moved from the English department to the school of education.

One-On-One, Iowa City Style:
Fifty Years of Individualized
Writing Instruction

by Lou Kelly

Our Writing Lab dates back to the 1930's. The University then admitted anybody who had a diploma from an Iowa high school and the English Department assumed they could all write. But in English 101 (Literature and Composition) at least one professor discovered some people who needed a little extra help.

Then, as now, the new grammar workbooks arrived from the publishers with far more certainty than the first or last spring thaw. But Carrie Stanley did not tell her writers-with-problems that grammar drills would turn them into good writers. Neither did she prepare or purchase modular units of individualized instruction on organization or invention for her students to complete at their own pace. Then, as now, individualized writing instruction at the University of Iowa meant talking with an individual human being, face-to-face, about his or her writing; it meant helping each uneasy writer become a more confident and competent writer by actually writing. Carl Rogers would have called Miss Stanley's kind of teaching "personal encounters" with her students. And for all of us who worked with her, he has provided the words we need to describe her attitude toward the underprepared:

> ... it is hard to know what term to put to it ... I think of it as prizing the learner, prizing his feelings, his opinions, his person ... accept[ing his fear] and hesitation ... as he approaches a new problem as well as accept[ing his] satisfaction in achievement ... accept[ing] the student's occasional apathy, his erratic desires to explore by-roads of knowledge, as well as his disciplined efforts to achieve major goals ... accept[ing] personal feelings which both disturb and promote learning ... as an imperfect human being with many feelings, many potentialities. (*Freedom to Learn,* Charles E. Merrill Publishing Company, p. 109.)

A teacher who prizes all her students may not be justly rewarded with salary increases and promotions. But Miss Stanley's unique talents were duly

Reprinted from *The Writing Center Journal* 1.1 (1980): 4-19. Used by permission.

acknowledged. More elitist Professors of English, less perceptive and less competent as teachers of writing, recommended her classes to their "bad" writers, who in turn told their friends about this empathetic but demanding teacher and the *laboratory* where they were *laboring* to improve their writing.

When the Communication Skills Program was established in 1945, Miss Stanley's Writing Laboratory gained official recognition and was given an official function: to provide instruction for the students whose placement themes did not meet departmental standards. For several years, four hours a week in the Lab was the "subfreshman" requirement. Later on, a new Coordinator of the Program decided to require "remedial" students to do their Lab work while taking their first semester of the required course. The next change made the "remedial" component "voluntary"—teachers were urged to send students to the Lab if they were consistently getting 1 or 2 on any of the categories on the theme rating blank. Some of these "volunteers" said they had been given a choice between two hours a week in the Writing Lab and an "F" in the course. Some people did indeed volunteer; they really wanted to become good writers. Others came because one of their professors had checked an item on a form the Coordinator had distributed. It offered help, but any generosity of tone was overshadowed by an imperious stance against unplanned and carelessly edited papers:

THE WRITING IN THIS PAPER IS UNACCEPTABLE

( ) It appears to suffer from carelessness. In the future, edit your papers carefully before you submit them.

( ) It is so poor that your grade has been affected. In the future, plan your papers before you begin writing, take more time to word them precisely, and edit them with care.

( ) Apparently you do not understand the process of writing well enough to improve your writing by yourself. Take this paper to your present or former instructor in Rhetoric and discuss it with him. If your former Rhetoric instructor is no longer available or if you had your writing instruction at some other institution, see the secretary in Room 4, OAT, who will arrange an appointment for you. Do this within the next week; then return this paper to me.

Obviously, Miss Stanley's accepting and caring interpersonal approach to the teaching of writing had been reshaped by institutional demands. But the personal conferences between student and teacher, the one-on-one responses to each student's writings survived, through all the curricula changes and all the new administrative officers who replaced the old. But for a quarter of a century, two hours a week in the Lab was the penalty imposed on everybody who did not pass the departmental theme exam at the end of one or two required semesters of Communication Skills (later called Rhetoric). So, for most teachers and students, working in the Lab was teaching to the test and practicing for the test; it was concentrating on organization and correctness; it was writing and reading hundreds of dull and mediocre papers.

As a beginning teacher I learned that teaching the attitude sentence outline was my most important function. When I returned to teaching fifteen years later, Lab instruction began with a lecture on how to write attitude sentences like the models on the chalkboard:

Subject	Linking Verb	Class	Attitude (dependent clause)
Joe Jones	is	a quarterback	who is versatile.
Mr. Finny	is	a high school English teacher	who has poor discipline.
X High School	is	a small school	which does a poor job of preparing its students for college composition courses.

During the second half of that Lab hour and all of the next one, each person sat alone in a carrel structuring sentences like the attitude sentence model. But before they were all checked by the teachers and restructured by the students, it was time for the lecture on how to construct attitude sentence outlines like the model on the chalkboard:

topic sentence
(attitude sentence)   I. Mr. Finney is a high school English teacher who has poor discipline.

body of paragraph   II. A. Practical jokes frequently disrupt his class.
      B. He does not insist that work be handed in on time.
      C. He allows students to talk while he lectures.

re-statement of   III. In the area of discipline, Mr. Finney is weak.
topic sentence

Students spent the next three or four sessions alone in their carrels writing attitude sentence outlines. Since they attended only twice a week, it was a slow-moving course. But finally they offered three outlines for their teacher's approval.

We were supposed to say something nice, find something to commend so they would feel less demeaned if not happy. And we were supposed to tell them what was wrong with their writing.

Like most English teachers in generations past, we saw the misspelled words and "bad" grammar first because that's easy. It was also easy to tell our students that they had not written complete sentences, then help them correct the fragments that would be 5-point errors on the test, and remind them to always imitate the sentences in the model. Explaining how their outlines failed to follow the prescribed model was also easy: the topic sentence does not include a word that expresses an attitude; the sub-topic sentences are not supporting reasons for the attitude, they don't explain why you think what you think about the subject; two sub-topic sentences may not be enough for a substantial paragraph, four is probably too many; A is a restatement of the topic sentence not a reason for your attitude; B or C merely repeats A or B; C is not clearly related to your topic sentence; the sub-topic sentences should be rearranged; III does not restate the attitude expressed in I, or III uses exactly the same words instead of restating the attitude sentence in different words.

That litany certainly indicates that following even a simplistic model may not be easy for writers-with-problems; that helping any one of them correct three outlines or trying to select the one that would be easiest to correct may take several conferences; that making the changes yourself instead of letting the student slowly work through them is a constant temptation. Even more frustrating, showing some of them how to correct their outlines was impossible because the causal factors underlying their attitude sentences, the actual personal experiences involved, were too complex to fit the simplistic model. But we all knew how to help them limit (i.e. simplify) their topics.

Back in their lonely carrels, they "fixed up" their outlines so they'd be more like the model. Then back they came—one, two days later—for teacher's OK. Then we sent them back to the carrels to "flesh out" their best outline with supporting details and examples.

By then, some of them had either stopped listening or were overcome with boredom. They merely copied the five sentences of their outlines, with Roman numerals and capital letters deleted. Others turned out more finished products. They added a couple of generalizations or a few facts and examples between the sub-topic sentences. If they saw the significance of the experience of the attitude stated in the topic sentence, if they had ever questioned the implications of the attitude stated in the topic sentence, the model had not permitted that much freedom of expression. So the collection of trivia we had to read bored us no more or less than the students were bored. And for most of them, and us, there was always the frustrating hassle with errors that would count against them on the "pass-out" exam.

But we had to move on to the longer paper because a passing theme was our goal. The next lecture told them how the paragraphs they had been writing were compositions-in-miniature, practice runs for the real thing. A 500 word theme. The final exam. So began another long and dreary practice run. Sentence outlines modeled after the one on the chalkboard. A conference about the outline. Then "fixing up" the outline. Then "fleshing it out." Another conference and more corrections. And after two or three weeks, sometimes longer, the product-oriented process started all over again.

Only their determination to pass the hated "pass-out" and the patient supportive work of a lot of caring teachers kept them at it. But for some, the meaningless grind and the constant threat of failure became intolerable. They took an "F" instead of attending. Or dropped out of college.

* * *

They arrived, hour after hour, my first week as head teacher, 170 of them, glum and hostile. I could see it in their rigid bodies and their taut faces. *This* was the Writing Lab, the slums of an affluent campus; they were the poverty-stricken in a rich intellectual community. I could feel it in the very air we breathed, their angry despair coming at me. Whatever I might say, they had heard it all before—

> Five years of language arts, five years of English, two semesters of rhetoric. Then somebody tells you you can't write. Somebody gives you a stupid departmental theme exam. Gives you a list of stupid subjects and says write. For two hours. 500 words. *I hate to write. I'm gonna flunk out of college because I can't write.*

It seemed only human to let them say, on paper, what I knew they were thinking. The first assignment:

> Forget the list of stupid subjects you couldn't write about on the exam. Forget about organization and spelling and grammar. Just try to put on paper what you're feeling and thinking right now. No matter how confused and angry it sounds. Use the words other English teachers might mark inappropriate or offensive, if you want to. Your paper will not be marked or graded. I really want to know what you think and feel about being here. And about failing the exam. Why *did* you? After all those years in English classes. Did *you fail* or did somebody somewhere along the way *fail you?* Whatever you think, whatever you feel, say it—on paper.

Given that freedom, being told, for a happy change, to simply write about what they were thinking about, they did not sit and stare at the empty pages, wondering what they could say on the assigned subject, or trying to stretch a couple of relevant ideas into the required 500-word theme. Even the students whose minds usually turn off when they pick up a pencil or pen began writing immediately, and continued, eagerly, to the end of the period. And they filled the pages with honest feeling and convincing support. There was none of the purposeless, formless rambling or the incoherent sentences so typical of their theme exams. Even the spelling and punctuation errors that had prevented them from "passing out" were surprisingly diminished. But even more important, the voice of a unique human being and the force of a personality came through in almost every paper.

The reasons are obvious to anybody who was involved: the purpose of the assignment coincided with the purpose for speaking out that was seething inside them; they had something to say and they had not been told to make their thoughts and feelings fit prescribed models of organization and correctness. But the freedom that released that kind of writing did not last. All of them would again face the theme exam at the end of the semester. They wanted only one thing from the Lab—The Word. On how to "pass-out." How to put together a product labeled 'theme,' a product that would pass somebody's inspection, so they would not be required to spend another semester in the Lab.

Our responsibility was clear: to help the students who had failed the last time succeed the next time. And the faithful did succeed, even though their themes were rated by two "objective" teachers who were also rating themes from students who were taking the test for the first time. At the end of every semester we could claim that we were maintaining the proud tradition of the Lab.

But my pride was mixed with a sense of failure. After the burst of eloquence on the first day, the students, with rare exception, found no joy in their Lab experience until the day they were told they did not have to return. After passing the exam, they still hated to write. Most of them would never write again except to get through some teacher's drudging assignment. And with rare exception, the part-time teaching assistants (new ones every year, most of them inexperienced) shared the students' attitudes toward rhetoric, impatiently looking ahead to next year when they hoped to teach literature. And they certainly would never teach "remedial" English unless they had to.

Asking why seems like a logical reaction to such a demoralizing situation, and I found my answers in my students' writings. When I confirmed their hostile reactions to a demeaning requirement and I responded to their human needs first, when I asked them to write about their immediate concerns, to talk to me as I had talked to them, their words flowed onto pages with ease if not grace; their attitudes toward English and rhetoric teachers, toward learning and teaching came through clearly and forcefully; the details and examples from their own experiences were indeed convincing. Were they teaching me how to become a more competent teacher? Were they telling me that they could become something more than writers of minimal competence if I could find some alternatives to the rigid models and dreary routines I had inherited?

As I read the first set of Lab papers twice a year, I continued to question the way I had been taught to teach writing. In required in-service sessions every week, we were told to "integrate" the communication skills—writing, reading, speaking, listening. But our training did not include a lecture on the parallels between writing and the actual communication, the talking that people do all the days of their lives. The student writing we were "integrating" with their speaking was only for learning how. For the written word has to be different—much more formal than talking, even when one is explicating informal subjects for informal situations. The written word is distinguished by sophisticated diction and long sentences with complex syntactic structures that enable one to clarify and qualify the assertions one is making. The written word maintains some detachment, some distance from the person even when one is expressing personal concerns about personal experiences. And learning to manipulate the written word is an academic necessity.

Given that concept of the human behavior called writing, it's easy to see why we were not told that our student writers should address a real audience. Their writing was for teacher's eyes only, and teacher's main function was grading. Listening was one of the "integrated" skills, but we were not taught to listen to our students' writings. For writing was a communication *skill*, not communication.

The ironies seemed even more apparent because the name of this skills program had been changed to rhetoric while the major thrust of instruction had remained unchanged. How could it be rhetoric when people were writing only to demonstrate that they had mastered certain organizational patterns, correct usage and punctuation? If we don't hear and respond to *what* our students are saying, can we teach them anything about dynamic interactions between writer-subject-audience? Can they understand or put into practice the basic rhetorical principles unless our assignments create evocative rhetorical situations which they can respond to in writing that communicates what they want to say?

Traditionally, of course, teaching has always meant *telling,* the imparting of knowledge or skills through explanations and lectures that rarely if ever involve a whole class. But when you sit down face-to-face with one troubled writer, one human being whose problems and potentialities are unlike anybody else's, the academic conference can readily become a personal encounter. Even though you're expected to talk about your attitude sentence outlines, you feel impelled to say something to make the situation less threatening, so this particular person will be able to hear and assimilate your comments and suggestions, to be able to do the best writing he or she is capable of. Given that attitude—of prizing and accepting our troubled writers—the conferring can become real communication, two people actually talking about a common concern. Maybe that's why it seemed natural to ask Lab students, who were sure they couldn't write, to talk to me on paper.

Reading their spontaneous personal responses to that invitation, comparing the tone, content, structure and syntactic forms in those papers with their exam themes and their attitude sentence themes, helped me see new possibilities, new directions for the individual instruction offered in the Lab. Gradually—cautiously—I began to move away from the prescribed exterior forms and the dummy run assignments, began to work my way into a promising alternative to the approach that had taken the eagerness and spontaneity out of my students and the fluency and life out of their writings.

Of course, abandoning an old idea or method before developing and testing a new one would be irresponsible. That may indeed explain why many educational alternatives fail. But when your students are writing more and better, when their negative attitudes toward writing seem to be changing, you keep on trying to understand and explain the pedagogy that's achieving the results you want.

* * *

During the fall semester I now offer a graduate seminar/practicum called Teaching in a Writing Lab. In addition to the weekly meetings, the students work in the Lab four days a week, first observing the Director and two teaching assistants selected from a previous class, then working with Lab students assigned to them. In the spring and summer, other people who have completed the course are appointed as teaching assistants for the Lab.

The individualized instruction we offer is for any student who feels uneasy or hopeless about the writing they know they'll eventually have to do; any student who feels inadequate when a professor hands out a writing assignment, or painfully embarrassed, even threatened when a set of papers is returned; any student who cannot accept the grades they consistently get after working for hours on all their papers. We also offer a two-hour credit course. But not at the end of the required sequence and not for people who have already failed the "pass-out" theme. (It was discontinued ten years ago because it was no longer valid or reliable, if indeed it had ever been.) With an in-class writing during the first week of the first semester course, we try to identify the people who seem to need intensive work toward the development of their basic writing abilities. Then we talk with the ones who need us, explaining how working one-on-one with a Lab teacher can help anybody— "including you"—become a better writer. We advise most of them to enroll in the Lab without credit; for some we add a gentle warning, "If you find you can't do well in the course, even though you work hard, you can drop it anytime and add the credit course we offer in the Lab." We urge a few to drop Rhetoric and add our credit course, "today if possible."

But this initial effort is not enough if you want to make sure that failure is not inevitable for some of the people in your required writing course. For some of the underprepared register late or miss the first writing and many of them are not easily convinced. They feel threatened, and they don't trust teachers. So, from the third to the tenth week of the semester, whenever it seems impossible for a student to achieve the level of writing expected in any one of our required Rhetoric courses, we tell them about the add-drop option that allows them to move to the Lab from the course they're failing. The aim: to try to address each person's particular needs, to try to help everybody in all our classes write enough—learn enough—succeed enough—to keep them writing, learning, and succeeding. Students may also enroll in the Lab for credit before or after taking the required Rhetoric course and before enrolling in the second semester of the two-semester sequence. Since our credit course offers individualized instruction, it may be repeated as many times as a student wishes, if the director of the Lab agrees that further Lab work is feasible. Any credit earned counts toward the minimum or maximum number of hours that can be earned in one semester, and the course grade becomes a part of a person's cumulative GPA. However, Lab credit counts toward graduation only for the person who earns no more than 6 other hours in Rhetoric.

Given such an open admissions policy, we get new students throughout the semester, from diverse educational and cultural backgrounds and with a wide range of writing abilities. Some of them already have one graduate degree as they work toward another one, while others are severely underprepared for college. But each one of them began using and responding to language, with varying degrees of success, even before they learned to talk. In the years since, their language experiences have been even more various. But in spite of all the differences, instruction can begin, in fact must begin, with the grammatical and rhetorical competencies each person already has. So every semester, over many years with many students, we've invited them to talk on paper as the original invitation is elaborated in *From Dialogue to Discourse* (Scott, Foresman, 1972, pp. 133-16). The metaphor still works.

While telling us what bad writers and nonwriters they are, most of them fill a page or two, apparently quite easily, and there's rarely a syntactic disjuncture or a strange word choice to interfere with meaning. But the ones who write less, if only 5 or 6 lines in a tiny cramped script, have not failed. After responding to whatever they've said, we usually ask a question which tells them we'd like to hear more on that subject; then we try to add a cheering comment, about writing or the weather, anything to affirm their existence, anything to encourage them to see us as a fellow human being; and then we talk a moment about the next writing we'd like them to do.

While reading the first writings, we find another kind of short paper—half a page or less with many highly visible crossoffs, almost illegible handwriting, frequent and strange misspellings, not a single smooth and coherent sentence. During their next Lab hour, as we give the writers of these papers our close but unobtrusive attention, we can see how terribly uncomfortable they are with the physical act of writing. For them, moving a pen or pencil across the page is slow, painful work. Making a list would even be difficult, for they are still struggling with the basic mechanics of writing, the performance skills that, for most of our students, have already become unconscious motor responses. And when they think of writing, they think of spelling. For them writing *is* spelling, and spelling is agony—word after word, letter by letter. They cannot compose sentences because their minds are focused on words, not in relationship to each other, but in confusing and frustrating isolation.

But penmanship and spelling lessons do *not* interrupt our opening series of writings. Instead, we talk with these people, one-to-one of course, and usually about something other than their writing. Though we may indeed have a positive response to a thought or feeling vaguely expressed or implied in their disjointed sentences, there's the danger of sounding condescending instead of making them feel comfortable enough to talk about what we know they're thinking about. If we're gracious and lucky enough, they do express some of their anxieties; if not, we must find some other nonthreatening and reassuring way to address their problems. For some of them a little kidding seems to be the answer. ("Well, your writing is certainly not boring. You'll have to write a full page if you want to bore me." [or] "You must've heard that tired eyes is a chronic complaint around here. Are you trying to give mine a little rest?") We assure them that we've seen—and read—all kinds of strange handwriting and that worrying about spelling is absolutely forbidden while talking on paper. We talk very briefly about copyreading—that totally separate and final stage of preparing a paper for somebody else to read. It's not really a part of writing, but a time for us to consider what we have already written, a time to ask if we have followed all the conventions of spelling, punctuation and usage, the conventions that make it easier for our readers to hear what we are saying. But for now we *insist* that they write as fast as they can, leaving every word the way they first write it and writing only part of a word, just the first letter when they get stuck. They must *not* let spelling disrupt or displace their composing processes as they talk to us on paper. And even the least literate, if they can produce the written symbols for most of the words they use when talking, can do the kind of writing we're asking for. And teachers can learn to read and respond to these writers even though they misspell many words, punctuate erratically if at all, and frequently use "bad" English.

Before students do their first writing for us, we tell them the book they're about to read is a *talking* book. It's the director of the Lab talking to them. And we want them to talk back—sharing what they think and feel about what I've said to them, sharing with the Lab teachers their perceptions of the world. We tell them our knowledge and understanding of human experience will grow as we read their writing, and their understanding of their own experience will grow as we respond to what they tell us. There is no assigned subject for the first writing. We ask only that they try to tell us what they are thinking and how they are feeling "at this very moment. Say, as honestly as you can, what is going on inside your head *right now.*" Responding to these first writings is usually easy, often delightful. But instead of encouraging anyone to talk at length during the first conference, we ask them to talk again on paper. If they didn't mention their writing problems, as most people do in their first writing, we tell them we'd like to hear anything that might help us understand why they, or their teachers and advisors, think they need individual instruction in writing.

Their answers to this question, and all the others that we ask during the first few weeks, are important—because *learning our student writers* is our first goal. If we know how they feel about their writing and how they write, and if we can learn something about them as persons and as students (without invading their privacy), then the learner-teacher dialogues can evolve from the context of *their* interests instead of the teacher's. So we have a collection of questions and suggestions—invitations to write—that express our respect and concern while asking them to share some of their self-knowledge with their Lab teachers. And as they respond, they tell us far more than we could ever learn by talking with them in person. Our conferences with them during the first two or three weeks are intentionally very brief because we want the dialogues to begin in writing—with them responding in writing to what I have said to them in writing. By the beginning of the third week we like to have about 8 short papers, half of them written during their Lab hours and half over the two four-day week-ends.

While they are telling us what we think we need to know so that we can help them become better writers, other instructional goals are also being addressed. By providing nonthreatening but challenging writing experiences for them, we are enabling them *to develop confidence* in the writing abilities they already have as they demonstrate—for self as well as teacher—the syntactic fluency they have been developing through a lifetime of using and listening to their native tongue. Very few if any of them could explain that they are putting words together in the patterns that create meaning; and as they fill the empty pages, they would be unable to name the kinds of verbal constructs they're using to express their thoughts. But they are indeed demonstrating that they have already mastered the basic grammatical structures they need for writing. And the writing we're asking them to do is enabling them *to develop more fluency.*

As we attempt to make their natural way with language the way to write, as we assure them by what we say and by what we *don't* do with a red pencil that we are listening to their writing instead of looking for errors, as they begin to perceive their writing as their side of a dialogue with a teacher who will accept and respect their ideas, they know—maybe for the first time in all their years of schooling—the exhilarating feeling that comes with *fluency.* If we measured their T-units or counted their embeddings, their syntactic maturity rating might be low, but that does not stop the words from flowing. From mind to pen to page. For somebody to read and respond to. That's syntactic fluency. The actual writing that develops syntactic maturity. The actual writing that should precede, accompany and follow any work in sentence combining.

They talk on paper about being embarrassed and ashamed, baffled and confused, scared and worried when sent to the Lab; about feeling good inside or still depressed about their writing, or about life in general. They're surprised to be saying things they've wanted to say for a long time, to be writing words, expressing ideas the principal might censor. They want to communicate the "great" ideas they think they have, they want "to write something good—so bad."

> . . . to do something important, something that really satisfies me.
> No, that's not it—I want someone else to say it's good.

They seem delighted to have a chance to get back at all the teachers who've made them feel inferior.

> It's pure hell to try to work out something the teacher wants—something that's up to par with the rest of the students—and finished before the deadline.
> Why do they have to limit us to a certain number of words? What happens if we run out of things to say before 500 words? Do I make up sentences just to reach 500?
> I've always had the problem of trying to fathom teachers who don't want to be fathomed.

Though other folks never hear our students' writings as we do, never think they sound as good as we do, there's no denying the note of confidence, the promise of growth through writing, the good feelings about this writing as they do it. And I think these writers were indeed trying to tell me something they wanted me to know. In fact, the invitation to write that we often use on the second day of class could be regarded as my response to all the unsolicited comments I've read about teachers:

> A request for advice: You've already spent a lot of time in school —about 6 hours a day, 5 days a week, 9 months a year for 12 years

or more. You've probably had between 20 and 30 different teachers. Given that much experience, we think you can tell us something that will help us become better teachers. In your opinion, what *is* a good teacher? What will we have to do to fulfill your expectations? You can answer these questions for us by describing the work of some of your favorite teachers. Or tell us about one very special teacher you would like us to use as a model. We also need to know about the teachers whose personality traits and teaching methods you want us to avoid. Again, think of this writing as *talking on paper.* We're just asking you to share what you know about teaching with the people who'll be working with you in the Lab this semester.

In all our requests for writing, we try to convey genuine interest in what they can tell, what they can teach us. The way they respond, though different, is fundamentally the way they've been responding all their lives to the dynamic rhetorical situations that are part of being human. We all know we're still in school and many of them may not believe that we really want to learn from their experiences, but almost all of them are willing, at least momentarily, to suspend their disbelief—at least long enough to talk on paper in response to the questions we ask them.

Because they all arrive full of self-doubt, apparently convinced they know nothing a teacher would value, we ask them very soon to write about what they know best. In many instances, that means something the teacher knows very little about. Like the skills and knowledge they've developed at work or play, or a special interest or talent they've studied and practiced for a long time. Again students become teachers. Explaining their special competencies. Answering our requests for more information, more facts, more experiential details. Trying to clarify the parts we don't understand. Seeing the need to rearrange some parts if we can't follow what they are trying to teach us.

Frequently the experiences our students share with us are so briefly told, so general, they do not engage our interest. But we don't send them back to the lonely carrel to "fill in" the supporting material. We tell them, in our total response to them and their writing, that we want to hear more. Specifically, we tell them we want to *see* what they saw. We want to *hear* what they heard. To help them recall the details and recreate specific moments of the experience, we ask specific questions.

Such learner-teacher dialogues help our writers at least begin to achieve the goal that is most basic to the pedagogy that has been developing, not only in the Lab but in my classes, for the last fifteen years: *to experience writing as learning.* Not learning to write in the traditional sense of merely acquiring basic writing skills through precept and practice, but learning *and* writing. That is, discovering new insights, new understanding, new ways of knowing as they write.

Lab teachers could huddle around the nearest coffee pot and complain that our students have no ideas to write about. Much of their "thinking" is indeed the recycling of unexamined opinions. But with a few well-focused questions we attempt to entice them to reflect on a promising generalization or assertion they have made. Asking why is always a good starting point. Why do you say that? Where did you pick up that idea? How did that notion become a part of your "world view"? Why would some folks disagree with you? How are our personal opinions related to the things/concepts we value? Where/how do we come to value the things/people/ideas that we do value?

Not a barrage like that, of course. Even one question, if it sounds intimidating, can shut off the fluency and confidence they have begun to develop. So again, we must try to challenge without sounding threatening, try to help them make their talking on paper about a specific experience, a reflection on the implications and significance of that experience. We pose our questions, one by one, give them a few minutes to reflect on each question *while* trying to say in writing what they are thinking. Their attempts usually yield fragmentary bits and pieces, embryo ideas emerging from the uneven, unending flow of mixed up thoughts and feelings going on inside them. If we told them to think it through clearly before writing, we might sometimes get more words but less substance, sometimes get nothing. The underprepared, far more than the rest of us, do not know (in clear precise sentences) what they think until they see what they have said. Even then, they need a sympathetic reader to talk with them about their incomplete, undefined and confused reactions; they need a teacher who can frame the next clarifying question for them to consider, again in writing.

What we are attempting to do is certainly not as easy as giving them a model to imitate, but there are many possibilities for us to choose from. For example:

> Why was this experience so important to you?
> How did it feel to be caught up in it?
> How did you react as it was happening? How did everyone else react?
> Do you understand your reactions? Theirs?
> Why did you do what you did? Why did they?
> What values are implicit in your behavior? in theirs?
> How can you encourage/prevent the recurrence of such an experience?

With questions like these we are helping them change the intent of their talking on paper from merely telling what happened to analyzing and explaining what happened. And as they try to do that, they are looking at the experience from a different perspective and seeing it in a different way. That enables them to come up with new insights; helps them formulate their own ideas. Not the brilliant insights or profound ideas teachers like to dazzle each other with, but certainly the beginnings of thoughtful prose, and certainly prose that is less boring than attitude sentence paragraphs.

When our writers are trying to explain why they value some concept, some ideal they have perceived only in general, abstract terms, our best comment may be, "But I don't see what you mean" with extra strong emphasis on *see.* For they can usually remember an anecdote or a visual image that conveys the meaning they feel but have not clearly expressed. Or when they say, "I just don't get it, what is it *really* like?" they, too, can sometimes think of analogies that help us understand. And sometimes, even the ones labeled slow come up with a striking metaphor any writer would be proud of.

Asking questions to enable students to analyze their own experiences makes any prescribed pattern of organization seem irrelevant because questions reveal the complexities of human experience. Reducing organization to a simplistic model is asking them to reduce their thoughts and feelings instead of exploring and extending all the possibilities. Such a reductionist view demeans their hopes of "improving" their writing so they can stay in school and "get a good education." Organizing our perceptions of experience, our ideas, is not an easy simplistic task for any of us. Because seeing the various aspects or parts of an experience or an idea is not easy. Because seeing the connections between all the interrelated and overlapping parts is not easy.

> It's a drag and a puzzle. I can't get my thoughts together on paper. In high school I won honors in other subjects that require a quick mind. But I can't write a simple paper like the ones a lot of simple people I know can. Please tell me the problem is not in my mind.

We told him it wasn't. We tell all our students that the life of the mind does not come packaged in neat and tidy topic sentences and 500-word themes. For even the best writers among us, creating logical forms for our confusing, sometimes chaotic thinking is more often than not a struggle.

So instead of penalizing our students for sketchy and disorganized thinking/writing, we respond to it. And while trying to address the questions our response raises, they are learning to ask their own questions for clarifying, shaping, and expanding their confused or undeveloped pieces of writing.

Our questions can also help student writers move from personal experience to a consideration of larger issues:

> What parallels do you see between your experience and the experiences of others—in this class? on this campus? in this or other local communities? in the nation? in the world?

Writing about the larger issues and the great ideas of Western thought does not, of course, guarantee thoughtful writing, as any election year or any professional conference demonstrates. In fact I think the worst papers I've ever read, as teacher and as editor of a teachers' journal, were written by folks who had mastered "the thinking man's" jargon but had never engaged in a thoughtful analysis of somebody else's ideas and had never learned how to formulate and develop their own ideas.

To help Lab students learn to think clearly about their simple everyday concerns and the "heavy" ideas they're into, we study their early writings, noting all the potentialities for further exploration and development. And from these writings we usually learn enough to keep them writing two or three times a week for the rest of the semester.

Near the end of the semester I distribute a final invitation to write, not an exam, just one more in-class writing, one more question that I want to know their answers to. When they return next time, we are not waiting with the good or bad news about the "pass out." Instead, I ask them to read the writing they did last time, then tell me what they think their teacher's response will be.

This is not a director's attempt at quality control. I've been reading course journals every week from the teachers enrolled in our seminar/practicum. They have told me how easy or difficult it has been for them to understand, accept and implement what is for most of them a new approach to the teaching of writing. They have responded, in writing, to the student writings I've distributed in class, and to the reading on theory and practice which I've asked them to do. I've kept up with the learner-teacher dialogues going on in the Lab through the teachers' dialogues with me—in their writings, in the conversations that fill all our free Lab moments, and in class discussions. They have shared their successes and failures with me and their classmates. They have made another semester a time of learning not only for themselves and their students, but also for each other and for the head teacher.

There's no hidden agenda when I ask students to read a piece of their writing and respond to it as they think their teacher will. For this request they do not need to suspend their disbelief. They all know that I want to know how much progress each of them has made toward achieving the final goal we have set for them: *to become a perceptive, critical reader of their own writing*—a reader who listens first for the questions other readers may ask, and then attempts to address those questions; a reader who listens for the sound of their own voice and the "flow" of their sentences; a reader who consciously looks for the mistakes they habitually make in punctuation, spelling and usage.

What I'm learning from my students these days is reassuring. Though our pedagogy has not yet been perfected, the patient supportive work of a lot of caring teachers continues to make our Lab a place where people—students and teachers—can learn to think of writing, not as a drudging academic requirement, but a fulfilling dynamic process of sharing their experiences with others; where they see their own writing, not as a product to be criticized and graded, but as a means of exploring and understanding their perceptions of the world; where they can hear their writing as the voice of the unique human being each of them is and is becoming.

What's Up and What's In: Trends and Traditions in Writing Centers

by Muriel Harris

In the mid-1970's when large numbers of writing centers were getting started, the most pressing question in the minds of new writing center directors was "What is a writing center?" Now that hundreds of writing centers have been in existence well over a decade, we have moved on to other questions such as "What's new in writing centers?" and "What kinds of traditions have we developed?" These questions suggest that we now have enough history to start taking a longer look at where we've been and where we are going. However, this raises the classic problem of using the term "writing center" as if there were a generic description. The idea of a generic writing center makes us uneasy because it is a truism of this field that writing centers tend to differ from one another because they have evolved within different kinds of institutions and different writing programs and therefore serve different needs. But by surfacing our traditions, we can formulate some general truths about similarities among different writing centers; and by looking for recent trends, we can consider whether we are headed in new directions.

The Short History of Writing Center Traditions

Perhaps the most obvious thing we can say about our traditions is that we don't have to search any dim, dusty records or reach back into archives that have been shelved for generations. Many of us now active in writing center organizations were the novices ten, twelve, or fourteen years ago who responded to the call for organizing tutorial centers to assist with declining writing skills. But if writing centers have only a short history, it is nevertheless a rather awesome one. In little more than a decade or so, literally hundreds of writing centers have been established and have become a vital part of composition programs in post-secondary institutions and in language arts programs in secondary schools. Writing programs without a tutorial component for one-to-one collaboration in some form of a writing center are seen to be "incomplete" or lacking. Moreover, national meetings such as the

Reprinted from *The Writing Center Journal* 11.1 (1990): 15-25. Used by permission.

annual Conference on College Composition and Communication, the National Council of Teachers of English conference, and the Writing Program Administration conference regularly have sessions on writing centers. Thus it seems that we can reasonably conclude that in a decade or so, we have indeed become an integral part of writing programs and are recognized as an interest group at conferences.

The Tradition of Sharing

As writing centers started, new directors—unsure of what constituted a writing center—consulted one another, offered advice, and shared what they knew and/or had tried out. And this continues to be true. Thus, one of our firmest traditions, in keeping with our pedagogical approach, is that of helping one another and sharing what we have learned. No special interest group among composition specialists has such an extensive history of visiting one another's facilities, phoning for advice, and interacting for the sole purpose of helping one another. Consider the long-standing tradition of materials exchange tables at regional and national writing centers. Similarly, the *Writing Lab Newsletter* began in 1976 at the end of a session on writing centers at the Conference on College Composition and Communication to help the participants of that session keep in touch and continue to exchange ideas and information. And the National Writing Centers Association began as a support group, a central umbrella to encourage regional groups and help them interact.

The tradition of sharing, of helping, of working together may well have been established because of the nature of many of the people who, attracted to the idea of a writing center, became involved in this particular area of composition instruction. It may be that writing centers attract those who are of a helping, nurturing bent anyway, who see themselves as providing ways for others to grow and develop their own skills. The pervasiveness of this can best be seen by some recent examples. At the 1988 conference of the Writing Centers Association: East Central, on the materials exchange table, there were copies of a cookbook put together by the tutors at the Indiana University of Pennsylvania Writing Center. Writing center directors who picked up copies didn't question why a book of recipes was lying among samples of handouts and publicity brochures. Instead, people admired the attractive format, browsed through the recipes, and were overheard to offer such comments as "I'll give this to our tutors, who are always bringing in such interesting food for our parties" or "Our staff meetings always focus on good food too—our tutors should put together a similar book." Every writing center may not be staffed by tutors who are gourmet chefs, but food or drink is often in view. There are coffee pots, dishes of candy, and open houses that lure students in with popcorn and doughnuts. Providing nourishment is a constant activity in writing centers, and all that flow of food seems like a natural accompaniment.

As further example of this mindset, the September 1988 issue of the *Writing Lab Newsletter* collected several articles on diverse topics—principles of tutor selection, the need for research in writing centers, and a perspective on drop-in tutorials, and the discussion in each article was cast in food metaphors. The response to that issue of the newsletter was immediate, hearty, and appreciative. Readers were apparently responding to some sense of "rightness" in these nurturing, nutritive analogies, and in doing so were reflecting some of what they see themselves as doing. If we were to cast about for various metaphors and analogies for the role of writing centers, we might instead try other stances such as being havens for students caught in impersonal, anonymous institutions or being liberators of students forced to conform to textbook and large group requirements. Perhaps such views (or others) exist, but they don't resonate through the literature of writing centers. Instead, there is a very noticeable tradition of perceiving writing centers as nurturing, helping places which provide assistance to other writing centers and sustenance to students to help them grow, mature, and become independent.

The Tradition of Mystifying Our Colleagues

The nutritive metaphor may be a tradition in writing centers, but it is a view from the inside, for there is another tradition that persists when we shift our point of view and look at writing centers from the outside. From this other perspective we are traditionally seen as somewhat of a mystery to our colleagues. What exactly is it writing centers do? Are we running only remedial centers, places to salvage some of the "boneheads" that have been permitted to enroll (for however brief a tenure) in our institutions? Are we band-aid clinics offering clean-up service for papers about to be handed in? Such questions persist with the tenacity of barnacles. We seem forever to be countering these and other equally limited notions. But why do we perennially have to keep explaining ourselves? And why do we keep doing it from a somewhat defensive posture? I certainly find myself explaining, year after year, what a writing center can and does do, and every fall at the start of the new academic year I have an hour to meet with new members of our composition staff. At that orientation session I usually pass around portfolios of materials. The cover letter is as positive as I can be, explaining the rationale for a writing center and the benefits to students and instructors, but buried in there is a section called "Some Myths About Writing Centers." Here I deal with all the old familiar misapprehensions: that using the lab is a sign of a teacher's incompetence, that only the "basket cases" and remedial writers need a writing lab, that a writing lab is only for grammar problems, that the tutors write the papers for the students and/or hand them the answers they should find themselves, that the tutors offer evaluative comments, and so on.

Such an effort is hardly unique. At Boise State University, where Richard Leahy, the Writing Center director, issues a monthly newsletter to the faculty, the September 1988 issue of his newsletter (reprinted in the *Writing Lab Newsletter)* was dedicated to correcting similar misunderstandings. Entitling the issue "Seven Myth-Understandings about the Writing Center," Leahy and his co-author Roy Fox attacked seven myths that prevail on their campus: 1) The writing center is a remedial service for poor writers, 2) The writing center is mainly concerned with competency exams, 3) The writing center is only for students in English classes, 4) The writing center does work for students that they should be doing on their own, 5) Faculty should require students to visit the writing center, 6) The writing center only helps with essays and term papers, and 7) The writing center is only for students. The recurring themes sound like a litany.

As a further example of what I mean about the persistence of misunderstanding, consider Stephen North's article in the September 1984 issue of *College English.* North begins with an explosion of emotion with which too many of us can and do identify:

> This is an essay that began out of frustration.... The source of my frustration? Ignorance: the members of my profession, my colleagues, people I might see at MLA or CCCC or read in the pages of *College English* do not understand what I do. They do not understand what does happen, what can happen, in a writing center. (433)

Deeply frustrated by the prevailing view among the faculty in his department that the writing center is a fix-it shop or a place for students with "special problems," North reminds us of the prevalence of this view in earlier books and articles and cites a study by Malcolm Hayward, who found that the primary criteria among faculty at his institution for referring students to the writing center were problems with grammar and punctuation. Those of us in writing centers may agree with North's explanations of what we are really about, but the point here is that in 1988 Richard Leahy is still busy explaining to the faculty at his institution what a writing center is. And Diana George, at the 1987 Midwest Association of Departments of English, was asked to speak to this group of department heads about writing centers. In an article based on her experience, George reports a very positive interest among the administrators to whom she talked, but doesn't overlook the "bad news: Many still do not know us, do not know what we can offer them, do not know how we work with students" (38). There seems to be a long and tenacious tradition of not understanding or misunderstanding what writing centers are about. As North laments, it is even more disappointing when the most blatant blindness and the most simplistic views are held by colleagues in our departments who are otherwise interested in and knowledgeable about the teaching of writing.

What, one wonders, causes this gulf between writing centers and teachers of writing? Why do they think we're merely band-aid grammar clinics for the terminally thick-headed? It may be that we operate within a different perspective of education—individualized instruction, a form of learning so far removed from the perspective of most teachers that they don't know how to begin to think about what we do. After all, most educators think of education in group terms. Students sit in classes, move in groups, pass through educational systems in large numbers. If someone uses the word "student," there is a generic student in mind. Classroom teachers of writing can talk about "the writing process" as if it applies universally to all writers, about textbooks that work for whole levels of students (e.g., basic writers, traditional freshmen, advanced composition, and so on). Yet, what writing centers are about is the antitheses of generic, mass instruction. We are committed to individualized instruction, to taking the student out of the group and to looking at her as an individual, as a person with all her uniqueness. Sitting down in a tutorial with a student, we know that our job, in North's neat phrase, "is to produce better writers, not better writing" (438).

Committed to working with the whole person, we train ourselves to ask about that particular person's writing processes, about her past history, about her perception of her assignment, about her particular problems, about her questions. When that student leaves, we know that the next person we work with will be equally unique. We know that the deadliest thing we can do is to treat two writers alike. Thus, we don't merely value the individual student; we focus on that student's individuality as a basis for whatever help we can offer. And therein lies the secret of some of our success. When large-group instruction isn't cutting it, when textbooks and classroom explanations evaporate into airy abstractions, when generalities fail to make connections to the specific writing task the writer is engaged in, then the tutor and student engage in dialogue that leads to making those connections. This kind of help assists writers in moving forward with a piece of writing. Another kind of help is that collaborative dialogue between writer and responding reader that helps the writer move beyond herself as composer to see what she is offering her readers. Collaboration, with the tutor serving as reader/responder, usually intermingles with the collaborative effort to help the writer compose more effectively. All of this goes on in the one-to-one setting of a tutorial as we know, but our colleagues outside the writing center don't seem to know it.

This tradition of misunderstanding is so persistent that it isn't likely to disappear unless we address the composition community in ways we haven't yet done, for writing centers also have a tradition of not speaking up effectively. There have been endless calls for research in the writing center, to validate and elucidate what we do, and it is a tradition that we keep on making those calls—and not answering them. Far too little research, especially research that will wake up and inform our colleagues, has been conducted in our writing centers. And there have been far too few articles presenting general theories of individualized instruction. We have, in fact, talked too much to ourselves in our journals and at our conferences (and in those phone calls and visits) and not enough to the world of composition outside. But it is most likely not a matter of more journal articles about what writing centers do (for North's article articulated that very well) or more campus newsletters explaining ourselves to our colleagues—we can see that these solutions haven't seemed to change matters much. Some more effective approach, stance, action, or method of explanation is apparently needed.

The Tradition of Being at the Bottom of the Totem Pole

A concurrent tradition to being misunderstanding is being undervalued. We traditionally have been the field hands waiting at the back door for a few scraps from the table of the real folk dining inside. Yes, we make jokes about "winging it" with no budget and too few tutors, about making midnight raids down the hall to "liberate" furniture from other facilities and offices, about having less clout than the night janitor. We tend to be grateful for minimal responses to our requests, and we lose people who see themselves as "moving up" when they go on to direct the freshman composition program or take some other administrative position. Believing in what we do, we tend to accept lower salaries, poorer working conditions, lower status.

The National Writing Centers Association position statement on writing centers, recently adopted by the National Council of Teachers of English, will help—and it is a major step in the right direction—but too many of us have a tradition of letting ourselves be sold short. We find our compensation in our work, knowing that what we do is effective and right, but that shouldn't deter us from taking stronger stances in demonstrating that the needs of our writing centers are legitimate and that our work should be valued as a major responsibility.

One way to see how others view the role of being a writing center director is to look at job postings. One that I recently received was from a university seeking someone with experience in writing assessment who could also teach undergraduate and graduate courses in rhetoric. And by the way, that person will be a half-time lab director responsible for training tutors, developing materials, etc. That may sound like a job that would best be filled by several people, but someone will take it. Writing center administration is still too often something we are supposed to do with our left hand while focusing our "quality time" on all of our other responsibilities.

The Tradition of Incorporating Collaborative Learning

It may seem that writing centers have some discouraging traditions that we've lived with for too long, but there are also other traditions that we can view far more positively. For example, writing centers from their first blossoming have a tradition of enriching the world of learning by adding a new dimension—collaborative learning—in which the writer and the tutor remove themselves from that other traditional world of teacher and student, the one in which the student is expected to remain passive and receive what the instructor gives him. We've added to traditional instruction this new dimension of students leading each other to greater understanding and enhanced skills. Peer tutors have a power—and responsibility—and a goal—of being other than a teacher. The students they work with are given encouragement and an opportunity to shake off their passive classroom stance and assume some responsibility for getting involved with their own learning. That's even more heretical than we might imagine as there is a general assumption that good teachers in classrooms also actively involve their students in responding to questions.

However, we can understand more fully why writing labs differ from classrooms and why students come in meekly expecting someone to give them the answer if we can see what is happening in classrooms. One study which lets us peer into a large number of classrooms was done by Carol

Barnes, and it indicates how little question-asking actually goes on in classrooms. For the study, Barnes surveyed forty college classrooms in large and small public institutions, large private universities, and small private colleges, in both beginning and advanced courses in a variety of disciplines. She found that the mean percentage of time spent on question asking is close to 3.65%. Of that tiny portion of class time spent on questioning, 63% of the questions were classified as cognitive memory questions, questions asking students to recapitulate, to clarify, or to offer factual information. Questions calling for other kinds of thinking were less frequently asked. And so we can see that the collaboration of the tutorial is indeed a very different mode of learning for students. The closest thing to compare it to in the classroom is the collaboration of peer response groups, but recent work on peer response groups has indicated some of the difficulties of this setting.

The Tradition of Tutors' Personal Enrichment

As a corollary to the tradition of active involvement in learning, of making the student a participant instead of a passive listener, writing centers have a tradition of offering a kind of experience for tutors that is not offered elsewhere in the academic setting. Through training courses, at conferences, and at work, tutors are developing skills and talents that enhance their own writing skills, their understanding of the learning processes, their interpersonal skills, their awareness of writing processes, and their employability. Contributing to the institutionalizing of tutoring, having students learn how to help others learn, is a tradition of which writing center directors have long been aware and can be proud. Educators concerned with the training of future teachers are beginning to recognize this additional kind of "field experience" for education majors and are making use of writing centers as teacher training grounds. Offering course credit for tutoring, as is done in many writing centers, is a means of recognizing what tutors learn as they tutor. As we note what tutors learn, it should not surprise us that they tend to be so evangelical about what they do. At tutoring conferences and in articles written by tutors, we don't hear negative voices or disillusioned sneers. Instead, these tutors have entered a realm they find exhilarating.

The Tradition of Being People-Oriented

One more tradition to add to this list of what has stayed constant in the short history of most writing centers is that they have remained people-oriented. When writing centers were beginning to define themselves and their roles, there was some concern that two models were developing, the writing center with people collaborating with people and the writing lab with rows of study carrels where students would be plugged into appropriate hardware, software, tapes, screens, and anything else that ran by itself with little or no human intervention. (See, for example, Muriel Harris, "Process and Product: Dominant Models for Writing Centers.") The problem of insufficient staff continues to plague some writing centers, and computers for word processing have become useful aids to revision in writing centers with funds for this type of resource. But writing enters have remained in the human realm of inter-action and collaboration, using machines as supplements, but never losing sight of the value of the tutorial. This may, in part, reflect the general trend away from self-instruction facilities and the generally disappointing lack of computer software that will do anything more pedagogically respectable than drill-and-practice. But it may also be that writing centers have defined themselves primarily as tutorial centers.

Trends in Writing Centers

While there are clearly traditions that delineate some of the consistent characteristics of writing centers, there are also accompanying trends, changes and new directions that also define writing centers. In one sense, there are always new directions because writing centers tend to grow, develop, change, respond to new challenges, try new services, shift gears when something bombs out, and add something that the director learned about from an article, conference talk, or visit to another center. There is no sense of stagnation in writing centers, surely, but there are also a few general trends in addition to the normal growth of writing centers within their own institutions as they respond to local needs.

1. Toward Greater Professionalism

One very definite trend is that there is a new sense of professionalism in the air. Ten or twelve years ago new directors were often selected solely on the basis of their interest or willingness to learn about writing centers, and directors continue to be hired with little or no prior experience. However, graduate programs in rhetoric and composition, which are flourishing in numerous institutions, are producing specialists in composition who have training and experience in writing centers. Job descriptions for writing center director are likely to list as necessary credentials for application advanced degrees in composition with some background and training in writing centers. Graduate students going out on the job market often have academic coursework, experience, and publications in the field to offer. Among peer tutors, there are English education majors who have gone on to set up or work in high school writing centers. This new professionalism is the result of writing center administrators having nurtured new people in the field who won't begin at ground zero, where directors usually began a dozen years ago. Dissertations are also being done on writing centers, and—the true mark of a burgeoning field of inquiry—there is such a huge body of literature about tutoring and writing centers (gathered in the annual bibliographies in the *The Writing Center Journal*) that it is difficult to keep up with it all.

2. Away from the Label of "Remedial Only"

Another trend, a heartening one, is that writing centers have weathered the backlash against remedial studies by no longer being generally viewed as nothing but remedial services. Yes, the myth persists, but it is not a universal one, and the variety of responsibilities writing centers have taken on help to dispel the simplistic view that students who need help with writing always have major deficiencies in basic skills. Having taken on more responsibilities with writing across the curriculum, with writing assessment, and with teacher training, writing centers have redefined themselves. There is still a tendency among too many teachers to think of the writing center as the place to work with students who have "problems," but at least there is a recognition even here that this can be ordinary students in freshmen composition, not just developmental students "with severe problems."

3. Growth in High School Writing Centers

Another healthy trend is the proliferation of writing centers in high schools. At the meetings of the National Council of Teachers of English, the National Writing Centers Association has sponsored sessions and all-day workshops for high school teachers who are starting writing centers; at regional writing center conferences there is a growing participation of high school writing center directors; and articles about high school writing centers appear almost monthly in the *Writing Lab Newsletter*. High school directors of writing centers are particularly involved with the integration of writing skills into courses other than English.

4. Toward Integration with Classrooms

Another trend is the melding of our pedagogy with classroom instruction in interesting new ways. There are writing centers that send peer tutors to classrooms to lead small groups in workshop classrooms, there are other centers where the peer response groups from the classrooms come to the center to work, and there are collaborative writing activities that tie classroom and writing lab together. As a way to help our colleagues learn about what we do, this may be a particularly encouraging trend. In addition it offers us some interesting new ways to expand the role of the tutor.

5. Toward Serving More Non-Traditional Students

Yet another trend is that in many colleges writing centers are serving a growing population of non-traditional students. We are hearing and reading more about writing centers that are adding interesting new services, such as courses taught through centers for older, returning students and part-time students from the community. We are beginning to find imaginative ways to serve the unique needs of this population, in offering them support, counseling, tutoring opportunities, and a place to work on skills that may have gotten a bit rusty. With 45 percent of the nation's college population now over 25, writing centers will become increasingly important as part of the system of support services these people need.

Some Conclusions and Speculations

But what can we make of all this? On one hand, there are traditions that define the very essence of writing centers. Given the endurance of these traditions, they are likely to continue as defining characteristics. It would seem a safe generalization to say that writing centers have defined their goals and unique approaches and that they have gained a sense of permanence and a level of professionalism that has established writing centers as integral parts of writing instruction. Moreover, while the wider field of composition seems subject to constant winds of change and trends that overtake the national conferences and journals, only to be swept aside in a year or two, writing centers seem on a steadier course. We have experienced growth and expansion but no major swings, shifts, or redefinitions of interests. While some of our traditions suggest that writing centers merely need to maintain a steady course, others indicate a need for more or different effort, particularly in the areas of educating colleagues and of doing the kinds of research that validate writing centers' claims of success and define what individualized instruction is. Only a concerted effort to explain what writing center instruction is and what writing centers are about will reduce our ever-present paranoia and sense of living at the periphery (or the bottom rung of the composition ladder).

The trends that are currently evident in writing centers point to continued growth and some additional services and students we can and are working with. We don't seem to be shifting course in any major way. If anything, we can probably say we are in a period of consolidation and on a steady course. In sum, we have traditions to be proud of and some trends that will keep us busy developing new services and moving in new directions. Clearly, we are still a growth industry—and that may be the best tradition of all.

Works Cited

Barnes, Carol. "Questioning in the College Classrooms," in *Studies of College Teaching,* ed. Carolyn Ellner and Carol Barnes. Lexington: Lexington Books, 1983. 61-81.
Freedman, Sarah Warshauer. "Response to Response Groups." Conference on College Composition and Communication. Atlanta, 20 Mar. 1987.
George, Diana. "Talking to the Boss: A Preface." *The Writing Center Journal* 9.1 (1988): 37-43.
Harris, Muriel. "Process and Product: Dominant Models for Writing Centers," in *Improving Writing Skills*, ed. Thom Hawkins and Phyllis Brooks. *New Directions for College Learning Assistance*. San Francisco: Jossey-Bass, 1981. 1-8.
Hayward, Malcolm. "Assessing Attitudes Towards the Writing Center." *The Writing Center Journal* 3.2 (1983): 1-11.
North, Stephen. "The Idea of a Writing Center." *College English* 46 (1984): 433-466.

What Do We Talk About When We Talk About Our Metaphors: A Cultural Critique of Clinic, Lab, and Center

by Peter Carino

My title evokes Raymond Carver's "What We Talk About When We Talk About Love," a short story in which two couples talk and drink an afternoon away discussing various experiences and definitions of love, searching for the elusive signified that would fill the signifier and render the word and their lives meaningful. Ultimately, meaning eludes them, and the narrative appears to reach closure as they run out of the gin that has lubricated the conversation. But this closure is undone in the last line of the story when the first-person narrator hears everyone's heart beating and metaphorically identifies the sound as "the human noise we sat there making" (154).

The indeterminacy of Carver's story provides an apt metaphor for examining the ways we have attempted to define the writing center. Though we have not been drinking gin, the various attempts at definition in our literature can leave one dizzy. As Thomas Hemmeter argues, discourse on writing centers continually begins with gestures of self-definition: "It is as if each theorist must begin anew the process of awakening the slumbering writing center profession to the urgent need for self-creation" (36). In one sense, this is how it should be. From a post-structuralist perspective on language, we accept that definition is always already tenuous, for to define is to symbolize, to create metaphors, to be in language. Situated thus, one might arrive at a definition like that which Hemmeter constructs. Playing off Stephen North he writes, "The writing center is an idea—in language." Pushing a bit further, he concludes, "The writing center *is* our words, a linguistic phenomenon" (emphasis original, 44).

I do not advocate a naive return to an uncomplicated view of language, but to borrow a term from Stuart Hall, the "experiential 'thickness'" (58) we confront daily in writing centers may make us uneasy with Hemmeter's reduction of them to "a linguistic phenomenon," even though we may support the post-structural premises informing this claim. Any attempts to define centers, it seems to me, should recognize them as both a culture unto themselves and as an activity in relation with larger cultures: the writing

Reprinted from *The Writing Center Journal* 13.1 (1992): 31-42. Used by permission.

program, the profession of English studies, the university, and the culture in general. I use *culture* here in two senses offered by Raymond Williams in *The Long Revolution.* The first, the social notion of culture, is "a particular way of life which expresses certain meanings and values . . . in institutions and ordinary behavior" (41). I take this sense to express the ineluctable welter of experience that confronts us daily in our centers, the experience that makes our history. The second sense "is the 'documentary,' in which culture is the body of intellectual and imaginative work, in which, in a detailed way, human thought and experience are variously recorded" (41). I take the documentary sense to express the ways in which our language constructs our history.

Writing centers, then, are social as well as linguistic, social in the sense of the praxis that goes on there, linguistic in the sense that all of that praxis is mediated by language both as it occurs and in any attempts we make to document it. As language, our documentation, our discourse, is always already interpretive. Have we arrived back at Hemmeter's position that "the writing center is our words?" Yes and no. Yes, to the extent that we can think and theorize the center culturally only in words. No, if we read our language through the lens of Bahktinian dialogic that deconstructs the boundary between Williams' social and documentary senses of culture. As Bahktin writes:

> The word, in language is half someone else's. It becomes "one's own" only when the speaker populates it with his own intentions, his own accent, when he appropriates the word adapting it to his own semantic and expressive intention. Prior to this moment of appropriation, the word does not exist in a neutral and personal language . . . but rather it exists in other people's mouths, in other people's contexts serving other people's intentions: it is from there that one must take the word and make it one's own. (293-94)

Bahktin here recognizes that we construct reality in language, but this recognition also accounts for the material conditions and political intentions inscribed in our constructions. From this perspective I would like to examine three metaphors by which we call and have called ourselves: clinic, lab, and center. Though not a comprehensive list, these metaphors have been the most widely used in the roughly twenty years since the advent of open admissions and the subsequent proliferation of facilities, by whatever name, providing one-to-one instruction in writing.

Calling such a facility a clinic was not uncommon in the early 1970s and has its origins long before. The *OED*, aside from its medical definition of *clinic*, lists one sense, designated chiefly American, as "An institution, class, or conference, etc. for instruction in or the study of a particular subject; a seminar" (328). In two of the quotations used to exemplify this sense of *clinic*, the word is appropriated euphemistically by economists and business people to elevate their activities to the scientific status of medicine. However, the final quotation comes from the January, 1951, issue of *College English*: "A 'composition clinic' has been set up by the college of liberal arts in the department of English of Wayne University... Once the student is enrolled there, his writing is diagnosed and he is given what ever treatment he needs" (ellipsis original, 328). The notable difference here is that while economics and business use *clinic* to name a context for solving abstract problems, this last definition begins with an abstract problem—writing—but shifts focus to a human subject—the student who is "diagnosed and given treatment." This sense of *clinic*, while garnering prestige for those who work there, degrades students by enclosing them in a metaphor of illness.

That this sense often persisted when facilities began to proliferate in the 1970s is not surprising when we consider that their growth is related to the advent and growth of open admissions policies. The cultural moment producing open admissions and writing centers is so thick that its outline would require volumes, but even a cursory examination of it reveals the complex sociopolitical forces surrounding the illness model implicit in the clinic metaphor.

Open admissions was not solely the result of a sudden humanitarian impulse by those in power. While in some quarters Johnsonian liberalism and the war on poverty likely contributed to the thinking of legislators and university officials, open admissions, I would argue, was as much the result of the struggles of the disenfranchised throughout the 1960s. As the civil rights, feminist, and anti-war movements questioned the prevailing ideology, their material struggles in the streets entailed a dialogic struggle for language, with the name and notion of democracy at stake. My tracing here is, I admit, an oversimplification. Consider also the advantages to organized labor of having a sizable, largely blue-collar segment of baby boomers, now reaching employable age, entering colleges and universities rather than vying for positions in the work force. One could go on.

But why clinic? It is one thing to let the rabble into the palace; it is another to make them comfortable there. Examining the institutional responses to basic writers for whom clinics were designed, Mina Shaughnessy identifies a stage she calls "guarding the tower." Writing in 1975 she states,

> during this stage the teacher is in one way or another concentrating on protecting the academy (including himself) from the outsiders, those who do not seem to belong in the community of learners. The grounds for exclusion are various. The mores of the times inhibit anyone's openly ascribing the exclusion to genetic inferiority, but a few teachers doubtless still hold to this view. (234-235)

Though focused on teachers, Shaughnessy's argument likely applied as well to a significant number of administrators who funded writing clinics. This is not to say that they consciously conspired to keep open admissions students in their places by adopting an illness metaphor to designate the place where these students could develop their writing. My point, rather, is that the intellectual and political climate, or to use Raymond Williams' term, the "structure of feeling" (48) of the times approximated that which Shaughnessy saw among her teaching colleagues.

Shaughnessy's second stage of response—"converting the natives"— also tells us much about the ideology operating in the clinic metaphor. In this stage, "Whether the truth is delivered in lectures or modules, cassettes or computers . . . the teacher's purpose is the same: to carry the technology of advanced literacy to the inhabitants of an underdeveloped country" (235). The colonial impulses Shaughnessy attributes to this response from teachers inform the pedagogical and ideological connotations of calling a center a clinic. Writing clinics were associated with drill and kill pedagogy, materially evident in file cabinets full of hundreds of worksheets, and theoretically underpinned by the residual influence of current-traditional rhetoric, with its emphasis on product, which, in turn, was underpinned by the objective notion of text prevailing in the largely New Critical bent of most English Departments. This pedagogy did not, however, consider that learning is a negotiation of new habits, values, expectations, turns of mind, strategies of representation, and the like. Ideologically, clinic pedagogy was informed by the belief that if we can only get them to talk and write like us, everything will be okay.

This position is evident in the sense of *clinic* as "an institution attached to a hospital or medical school at which patients received treatment free of cost or at reduced fees" (OED, 328). In this definition, we can see contending both the humanitarian impulse of offering help to students and the connotation of reduced circumstances for the facility itself and the students and staff working there. Fortunately, the metaphor of the clinic neither lasted long nor persisted—only one facility carried this designation in the *1984 Writing Lab Directory* and none in 1992 directory—but its residue touched and still touches our designations as labs and centers.

While the clinic metaphor contained both a misguided humanitarianism and a tacit reactionary politics, the metaphor of a writing *lab* constituted a powerful counter narrative, advancing a cultural ideology more akin to the ways we perceive ourselves today. Whether called clinics, labs, or centers, the development of facilities providing one-to-one writing instruction paralleled the paradigm shift in composition studies from the current-traditional emphasis on product to the focus on writing as process, but this growth has particular bearing on the metaphor of a lab. By the 1970s the then new process approach, growing out of the 1967 Dartmouth conference, was influencing facilities for student writers. Even in some of the so-called clinics, directors and tutors were ignoring the worksheets and "diving in," to use a third of Shaughnessy's metaphors. In this response, the teacher makes "a decision to remediate himself, to become a student of new disciplines and of his students themselves in order to perceive both their difficulties and their incipient excellence" (238). Judith Summerfield describes this period as a time of excitement, experiment, and collaboration: "One day we were working there alone, and the next day we were all engaged—instructor, student, administrator, tutor—in collaborative *doing*. Nothing seemed impossible . . . the maps had not yet been drawn" (4-5).

Despite this optimism, the metaphor of the lab came to signify a place as marginal as most clinics. Summerfield attributes this development to the triumph of post-sixties reactionary politics: "The *no* I kept hearing had to do with the times, with going back, with pulling back, with the Nixons of the time saying watch out for those who assemble. . . . Danger lurks when teachers gather in the halls or when they engage in talk . . . " (emphasis original, 9). This is a fine piece of rhetoric, but it is an oversimplification. Granted the Nixon administration carried an ideology repressive to the chaotic spirit of the times out of which open admissions was born and writing labs proliferated. However, we need a thicker description if we are to begin tracing the ideological and cultural pressures contending in the lab metaphor.

As Shaughnessy's and Summerfield's statements indicate, in the context of open admissions and the paradigm shift in composition, those working in labs probably perceived their efforts in the connotation of *lab* as a place to experiment, to pose questions, and seek solutions to problems. For other constituencies, the lab metaphor took on different meanings. In the larger culture of the institution, its experimental connotation fit nicely with the experiment of open admissions. Also, there was a tradition of having labs for various disciplines—biology or physics labs, for example. This tradition must have been unconsciously bracing to those working in writing labs, but it would soon contribute to their marginalization.

For what probably was a limited number of writing programs, the metaphor of the lab as experiment offered a way of organizing themselves in the paradigm shift by coordinating lab and classroom instruction and by using the lab for research. But probably for most writing programs, excited but still anxious about the paradigm shift, the lab became the place to do the dirty work of grammar that would free classroom teachers to concentrate on the new process pedagogy. This was not a conspiracy but a culturally specific reading of the metaphor; that is, in colleges and universities labs used by undergraduates are primarily course supplements. And likely some lab personnel, to a greater or lesser degrees, bought into this interpretation. As Lester Faigley has written, "words carry with them the places where they have been" (535).

Already seen as supplements to writing courses, the designation writing *lab* suffered pejoration because students went to the lab only because they wanted to or because instructors in the regular first-year composition course singled them out for remediation. Also, they went there to be *tutored* (a term beyond the scope of this paper but carefully examined by Lex Runciman). Required lab work, which would have put writing labs at least on par with science labs, was only for remedial courses. In other words, to grasp principles of physics or biology, a student needed a lab, but classroom instruction was sufficient to teach students to write unless they were basic writers, an already marginalized group in need of remediation. We can thus trace a double-bind organization in the lab metaphor. Not to require all students in all writing courses to work in the lab was to deny that the kind of instruction it offered is integral to learning to write. To require the lab of only basic writers was to infuse the metaphor with connotations of punishment meted out to those who dared to be ungrammatical.

This pejoration of the metaphor seems to have a certain logic. Certainly, millions of people have become accomplished writers without working in the institutional entity we call a writing lab. However, this logic breaks down if we consider that few have learned to write well without ever having done the things writers do in writing labs: talking with another about writing, discussing risks, making and recovering from false starts—in short, collaborating. One might consider, for instance, Ezra Pound's work with T.S. Eliot on *The Wasteland* or Max Perkins' correspondence with F. Scott Fitzgerald as great moments in peer tutoring. Unfortunately, as we know, *lab* as in writing lab came to connote a marginal place where the marginal student attends to the teacher's marginal symbols on grammar errors. In such a relation, we see the beginnings of the binary split Thomas Hemmeter traces whereby the classroom is privileged and the lab subordinated.

One might imagine an alternate history in which writing programs and writing labs integrated themselves to form a pedagogy by which all students in all writing courses spent time in both classroom and lab, with the lab as a place where students worked on the same things they worked on in class but differently. In most cases, this alternate history did not occur because, among other reasons, knowledge about collaborative learning was neither as plentiful nor as widespread as it is today. But in a limited sense it did occur because lab personnel refused to see themselves as grammar grinds. However, these efforts went on covertly, the lab folk reading the lab metaphor one way, the writing program reading it another. Thus, the lab, both as signifier and signified, was the site of conflicting pedagogies, ideologies, and intentions that persist today, though increasingly in less pronounced forms as a result of the work on collaborative learning.

Still larger forces than writing program/writing lab skirmishes contributed to the pejoration of *lab*. First, the post-war economy of the late 1970s was a time of economic recession. With staggering inflation and U.S. industrial and economic power declining in world markets, federal and state governments collected and allocated less funding for higher education. Add to the recession the resulting unemployment rates, which often drove the unemployed to school, and one can argue that even had university administrations, writing programs, and writing labs been in accord, it is unlikely that the funding would have been available to fulfill the most optimistic vision of the lab metaphor. With neither funding nor agreement on what labs should be, they were allocated the dowdy facilities often misguidedly romanticized in writing lab literature.

These digs sometimes seemed appropriate to those in English Departments because anyone who had studied a literature specialty but could not find a job could be suspected of deficiencies, despite a glutted market of Ph.D.s (itself a condition of multiple sociohistorical forces). That these people were willing to teach remedial composition, or even worse work in writing labs, often without promise of tenure, placed them on the academic margins. This tale of woe has been told too many times. In the worst cases, directors in this situation saw the position as a way to get a foot in the door of academe and were content to leave students to work on drill exercises, audio cassettes, or computer terminals while they themselves worked to publish in their literature specialties in hopes of either earning teaching assignments in literature or moving on to other institutions. In contrast, many others made writing labs their specialty, writing and researching in the field, working to establish writing lab publications and organizations, and building labs that might begin to fill their version of the metaphor.

This cultural sketch of the 1970s, a thumbnail history of the forces resulting in marginalization, applies to writing centers whether we call them clinics, labs, or centers, but I think it has more bearing on the designation *lab*. The idea of experimentation and innovation, multiple possibility and productive chaos, which informed the metaphor for those who chose to call their enterprises labs persists today as many of them have largely succeeded in maintaining this sense in the praxis of their labs as microcultures. For this reason, I believe the lab metaphor has not gone the way of the clinic metaphor. Still, for those who read the metaphor pejoratively, it is a short step to making jokes about students being dissected in the writing lab or tutors creating Frankenstein monsters.

The historical and cultural contexts contained in the lab metaphor at once parallel and vary from those contained in the notion of a writing center. The writing center metaphor likely has connotative affinities with such compounds as convention center or community center, with *center* defined as "the main area for a particular activity or interest, or the like" (*OED*, 1036). This definition evokes the communal aspect of the center as a microculture in which camaraderie replaces the competitive atmosphere of the classroom. But as with the lab metaphor, other academic cultures had their own readings, seeing the metaphor as a euphemism for clinic or lab. We see this notion at work when *center* is used to form such compounds as English Skills Center, Basic Skills Center, or even Writing Skills Center, for *skills,* as Christina Murphy points out, connotes "a mechanistic model of parts being put together to make a whole" (277). In contrast, yoked simply with *writing, center* forms a bold and audacious metaphor aspiring to powerful definitions as in "the center of a circle, of revolution, of centripetal attraction; and connected uses" (*OED,* 1035). In this broad sense, for writers of the 1920s, Paris was a writing center.

Aspiring to this sense on campus is to move toward empowerment, not only by claiming to be central to all writers but also through such activities as the training of teaching assistants, faculty workshops for writing across the curriculum, credit courses, grammar hotlines, and tutoring for standardized tests such as the NTE and GRE. Increasing both the profile and prestige of the writing center, these efforts aspire, in Stephen North's words, to "make writing centers the centers of consciousness abut writing on campus, a kind of physical locus for the ideas and ideals of college or university or high school commitment or writing" (446). While certainly facilities called labs may hold and fulfill similar aspirations, the center metaphor encompasses them.

But this sense of the metaphor carries the dangers of assimilation as well as the potential for empowerment as it further imbricates writing centers in university culture, defining them beyond the nurturing communities they often see themselves as. For some, this is reason for trepidation. North, though supporting expansion, argues that writing centers must be valued "on their own terms, as places whose primary responsibility, whose only reason for being, is to talk to writers" (446). He worries that broader services make centers like "some marginal ballplayer... doing whatever it takes to stay on the team" (446). Summerfield expresses her astonishment and suspicion at the plush facilities of some of today's writing centers (9), implying that they are allowing themselves to be co-opted by the powers that be. Warnock and Warnock have argued that to some degree "it is probably a mistake for centers to seek integration into the established institution" (22). While the Warnocks do not advocate a lack of involvement, they advise that maintaining a certain sense of marginality will enable centers to retain a necessary "critical consciousness" (22).

Maintaining critical consciousness is indeed necessary. As we enter into alliances in the macroculture of the institution, we should examine them carefully. For instance, in some institutions the writing center's role in writing across the curriculum often translates into grammar across the curriculum, leaving us back at square one, clinics by another name. Likewise, in preparing students for standardized tests, such as the PPST or NTE, we risk assimilation if we do so uncritically.

Equally important, as Irene Lurkis Clarke has argued, we must maintain critical consciousness about ourselves. Reports by Diana George, Karen Rodis, and Lea Masiello and Malcolm Hayward all tell us prejudices toward and misconceptions about writing centers still exist. Even without this documented history, we need only cite examples in job advertisements for directors to know that in many quarters centers are still perceived as remedial fix-it shops run by the underpaid who cannot find jobs elsewhere. These prejudices and misconceptions hurt, especially since they have persisted for a long time.

One response is to draw angrily inward, to buy into the metaphor of the center as enclosed, to set up a we/they binary in which those not affiliated with writing centers are vilified and martyrdom becomes a dogma by which we comfort and elevate ourselves by rationalizing that we accept these conditions because we are so dedicated to and believe so strongly in what we do. When we feel this way, we withdraw into the microculture of the center, taking solace in the spirit of community we enjoy in working closely with our tutors and the students frequenting the center. Situated thus, we emphasize our differences, alienating ourselves and others.

This perspective leads to what Hemmeter has identified as "a discourse articulated in dualities" (37) opposing the center and the classroom. One could expand these dualities to oppose center and writing program, center and institution. This binary logic has often reified administration as a Dickensian chancery, vilified classroom teachers as current-traditionalist Gradgrinds, but sanctified writing center folk as kind, liberal, nurturing, and theoretically hip advocates of the poor, oppressed student.

Granted these characterizations may sometimes hold true, but probably more often they do not. Masiello and Hayward report, for instance, that between 1984 and 1987 at Indiana University of Pennsylvania, teachers' perceptions of the writing center increasingly matched those of center personnel. In "Talking to the Boss," Diana George informs us that "Department chairs are much more interested in the workings of writing centers than we think they are" (38).

I am not advocating that we forget our heritage on the margins. But while remembering our marginalization, we should avoid romanticizing tutoring on torn couches in paint-peeled rooms. As Gary Waller writes,

> in order to speak meaningfully to and within a dominant discourse, we must be inserted within it instead of trying to create an alternative outside. Deliberately choosing to be marginalized is a kind of masochism, the root of martyrdom. . . . Discursive structures do change, but they do so from within a given state of affairs. (11)

Like Waller, I would argue that only from the inside can we define our own metaphors to make what others talk about when they talk about writing centers and our talk about them one and the same.

This goal, however, will always remain elusive, and though to pursue it is to continually empower ourselves, to achieve it would be to arrive at definition, a comfortable but naive position. As Muriel Harris reminds us, "the idea of a generic writing center makes us uneasy because it is a truism of this field that writing centers tend to differ from one another because they have evolved within different kinds of institutions and different writing programs and therefore serve different needs" (15). Here Harris recognizes the cultural situatedness of particular centers. And though I have attempted to place our defining metaphors in historical contexts, I recognize the illusory elements in diachronic approaches to history. Culture and history are synchronous. Put concretely, for a writing center at one school it may be 1991; for a center at another it may be 1970. As Stuart Hall argues,

> In serious, critical intellectual work, there are no "absolute beginnings" and few unbroken continuities. Neither the endless unwinding of "tradition," so beloved on the History of Ideas, nor the absolutism of "epistemological rupture," punctuating Thought into its "false" and "correct" parts . . . will do. What we find, instead, is an untidy but characteristic unevenness of development. (57)

Though Hall is writing of culture in total, his comments apply equally to our attempts to define writing centers. From this perspective, our attempts at definition, though constantly necessary, are always already doomed to fail. This thought, however, should not be depressing but invigorating, for the notion of definition, a word etymologically rooted in *finish* and *finite* smacks of closure, of completion, of death, while the "human noise" we make in our centers and in writing center discourse is clearly a vital sign of life.

Works Cited

Bakhtin, M.M. *The Dialogic Imagination.* Ed. Michael Holquist. Trans. Caryl Emerson and Michael Holquist. Austin: U of Texas P, 1981.

Carver, Raymond. *What We Talk About When We Talk About Love.* New York: Knopf, 1981.

Clark, Irene Lurkis. "Maintaining Chaos in the Writing Center: A Critical Perspective On Writing Center Dogma." *The Writing Center Journal* 11.1 (1990): 81-93.

Faigley, Lester. "Competing Theories of Process: A Critique and Proposal." *College English* 48 (1986): 527-542.

George, Diana. "Talking to the Boss: A Preface." *The Writing Center Journal* 9.1 (1988): 37-44.

Hall, Stuart. "Cultural Studies: Two Paradigms." *Media, Culture, and Society* 2 (1980): 52-72.

Harris, Muriel. "What's Up and What's In: Trends and Traditions in Writing Centers." *The Writing Center Journal* 11.1 (1990): 15-25.

Hemmeter, Thomas. "The 'Smack of Difference': The Language of Writing Center Discourse." *The Writing Center Journal* 11.1 (1990): 35-48.

Masiello, Lea and Malcolm Hayward. "The Faculty Survey: Identifying Bridges Between the Classroom and the Writing Center." *The Writing Center Journal* 11.2 (1991): 73-79.

Murphy, Christina. "Writing Centers in Context: Responding to Current Educational Theory." *The Writing Center: New Directions.* Eds. Ray Wallace and Jeanne Simpson. New York: Garland, 1991: 276-288.

North, Stephen. "The Idea of a Writing Center." *College English* 46 (1984): 433-446.

The Oxford English Dictionary. 2nd ed. Vols. 2,3,8. 20 Vols. Oxford: Clarendon Press, 1989.

Rodis, Karen. "Mending the Damaged Path: How to Avoid a Conflict of Expectations When Setting up a Writing Center." *The Writing Center Journal* 10.2 (1990): 45-57.

Runciman, Lex. "Defining Ourselves: Do We Really Want to Use the Word Tutor." *The Writing Center Journal* 11.1 (1990): 27-34.

Shaughnessy, Mina P. "Diving In: An Introduction to Basic Writing." *College Composition and Communication* 27 (1976): 234-239.

Summerfield, Judith. "Writing Centers: A Long View." *The Writing Center Journal* 8.2 (1988): 3-9.

Waller, Gary. "Working within the Paradigm Shift: Poststructuralism and the College Curriculum." *ADE Bulletin* 81 (Fall 1985): 6-12.

Warnock, Tilly and John. "Liberatory Writing Centers: Restoring Authority to Writers." *Writing Centers: Theory and Administration.* Ed. Gary A. Olson. Urbana: NCTE, 1984: 16-23.

Williams, Raymond. *The Long Revolution.* London: Chatto and Windus, 1961.

Writing Center Directors:
The Search for Professional Status

by Gary A. Olson and Evelyn Ashton-Jones

During the past decade, the pages of *WPA* and other journals have recorded our efforts to define our roles as writing program administrators. In the last few years in particular, we have begun to experience a period of intense self-scrutiny, evidenced by a sharp increase in the number of books and articles published on the subject. However, preoccupied with our roles in managing university-wide writing programs, we have perhaps paid too little attention to the one writing program administrator who could benefit most from our understanding: the writing center director.

The role of the writing center director has never been adequately defined, and center directors are thus experiencing a kind of identity crisis. The lack of consensus about the center director's role is unfortunate, since the writing center is an essential complement to any comprehensive writing program.[1] Given current composition theory's emphasis on the process of composing and on the social context of language and knowledge, the writing center embodies what current theory says is most important about writing about pedagogy. If, in fact, as most compositionists argue, addressing individual writers' processes rather than a "text" is the way to help writers produce better writing, and if language and writing are social in nature, then the writing center very well may be the purest form of theory put into practice.[2] Thus, it is particularly unfortunate that the writing center director's role is so ill-defined.

Certainly, it is a difficult role to define because, like freshman English programs, writing centers are institution-specific in structure and function. Nevertheless, certain responsibilities and objectives of centers and their directors do remain constant, and identifying and analyzing these similarities will help us move toward a useful definition of the director's role. One step in defining this role is to explore how it is perceived by freshman English

---

Reprinted from *WPA: The Writing Program Administration*, Vol. 12, Nos. 1-2, Fall/Winter, 1988. Used by permission.

[1] This lack of consensus is reflected in the diverse institutional settings of writing centers. To get a sense of the great variety of writing center programs and their administrative relationships to university writing programs, see Connolly and Vilardi, Haring-Smith, Hartzog, and especially Kail and Trimbur.

[2] For one of the finest theoretical rationales for the efficacy of peer tutoring and writing center pedagogy, see Bruffee. See Trimbur as well as an excellent bibliographical survey of collaborative learning theories ("Collaborative Learning").

directors—those who on most campuses direct the overall writing program, or at least its largest component. Freshman English directors' conception of the status and responsibilities of the center director is especially important because both directors share a common goal: to provide quality writing instruction to students across the university. In addition, freshman English directors' perceptions provide a partial indication of how writing center directors are perceived by the faculty in general. To discover their perceptions, we surveyed 188 freshman English directors across the nation. (See the appendix for a description of this survey.)

Because the role of center director varies from institution to institution, the respondents' perceptions were not always unanimous; nevertheless, several clear patterns emerged in the responses. Overall, what we found is that freshman English directors are more likely to view the writing center director simply as an administrator, not as a teacher, a scholar, or even a writing specialist.

Teacher, Scholar, or Administrator?

For example, of twenty items listed on our questionnaire, the five rated most "essential" relate to the director's role as an administrator. Here are those five activities, followed by the percentage of respondents who consider them "essential":

- training tutors (84%)
- possessing strong communication skills (81%)
- monitoring the quality of the staff's tutoring (80%)
- communicating with the composition director (70%)
- recruiting and hiring tutors (69%)

Understandably, the respondents' most central concern is the director's role in recruiting, hiring, training, and monitoring tutors. In fact, in response to the open-ended questions supplementing the twenty-item rating scale, over 67 respondents (36%) identify one or a combination of these activities as the "*most* important aspect" of the director's job. As one respondent puts it, the writing center director is "above all responsible for ensuring that students have access to state-of-the-art tutoring."

Nor is it surprising that strong communication skills and regular communication with the composition director should rate so highly. The ability to communicate effectively would indeed seem to be essential for training and monitoring tutors and for working in conjunction with the composition director. In fact, in their prose remarks, many respondents link communication with interpersonal skills, saying these are "indispensable" for running a successful center. One respondent writes that the director must be able to interact effectively not only with the composition director but with "everyone from entering students to the Dean." Another sums up how crucial interpersonal skills are to the position: the writing center director must be "a specialist in constructive human relations."

While freshman English directors perceive the center director as an administrator, they are less inclined to see him or her as a "teacher," or at least this role is of lesser importance. For example, these five activities are among those that received the *lowest* "essential" rating:

- teaching writing courses (32%)
- receiving outstanding teaching evaluations for classroom teaching (23%)
- teaching courses in tutoring and composition pedagogy (21%)
- conducting writing workshops for the university community (15%)
- familiarizing faculty with new developments in composition (12%)

Clearly, of all twenty items, lowest in priority are those activities that involve teaching and interacting with people beyond the confines of the center. Classroom teaching is de-emphasized, especially teaching composition and pedagogy courses and receiving outstanding evaluations. For instance, fewer than a third of the respondents agree that it is "essential" for the director to teach writing courses, and only 15% that the director conduct university-wide workshops. Also, activities related to faculty development—being a teacher of fellow teachers—rank lowest of all. Only 12% of the respondents believe the director should "familiarize faculty with developments in composition."

While the center director's numerous responsibilities within the center might explain why composition directors de-emphasize classroom and workshop teaching, there is a surprising amount of disagreement about the center director's role as a teacher even within the center. Whether the center director should teach is uncertain. For example, a large number of respondents (40) don't believe the director should participate in tutoring—the center's version of teaching. Of the significant number who do believe the director should tutor students, many qualify their responses: the director should tutor "just enough to have a feel for students' needs" or "simply to remain in touch."[3] More importantly, it appears that not many respondents view tutoring students or training tutors as "real" teaching; even though they perceive tutor training as the single most important responsibility of the center director, their responses indicate that they do not define this activity—or tutoring students— as "teaching." John Trimbur, writing in *WPA*, describes this attitude as a product of "the academic caste system" and attributes it to the "traditional academic hierarchy's scale of values." According to this value system, Trimbur claims, the "writing center's time is less valuable than a faculty member's" ("Students" 34).

If freshman English directors do not recognize the center director as a "teacher," they appear equally disinclined to see the director as a "scholar" or as a "trained specialist." Only 33% say it is "essential" that the director "maintain scholarship." One respondent comments that scholarship might be

---

[3] Murray and Bannister asked center directors to rank their daily responsibilities in order of frequency; teaching and tutoring ranked low on the scale, well below advertising center services, handling public relations, and developing instructional exercises (11). Not only are center directors not perceived as teachers, but evidently they do, in fact, spend most of their time and energy in routine administrative activities.

"helpful if he or she has the time," and another explains that scholarship is not necessary because the director is a TA. To be fair, some respondents (three to be exact) mention that the director should possess "knowledge of current composition theory," and one states that the director should have a "national reputation as researcher"; but the great preponderance of respondents do not find scholarship to be important for center directors.

Of course, it can be argued that the writing center director does not need to be a scholar (or even a teacher) to run an effective center; that is, the director's position can be defined as purely administrative. And there may be some truth to this argument. But the center director's status reflects and represents the status of the center itself, and status in academe derives from scholarly credentials. Typically administrators—university provosts, department chairs, even freshman English directors—all prove themselves *first* as competent scholars *before* being given the responsibilities of administration. To the extent that these values do not apply to writing center directors, we can assume that the center director and the center itself are not valued in the academic community. And, perhaps more importantly, unlike many high-level administrative positions in the university, the position of writing center director is discipline-specific. Not only is it inextricably linked to an academic discipline—composition—but writing center direction itself is recognized as a legitimate "field," complete with an NCTE-sanctioned association, a professional journal and newsletter, and books on writing centers published by reputable houses, including NCTE. Thus, it seems unfair to suggest that center directors should remain purely "administrative" and, in so doing, to deny writing directors the same kind of professional recognition afforded most academic administrators and *all* other writing program administrators.

In addition, when asked whether the director should be a trained composition specialist, nearly a fourth said "no" or it "doesn't matter." One respondent writes, "It would be helpful if the director is a trained specialist, but above all she must be an administrator." This attitude sums up our main point: freshman English directors see center directors primarily as administrators and only secondarily, if at all, as teachers or scholars. As one respondent writes, "Other things are more important."[4]

In fact, many freshman English directors do not seem to view the director as a full faculty member who teaches and engages in scholarly research; this is reflected in answers to survey questions about the director's professional status. While it is true that 113 respondents believe the director should hold a tenure-track appointment—as most faculty do—the remainder (75) state that the director's appointment should be nontenure-track, joint faculty/staff, staff

---

[4] In fact, it seems that directors are perceived more as *supervisors* than as *administrators*. For example, the respondents most often describe the directors' activities in terms associated with "supervision": *oversee, maintain, run, coordinate, serve, compile, schedule*. Such terms appear much more frequently than do terms associated with active administration: *establish, develop, create, determine*. Even the jargon of the field reinforces this attitude: center directors, for instance, do not "teach" but "train"; their "tutors" are called "staff" or "personnel"; their students are "clients" or "tutees."

only, or that it does not matter at all. Few respondents write emphatically that the director's position should be "defined as a staff position." Others comment that because TA's direct their centers the question is irrelevant, and 17 write that "it doesn't matter; tenure or nontenure track—either could work." Thus, a substantial number of respondents do not acknowledge the director as fellow member of the faculty or simply are unconcerned.[5]

Teachers Without Voices: A Paradox of Power

What do the survey data tell us in general about the writing center director? In a way, they suggest that the center director is perceived as a kind of *wife*. Like the idealized support-mate Judy Syfers describes in her well-anthologized essay, the director is expected to keep a good house, to make sure the center "runs smoothly." She—and, incidentally, a substantial number of respondents use the generic "she"—even has a certain amount of power within her house, enough, at least, to make sure her charges behave. But her influence is confined within four walls; outside, she is voiceless, unable to participate as a full member of the large community. She is not encouraged to "work" as the real members of the academic community do, and when she is allowed to, she is certainly not compensated fully for her labor, since her labor is not truly valued by the community. In short, her place is in the home.

If this wife metaphor seems a bit forced, consider these representative responses to the question, "What important qualities and responsibilities are not listed on this questionnaire?":

- the writing center director should be "nice!" (The respondent included the exclamation point.)
- she should "know her place in the chain of command and respect it"
- she should be "friendly, cooperative, and have lots of personality"
- she should be "supportive but not critical"
- she should not only be "sensitive to the needs of others," but be able to "recognize what needs are not being met" and "respond to the needs of the university whatever they become"
- she should "maintain an inventory of equipment and supplies" (kitchen utensils, no doubt)
- and (believe it or not) she should "provide chocolate chip cookies to writing center clients"

Amusing? Perhaps on the surface. But the attitude underlying these remarks subtly helps prevent center directors from fulfilling their potential as teachers, scholars, and program administrators, and it keeps centers themselves from achieving their mission. As we all know, composition theory

---

[5] Over two-thirds of the center directors responding to Murray and Bannister's survey held nontenure track appointments (10).

stresses that the most effective pedagogy is one in which teachers interact with their students, in which teachers help writers find their own voices, their own *authority* to construct texts. Such theory also emphasizes that meaning-making is a communal, social activity. In no other place in the university is there a better opportunity to engage in this kind of interaction than in the writing center. Interactive learning is much more likely to occur during one-on-one or small group instruction in the center than in the typical teacher-centered classroom, or even in a class utilizing the workshop approach. Yet, it is sadly ironic that writing center directors, the very persons charged with empowering students to find their own voices, are themselves constrained from having a full voice in the academic community of their peers—thought of not as teachers, not as scholars, but simply as administrators.

We must make clear that in no way are we attempting to vilify freshman English directors. In fact, our experience is that by and large freshman English directors are generally supportive of center directors, especially since both program directors share mutual professional concerns. Rather, we interpret these survey data as indicative of the general perception of writing center directors within English departments. If anything, freshman English directors are probably more inclined to view center directors as fellow professionals than are typical faculty members who are not compositionists. And it is reasonable to assume that if freshman English directors have difficulty perceiving center directors as full colleagues, then non-composition faculty are even more likely to have trouble doing so.

Joining the Professional Conversation

If the writing center is ever to accomplish what it is designed to accomplish, these perceptions of center directors need to change. Directors should no longer be isolated within the non-threatening four walls of a "lab." Their position should be redefined so that they are recognized as true members of the academic community: as teachers, scholars, and administrators.

This goal can be achieved in several ways, and most successfully so, with the input and support of freshman English directors. First, the writing center director should be required to be a rhetoric and composition specialist, a person well-versed in theory of and research in both composition and writing centers. Second, along with NCTE and the National Writing Center Association (see Simpson), we believe the director should hold a tenure-track appointment and receive teaching credit for tutoring and training tutors, as well as release time for directing the center. Further, we believe that as a composition specialist, the director should participate fully in all aspects of the larger writing program, assisting in faculty development and policy-making. In fact, as a specialist in writing center administration, the director should be recognized as a co-equal of the freshman English director—both directors administering their own different but complementary writing programs.

The future of the writing center and the integrity of the larger writing program are directly linked to the professional status accorded their directors.

In order to ensure that our programs are coherent and effective, we should more fully integrate the center into the larger writing program, and its director into the academic community. Writing centers can then become, as Stephen North suggests in *College English*, "centers of consciousness about writing on campus, a kind of physical locus" for an institution's "commitment to writing." This is a status, North says, "they can achieve" (446).

That is, we should add, if we allow them to.

Appendix

To determine how composition directors perceive the role of the writing center director, we distributed a questionnaire during the winter of 1988 to freshman English directors across the nation. Targeting a range of institutions from medium-small to large, we selected 275 of these institutions at random, making sure, however, that every state was represented. One hundred eighty-eight directors (68%) completed and returned the questionnaire.

The questionnaire (printed on pages 54-55) solicits data about the tasks and responsibilities of directing a writing center. It asks respondents to rate twenty items on a four-point scale from "essential" to "unimportant." This continuum enabled the directors to rate the importance of each item, giving us a sense of their priorities. More importantly, however, the directors' priorities allowed us to determine the relative level of status writing center directors have or are expected to have. The remaining questions solicit brief answers.

Works Cited

Bruffee, Kenneth A. "Peer Tutoring and the Conversation of Mankind." *Writing Centers: Theory and Administration.* Ed. Gary A. Olson. Urbana: NCTE, 1984. 3-15.

Connolly, Paul, and Teresa Vilardi, eds. *New Methods in College Writing Programs: Theories in Practice.* New York: MLA, 1986.

Haring-Smith, Tori, ed. *A Guide to Writing Programs: Writing Centers, Peer Tutoring Programs, and Writing-Across-the-Curriculum.* Glenview, IL: Scott, 1985.

Hartzog, Carol P. *Composition and the Academy: A Study of Writing Program Administration.* New York: MLA, 1986.

Kail, Harvey, and John Trimbur. "The Politics of Peer Tutoring." *WPA: Writing Program Administration* 11.1-2 (1987): 5-12.

Murray, Patricia Y., and Linda Bannister. "The Status and Responsibilities of Writing Lab Directors: A Survey." *Writing Lab Newsletter* 9.6 (1985): 10-11.

North, Stephen M. "The Idea of a Writing Center." *College English* 46 (1984): 433-46.

Simpson, Jeanne H. "What Lies Ahead for Writing Centers: Position Statement on Professional Concerns." *Writing Center Journal* 5-6 (1985): 35-39.

Syfers, Judy. "I Want a Wife." *Ms.* Apr. 1972: 56.

Trimbur, John. "Collaborative Learning and Teaching Writing." *Perspectives on Research and Scholarship in Composition.* Eds. Ben W. McClelland and Timothy R. Donovan. New York: MLA, 1985. 87-109.

_____. "Students or Staff: Thoughts on the Use of Peer Tutors in Writing Centers." *WPA: Writing Program Administration* 7.1-2 (1983): 33-38.

Questionnaire

DIRECTIONS: The first 20 statements relate to activities and responsibilities of the writing center director. Please rate each one by checking the appropiate box. The remaining questions ask for brief answers.

	Essential	Important	Helpful	Unimportant
1. Recruits and hires tutors	☐	☐	☐	☐
2. Trains tutors	☐	☐	☐	☐
3. Publicizes center services	☐	☐	☐	☐
4. Has access to administrators beyond the English dept.	☐	☐	☐	☐
5. Maintains his or her own scholarship	☐	☐	☐	☐
6. Teaches courses in tutoring and composition pedagogy	☐	☐	☐	☐
7. Possesses strong communication skills	☐	☐	☐	☐
8. Creates writing center policy	☐	☐	☐	☐
9. Controls writing center budget	☐	☐	☐	☐
10. Expresses policy in written documents	☐	☐	☐	☐
11. Stays current with pedagogical applications of computers	☐	☐	☐	☐
12. Conducts writing workshops for the university community	☐	☐	☐	☐
13. Familiarizes faculty with new developments in composition	☐	☐	☐	☐
14. Teaches writing courses	☐	☐	☐	☐
15. Receives outstanding evaluations for his or her own classroom teaching	☐	☐	☐	☐
16. Monitors quality of staff's tutoring	☐	☐	☐	☐
17. Remains current with developments in the field	☐	☐	☐	☐
18. Communicates regularly with composition director	☐	☐	☐	☐
19. Communicates regularly with department chair	☐	☐	☐	☐
20. Remains accessible throughout the workday	☐	☐	☐	☐

Questionnaire
(continued)

21. What important qualities and responsibilities are not listed on the previous page?

_____

_____

_____

_____

22. Who should be the primary policymaker for the writing center?

☐ writing center director   ☐ freshman English director

☐ department chair   ☐ other

23. What is the *most* important aspect of the writing center director's job? _____

_____

_____

_____

_____

24. Should the center director be a trained composition specialist?

☐ yes   ☐ no   ☐ doesn't matter

25. Should the director participate in tutoring?

☐ yes   ☐ no

If so, how many hours per week?

26. What kind of appointment should the center director have?

☐ tenure track   ☐ non tenure track staff   ☐ joint staff/faculty   ☐ other

27. Should the director have release time for directing the center?

☐ yes   ☐ no

If so, how much? _____

28. In your department, whom does the writing center director report to? _____

_____

_____

_____

What Lies Ahead For Writing Centers: Position Statement on Professional Concerns

by Jeanne H. Simpson

The existence of a National Writing Centers Association and half a dozen regional writing center organizations suggests that the idea of writing centers has matured. We have a growing library of writing center books available to us, two publications, and an annual round of meetings and workshops. All this evidence that writing centers have arrived may lead us into complacency, into the relief felt after a battle has been won. We should be wary of that complacency and ask ourselves just where we are and where we go from here?

The evidence indicates that we have achieved a kind of legitimacy: writing centers have become academically respectable programs. Even though Stephen North must remind the world that its perceptions of writing centers are often wrong, the fact is that the academic world now accepts writing centers.

The writing center movement has expanded because writing center people have learned to communicate—to form a network, to transmit information, and to exchange assistance. Thus the isolation of individual writing centers has ended.

Great. Now what should we do and what should we not do with what we have created?

First, we should not assume that our work is over—that now we can glide easily along, meeting a couple of times a year, giving or attending a workshop here and there, assuming that writing centers are now a permanent part of the academic scene. The changes in writing centers—in what they mean and how they have been used, funded, and administered over the last decade—should tell us that fluidity is a fact we must accept. Writing centers unquestionably will continue to change. We must be careful to use the structure we have built as a way of detecting those changes, of evaluating them and of adjusting to the changes that represent improvement and working to prevent those we consider harmful.

In the past, the writing center movement has operated largely as a support system, a way of keeping lots of worried people afloat. That function will

Reprinted from *The Writing Center Journal* 5.2/6.1 (1985): 35-39. Used by permission.

continue, but it seems likely that the movement, with its publications and meetings, will increasingly function as a system for addressing issues. For instance, I find many writing center people who see no problem with giving a writing center a strictly remedial focus. To me, that approach is anathema. But we have to understand each other; we have to listen to each other, or we will both lose. Similarly, I oppose the idea of incorporating writing labs into larger "learning centers" in which tutoring for several disciplines occurs. Yet people whose work I admire and whose centers have been models for mine are moving in this direction. We need to make opportunities to listen to each other, to ask questions, to examine arguments for both sides.

These are issues within the writing center movement. At the same time, we need to continue the dialogue between writing center people and others, especially administrators—those who control our budgets. In that dialogue, we still have much to accomplish. One effort obviously will be directed toward improving the conditions under which we work. Although the idea of writing centers may be firmly established, writing center directors still face a struggle to move out of positions of relative powerlessness. One of the immediate purposes of having a national organization is to lend the strength of the organization to the struggle for control of writing centers. At the same time, the existence of the organization implies a sense of professionalism. If we demand working conditions that encourage the best from us, we must also be willing to listen and make reasonable compromises. The situation is a reciprocal one—the more professional we are, the more we can ask for; the more we ask for, the more likely it is that we will be recognized as professionals.

Presenting writing center directors as professionals is, in fact, one of the most important tasks facing the writing center movement. The National Writing Centers Association has been collecting ideas from the membership on this subject, and the results are reported below as a position statement on the professional concerns of writing center directors. The statement explains the need for appropriate preparation for writing center directorships, asks for clear job descriptions, outlines the ideal conditions of a directorship, and suggests guidelines for directing a writing center. The statement is intended to guide both writing center directors and administrators who hire and supervise them.

Although most of us are unlikely to encounter working conditions as ideal as those suggested by the position statement, we can regard the statement as a "basis" for negotiation. Often, writing center directors work in dreadful situations not because administrators are intentionally making things difficult but because no one has a clear idea of how things should be. The existence of a position statement endorsed by our national organization should encourage a trend toward graduate programs that provide specific training for writing center directors. Surely it is our obligation to foster such programs since they will be a source of our future leadership.

The statement is the product of effort by the Executive Board and the Professional Concerns Committee of the National Writing Centers Association, dozens of writing center directors who participated in NWCA workshops and who answered our letters, and individuals who took time to answer my questions.

Position Statement on Professional Concerns of Writing Center Directors

The directorship of a writing center is a professional position, one that requires specialized preparation and administrative experience. It should be recognized as such and should carry the same rights and responsibilities as other professional faculty positions.

The National Writing Centers Association opposes the hiring of part-time faculty as directors unless they are given full access to the rights, privileges and services available to regular faculty. The National Writing Centers Association opposes the practice of establishing temporary directorships and filling them with temporary or unprepared personnel. Establishment of a writing center should be a long-term, fully budgeted commitment on the part of an institution, since these conditions are necessary for a writing center to meet any but the most modest goals.

Therefore, the National Writing Centers Association recommends that institutions employing writing center directors provide the following working conditions:

1. Establishment of a directorship should begin with a definition of appropriate preparation for the position.

2. Directorships should carry sufficient stability and continuity to provide for sound educational programs and planning.

3. Directorships should not be assigned to persons against their will.

4. Directorships should be considered faculty and administrative positions rather than staff positions.

5. Directorships should include access to promotion, salary, tenure, and travel funds equivalent to that provided for other faculty and administrators.

6. Requirements for retention, promotion and tenure should be clearly defined and should take into consideration the particular demands of the position.

7. Directorships should be established with clear formulas for determining equivalencies, such as released time for administration and tutor training. The National Writing Centers Association recommends that, where it is appropriate, tutor training programs should be considered courses and should have credit units assigned to them.

8. Directorships should be established within a clearly defined administrative structure so that directors know to whom they are responsible and whom they supervise.

9. Directorships should include access to administrative support—such as clerical help, computer time, and duplicating services—that is equal in quality to that available to other program directors.

10. Evaluation of writing center directors should be conducted by persons in the same area of specialization.

The National Writing Centers Association offers institutions the following
guidelines for developing job descriptions for writing center directorships and
for evaluating the credentials of applicants for these positions:

1. Essential preparation for a writing center director should include the
following:

- experience in teaching composition and rhetoric
- knowledge of theories of learning
- knowledge of research methods
- knowledge of evaluation methods
- experience in developing and evaluating materials

2. In addition, academic preparation or experience in the following areas
should be considered appropriate credentials:

- accounting
- basic business administration
- psychology
- personnel management
- information systems
- computer technology
- records management
- decision making
- writing experience
- grant writing and administration
- curriculum design
- methods of teaching English as a second language

3. The responsibilities of a writing center director should be the following:

- to provide and preserve a sense of direction for the writing center
- to shape the curriculum of the writing center
- to teach in the writing center's programs
- to prepare and/or purchase materials needed in the writing center
- to consult with writing center staff and with faculty on writing
  instruction
- to select and train tutors
- to supervise tutors
- to evaluate tutors regularly
- to keep careful records that are made available as required to students, teachers, tutors, and administrators
- to administer budget allocations responsibly
- to ensure continuous funding of the writing center
- to publicize the writing center
- to maintain communication with the institution's other writing programs
- to work with faculty in writing-across-the-curriculum programs
- to continue professional growth through appropriate reading, courses,
  studies, research, and participation in professional organizations and
  workshops

- to organize all activities of the writing center
- to provide for regular reports on the activities, progress, and problems of the writing center
- to provide for regular and thorough evaluation of the writing center's program.

The National Writing Centers Association offers the following basic guidelines for operating a writing center:

1. Because writing is a skill used in all subjects and at all levels of the educational process, a writing center should be considered a support service for the entire institution rather than simply for a single department. Although the budget and staff of a writing center may come from a single department, the mission of the center and its constituencies should encompass the entire institution.

2. Regardless of its organization and design, a writing center should be based on the idea of individualized instruction. Therefore, materials and methods chosen for writing centers should be adjusted to individual needs.

3. Access to the writing center should not be limited by a student's level of preparation or physical capabilities.

4. The writing center should have instructional goals that are clearly understood by tutors and students.

5. Writing center records should provide for continuity of instruction regardless of how its staff is organized.

6. A writing center should have clearly stated, consistent, and ethical principles to guide its tutors. The National Writing Centers Association suggests the following:
- Tutors should be provided clear explanations of writing center procedures.
- Tutors should neither directly nor indirectly offer criticism of a teacher's assignments, methods, or grading practices.
- Tutors should be given guidelines for defining acceptable and unacceptable intervention in a student's writing process.

The spirit of this statement is one of professionalism. The writing center movement has gone beyond the "can do" stage of scrounged materials and informal communications. However, we must not lose either the energy or the commitment that characterized our initial stages. A change in style need not affect our basic purpose of making writing centers exemplary programs that offer students an opportunity to develop as writers.

Works Cited

North, Stephen. "The Idea of a Writing Center." *College English* 46 (1984): 433-46.

Writing Centers: A Long View

by Judith Summerfield

William James says that we live our lives engaged in two fundamentally distinctive activities: *flights* and *perchings*. When we are in *flight,* we are doing, making, surviving, carrying on the work we need to do to stay alive. In James Britton's terms, we are *participating* in the work of the world. We are participants.

When we *perch*, we step back and look at what we have made, how we have done our work, what in fact worked and what didn't, what we would do over again, what now makes sense, what doesn't. Our primary mental activity now is *evaluating*, making sense of, interpreting, criticizing. We are now *spectators* of our own lives, of our makings and doing.

These two activities characterize my involvement with writing centers. For nearly all of the Seventies, I was a participant: doing, making, creating a writing center, paving new ground at the college, establishing satellite programs at local "feeder" high schools—all that is involved in *doing* a writing center. For the past five years or so, I've had the opportunity to take a long perching, a long view, to think about what writing centers are all about, to be a spectator.

About five years ago, I was asked to retire from the writing center at my college. I suppose I had been too noisy, too demanding, too persistent. I kept repeating myself. Parrot-like, I kept asking *why*? And *why not*? Why isn't there more money? Why can't we hire more tutors? Why can't we set up a course for tutors? Why can't we extend hours? Why can't we pay our tutors more? Why can't we get a larger room? Why can't we paint the walls?

At that time, the paint on the walls had dramatically chipped away—the hospital green looked shabbier and shabbier, and with the prospect of increased budget cuts, our spirits reflected those drab walls. I thought a coat of paint might brighten us, as well as the room—a converted class-room that was bursting at the seams.

The bureaucratic machinery opposed the new paint: every turn we took, we hit a stone wall. No, we could not get the writing center painted. When we decided to paint the room ourselves, we heard that the college regulated against using anything but college paint. Finally, after two years, the walls were painted—a shocking, blinding aqua-blue—the only paint, they told us, that was available at that time. Take it or leave it, we were told. We took it.

Reprinted from *The Writing Center Journal* 8.2 (1988): 3-9. Used by permission.

In short, I guess, I was a nuisance. I wouldn't take *no* for an answer. At one point, I suggested that the Writing Center break from the particular administrative, bureaucratic position we were in. I had called for civil war, secession, independence. I received a polite letter, saying something about the fact that institutions benefited from "rotation of administrators." I was to be *rotated*.

So it has been five years since I've set foot in the writing center. The message was clear—get out and stay out, and don't give the new directors any ideas. *Behave*. A time of nay-saying had set in.

It had been a time of yea-saying when the writing center had been created in 1972. The Writing Workshop (directed at the outset by Sandra Schor; I, one of her assistants, took over the directorship in 1974) had grown up and out of the great social experiment of Open Admissions at the City University of New York. In those years, we were in the hot-seat of school change. The University made a commitment to the under-classes of New York City: we would open our doors to all who wanted to attend. We would make it possible for them to pursue their own American dreams. We would open *new* doors. In those early experimental, exhilarating years, the writing center, its actual establishment, was seen as integral to these political, social, and pedagogic experiments.

It had been this social context that had induced the work of Mina Shaughnessy, Robert Lyons, Donald McQuade, Marie Ponsot, and Kenneth Bruffee. A new population of students demanded that we look at what we had been doing traditionally, habitually, in the college classroom. The spirit of innovation, of daring, of saying "*Yes*—it's possible"—was everywhere. It was a time when instructors opened the doors of their classrooms. Instructors who were faced with a new population of college student left the privacy, and the virtual isolation, of the classroom and peeked out into the halls and asked for support from their colleagues. "What can I do?" they asked each other, and the pronoun shifted to *we*—"What can *we* do?"—as a spirit of collaboration was born, it seems, almost overnight. One day we were working there alone, and the next day we were all engaged—instructor, student, administrator, tutor—in collaborative *doing*. Nothing seemed impossible.

We began to school ourselves: the maps had not yet been drawn. The territory was new. There were voices we called upon: Jerome Bruner on learning, James Moffett on the universe of discourse, William Labov on Black English, Noam Chomsky on transformational-generative grammar, but those were the days before ethnography, word-processing, collaborative learning, writing across the disciplines. I suppose that some administrators expected us to do no more than help students write correct sentences. But we weren't satisfied. We read all the grammar books we could find: transformational-generative, structural, Allen's X-word grammar, and traditional grammars. We read social histories, to try to place ourselves. We set up informal seminars for ourselves: one summer some of us decided to read James Britton's *Language and Learning* and *Writing Abilities*. We read and read, and when we had the time, we talked about what we had read.

Mostly, we *did*. We taught courses and ran tutor-training sessions and tutored students ourselves. We recognized that the tutors were key to the whole enterprise, that we were schooling a generation of teachers, some of whom are still the best teachers in our writing program. We started a weekly newsletter. We printed collections of students' writing. Of tutors' writings. We read each others' works. We put tutors in the classroom. We brought classes to the writing center. It was an extraordinary time of learning for all of us—and for many of us, even though we may not be directly related to writing centers now, the spillover still lasts, for it is in the writing center that many of us cut our teeth on a *kind* of doing that we still do. It is that which I will focus on now—what is it that we still do that is worth doing? What is it that is worth preserving? What is it that came out of these early experiments with writing centers?

The *it* can be summarized in a clause: that all teaching, tutoring, writing, reading, indeed, all languaging acts, are ineluctably social. The workshop experiment forced that upon us. Taking the long view, we might say that there have been two stages in this process:

1) The first was the focus on the individual, on the individual *process*.

2) The second is a focus on the individual in context, or to use Vygotsky's term: *The Mind in Society*.

Let me reflect on the first stage. What we began to recognize, particularly through the one-to-one encounter in tutoring was that we are all different. There are different ways of composing, of reading, of experiencing the world. Different minds, different experiences. Those of us who came to tutoring from teaching quickly realized that we could no longer construe our students as a homogeneous blob. Our perceptions and experiences of teaching and learning and language had fundamentally changed, not only in degree, but in kind. These shifts we see reflected in just about every textbook in the field: the shift from something called *product* to *process*. The focus on revision, on collaborative-learning, on peer-editing all began to make its way into our jargon under the catch-word *process*.

At its best, researchers began to explore the ways writers compose, revise, construct meaning. We all now take for granted that writing is *recursive*, a move back and forth, a taking in of what has been generated as we consider what is to come next. We know, for example, from Sondra Perl's research that inexperienced writers stop themselves, as they go back over the words they have already written, crossing out, correcting, rewriting the surface features, and not allowing themselves to write long stretches of discourse.

At its worst, the process of *process* has become reified, so that those who have not plumbed the depths of what it means to compose, to construct meaning, make *static* a fluid act. Look to the textbooks now that offer process in *stages*: first pre-write, then draft, then revise. At its worst, process has become institutionalized—one institution I know dictates that all students in all composition courses *must* write a certain number of drafts. The writer who does, in fact, get *it* all down in a first/final draft is highly suspect. Revision, institutionalized in these ways, is just as suspect as any other description that turns prescriptive.

When I hear a program or a text described as taking a "process-approach," I am immediately suspicious. And what I often find is that the emperor is not wearing any clothes, even though he claims to have a new wardrobe. My bet is that those who talk in these ways have had nothing to do with writing centers (or teaching), that they claim to understand what composing is all about, but their agenda is pre-emptive: it is an agenda. In the same way, I now see textbooks advertised as promoting a *workshop* approach—what precisely that means must be questioned. We must become skeptical, to make certain that the *workshop approach* does not become reified, institutionalized, and therefore, neutered, as *process* has become.

What is truly valuable about the experiment of writing centers/workshops has to do with the second stage, with the recognition of the social nature of language and learning. A genuine workshop is one that builds a community of writers, readers, listeners, talkers, thinkers, who are encouraged to understand how they write as individuals, but equally important, as members of a community. The process-approach lays on the individual student a method. The true workshop approach inquires into the mind working in society.

In a genuine workshop, writing is an interactive engagement between writer and reader. It is not a one-dimensional focus on what the writer does. Rather, writing is seen in terms of what it does *to* a reader, or better, to *readers*. In this dynamic interaction, the words a writer writes come to life as they are received, reacted to, by a live reader(s) who reads not only out of her own personal preferences, biases, associations, memories, but also, out of what Stanley Fish calls interpretive communities. We do not write in a social vacuum. Nor do we read in a social vacuum. And the writing center, given its constraints of grades and exams and institutional requirements, allows us to make our own courses—to construct what Robert Scholes calls a "local curriculum" which grows out of the students' needs and interests and the instructor/tutor's awareness of those needs. In the context of schooling in the academy, the workshop offers an extraordinary freedom. The agendas can be ours. We do not need to be cut off from students at the ends of semesters. Our courses can continue. Even for years. And when it works, we find a possibility for growth, for a kind of recycling: students become tutors become teachers. I have seen it happen.

The nature of the writing center, then, is community—and that is precisely why it can become problematic. Institutions don't necessarily *like* little communities within their walls, for there is power in numbers. As students come together, they can ask *why* and *why not?* "Why is my reading of this poem *wrong?"* Why is this phrase *awkward*? What does this grade mean? Why can I revise in this class and not in that one? Why did instructor X give this paper an A and instructor Y give the same paper a C-? How can you write a journal if it's graded? Who am I writing for? How can writing be "free"? Tutors and students question together. They often conclude that teachers in classrooms take particular stands in order to keep control, in order to manage behavior. These conversations challenge the "nature" of authority and expose underlying values, politics, ideology, and epistemology.

For we are talking about nothing less than this—about ways of knowing the world, about ways the dominant culture works (in the schools), about domination and subjugation, in the complex arena of writing and reading texts. If I, teacher Z, say that *this* is what this text means, then who are you to disagree with me? And if you persist, just remember that it is I who give the grade. (I grow uneasy with the loose usage of the word *power:* if we, as teachers set assignments, evaluate texts, and *give grades,* then we are the primary holders of power; to deny so is to deny the fundamental "nature" of schooling in the culture.)

As I look back now, from my long perching, I revise the evaluations that I began with when I started this text. For some time, when I stopped to think about my ousting from the writing center, I construed it personally. I had annoyed the authorities. I had asked too many questions, demanded too much. I had been made to feel that I hadn't *behaved* properly. But this is a personal reading. There's more I see now, with my advantage of spectatorship, my advantage of time. I can talk about this personal story within a public context, a history.

The history has to do with what happened to CUNY and its budget crises of the mid- to late-Seventies, with the fact that yea-saying had turned, overnight, into nay-saying. It was money—economics—that changed the environment from positive to negative. But it is not just CUNY that we must talk about; we must take a hard look at what happened to the experiments of the Sixties, with the fact that the doors that had been opened now began to close. You could see it happening. Open Admissions faded into the woodwork. The impetus to interact with colleagues turned sour as jobs were cut. The Sixties had brought Directors of Writing Programs together to form CAWS (the CUNY Association of Writing Supervisors) and had led to WPA (Writing Program Administrators)—these are the direct outgrowths of those times. But the energies that had been poured into collaboration now began to shift. The history of this experiment has not yet been written: perhaps we're still too close. And some of us have not yet given up some of the battle.

But it's clear to me that energies are now being directed to two areas: testing and computers. If you look at each—testing and computers—if you read these "new" movements politically, you'll see that each calls for the individual to confront his situation alone. One, the individual student facing a test that will determine whether or not she will be allowed to earn a college degree. Each man for himself because that is the nature of the beast. No collaborative activity is admitted when one is *taking a test.* That is the ineluctable fact.

In the same way, while the computer/word-processor may make writing and revision easier, it CAN threaten the community of the writing center. I know that much of the time now spent in the writing center at my school is spent on tutoring students to pass the CUNY Writing Assessment Test: that is the first order of business. I know, as well, that we are fortunate in having a director who is using computers in ways that do not threaten the collaborative community of the writing center. But I know, too, that the temptation must be great to call up a software program and call that tutoring.

I wasn't fighting for blue walls, for new paint, for more money: I was fighting for a *context*. The more I explored it, the richer it became, and the possibilities for an epidemic, an explosion of this kind of learning and languaging, made me dizzy. And the corresponding movements in other fields—of reader-response theories, of semiotics, cultural anthropology, sociolinguistics, of ethnography itself—all seemed to point in a direction that was, indeed, revolutionary. Shirley Brice Heath talks about the same kind of spirit in her seminal work, *Ways With Words,* in which she describes the community spirit and activity that sparked a small Southern town in the late Sixties, early Seventies, where school officials, teachers, parents, business-men, children, clergymen, were working together on the *possibilities* of integration. Her epilogue, however, tells us that the participants mostly gave up or were pushed out, as money dried up, as government grants ended, as disillusionment set in, as the realization became clear—that the system would need to be dynamited in order for it to change. She had spent ten years there. Now she is a spectator of that past, just as we all are when we look back on the past and try to make sense of it.

Now that I come to the end of this text, I see the past a little more clearly—for the moment. The *no* I kept hearing had to do with the times, with going back, with pulling back, with the Nixons of the time saying: watch out for those who assemble. There is power in numbers. *We* must divide to conquer. *We* must send those noisy schoolteachers back into the recesses of their classrooms and insist that they keep their doors shut. Danger lurks when teachers gather in the halls or when they engage in talk, in something new that seems to be cropping up all over the place—something called a *writing center. Decentralize.*

I have visited some writing centers of late. Some astonish me. They are plush, with luxurious carpets, modern (or post-modern) prints on the walls, secretaries, computer terminals, stocked libraries, spacious surroundings—and *cubicles*. I say watch out for cubicles. Watch out for computer terminals. Watch out for all evidence of attempts to break down the gathering of minds.

Part 2:
Theoretical Foundations

The Idea of a Writing Center

by Stephen M. North

This is an essay that began out of frustration. Despite the reference to writing centers in the title, it is not addressed to a writing center audience but to what is, for my purposes, just the opposite: those not involved with writing centers. Do not exclude yourself from this group just because you know that writing centers (or labs or clinics or places or however you think of them) exist; "involved" here means having directed such a place, having worked there for a minimum of 100 hours, or, at least, having talked about writing of your own there for five or more hours. The source of my frustration? Ignorance: the members of my profession, my colleagues, people I might see at MLA or CCCC or read in the pages of *College English*, do not understand what I do. They do not understand what does happen, what can happen, in a writing center.

Let me be clear here. Misunderstanding is something one expects—and almost gets used to—in the writing center business. The new faculty member in our writing-across-the-curriculum program, for example, who sends his students to get their papers "cleaned up" in the Writing Center before they hand them in; the occasional student who tosses her paper on our reception desk, announcing that she'll "pick it up in an hour"; even the well-intentioned administrators who are so happy that we deal with "skills" or "fundamentals" or, to use the word that seems to subsume all others, "grammar" (or usually "GRAMMAR")—these are fairly predictable. But from people in English departments, people well trained in the complex relationship between writer and text, so painfully aware, if only from the composing of dissertations and theses, how lonely and difficult writing can be, I expect more. And I am generally disappointed.

What makes the situation particularly frustrating is that so many such people will vehemently claim that they do, *really,* understand the idea of a writing center. The non-English faculty, the students, the administrators—they may not understand what a writing center is or does, but they have no investment in their ignorance, and can often be educated. But in English departments this second layer of ignorance, this false sense of knowing, makes it doubly hard to get a message through. Indeed, even as you read now, you may be dismissing my argument as the ritual plaint of a "remedial" teacher

---

Reprinted from *College English,* September 1984. Copyright (1984) by the National Council of Teachers of English. Reprinted with permission.

begging for respectability, the product of a kind of professional paranoia. But while I might admit that there are elements of such a plaint involved—no one likes not to be understood—there is a good deal more at stake. For in coming to terms with this ignorance, I have discovered that it is only a symptom of a much deeper, more serious problem. As a profession I think we are holding on tightly to attitudes and beliefs about the teaching and learning of writing that we thought we had left behind. In fact, my central contention—in the first half of this essay anyway—is that the failure or inability of the bulk of the English teaching profession, including even those most ardent spokespersons of the so-called 'revolution' in the teaching of writing, to perceive the idea of a writing center suggests that, for all our noise and bother about composition, we have fundamentally changed very little.

Let me begin by citing a couple of typical manifestations of this ignorance from close to home. Our writing center has been open for seven years. During that time we have changed our philosophy a little bit as a result of lessons learned from experience, but for the most part we have always been open to anybody in the university community, worked with writers at any time during the composing of a given piece of writing, and dealt with whole pieces of discourse, and not exercises on what might be construed as "subskills" (spelling, punctuation, etc.) outside of the context of the writer's work.

We have delivered the message about what we do to the university generally, and the English department in particular, in a number of ways: letters, flyers, posters, class presentations, information booths, and so on. And, as along as there has been a writing committee, advisory to the director of the writing program, we have sent at least one representative. So it is all the more surprising, and disheartening, that the text for our writing program flyer, composed and approved by that committee, should read as follows:

> The University houses the Center for Writing, founded in 1978 to sponsor the interdisciplinary study of writing. Among its projects are a series of summer institutes for area teachers of writing, a resource center for writers and teachers of writing, *and a tutorial facility for those with special problems in composition.* (My emphasis)

I don't know, quite frankly, how that copy got past me. What are these "special problems"? What would constitute a regular problem, and why wouldn't we talk to the owner of one? Is this hint of pathology, in some mysterious way, a good marketing ploy?

But that's only the beginning. Let me cite another, in many ways more common and painful instance. As a member, recently, of a doctoral examination committee, I conducted an oral in composition theory and practice. One of the candidate's areas of concentration was writing centers, so as part of the exam I gave her a piece of student writing and asked her to play tutor to my student. The session went well enough, but afterward, as we evaluated the entire exam, one of my fellow examiners—a longtime colleague and friend— said that, while the candidate handled the tutoring nicely, he was surprised that the student who had written the paper would have bothered with the Writing Center in the first place. He would not recommend a student to the Center, he said, "unless there were something like twenty-five errors per page."

People make similar remarks all the time, stopping me or members of my staff in the halls, or calling us into offices, to discuss—in hushed tones, frequently—their current "impossible" or difficult students. There was a time, I will confess, when I let my frustration get the better of me. I would be more or less combative, confrontational, challenging the instructor's often well-intentioned but not very useful "diagnosis." We no longer bother with such confrontations; they never worked very well, and they risk undermining the genuine compassion our teachers have for the students they single out. Nevertheless, their behavior makes it clear that for them, a writing center is to illiteracy what a cross between Lourdes and a hospice would be to serious illness: one goes there hoping for miracles, but ready to face the inevitable. In their minds, clearly, writers fall into three fairly distinct groups: the talented, the average, and the others; and the Writing Center's only logical *raison d'etre* must be to handle those others—those, as the flyer proclaims, with "special problems."

Mine is not, of course, the only English department in which such misconceptions are rife. One comes away from any large meeting of writing center people laden with similar horror stories. And in at least one case, a member of such a department—Malcolm Hayward of the Indiana University of Pennsylvania—decided formally to explore and document his faculty's perceptions of the center, and to compare them with the views the center's staff held.[1] His aim, in a two-part survey of both groups, was to determine, first, which goals each group deemed most important in the teaching of writing; and, second, what role they thought the writing center ought to play in that teaching, which goals it ought to concern itself with.

Happily, the writing faculty and the center staff agreed on what the primary goals in teaching writing should be (in the terms offered by Hayward's questionnaire): the development of general patterns of thinking and writing. Unhappily, the two groups disagreed rather sharply about the reasons for referring students to the center. For faculty members the two primary criteria were grammar and punctuation. Tutors, on the other hand, ranked organization "as by far the single most important factor for referral," followed rather distantly by paragraphing, grammar, and style. In short, Hayward's survey reveals the same kind of misunderstanding on his campus that I find so frustrating on my own: the idea that a writing center can only be some sort of skills center, a fix-it shop.

Now if this were just a matter of local misunderstanding, if Hayward and I could straighten it out with a few workshops or lectures, maybe I wouldn't need to write this essay for a public forum. But that is not the case. For

---

[1] "Assessing Attitudes Toward the Writing Center," *The Writing Center Journal*, 3, No. 2 (1983), 1-11.

whatever reasons writing centers have gotten mostly this kind of press, have been represented—or misrepresented—more often as fix-it shops than in any other way, and in some fairly influential places. Consider, for example, this passage from Barbara E. Fassler Walvoord's *Helping Students Write Well: A Guide for Teachers in All Disciplines* (New York: Modern Language Association, 1981). What makes it particularly odd, at least in terms of my argument, is that Professor Walvoord's book, in many other ways, offers to faculty the kind of perspective on writing (writing as a complex process, writing as a way of learning) that I might offer myself. Yet here she is on writing centers:

> If you are very short of time, if you think you are not skilled enough to deal with mechanical problems, or if you have a number of students with serious difficulties, you may wish to let the skills center carry the ball for mechanics and spend your time on other kinds of writing and learning problems. (p. 63)

Don't be misled by Professor Walvoord's use of the "skills center" label; in her index the entry for "Writing centers" reads "See skills centers"—precisely the kind of interchangeable terminology I find so abhorrent. On the other hand, to do Professor Walvoord justice, she does recommend that teachers become "at least generally aware of how your skills center works with students, what its basic philosophy is, and what goals it sets for the students in your class," but it seems to me that she has already restricted the possible scope of such a philosophy pretty severely: "deal with mechanical problems"? "carry the ball for mechanics"?

Still, as puzzling and troubling as it is to see Professor Walvoord publishing misinformation about writing centers, it is even more painful, downright maddening, to read one's own professional obituary; to find, in the pages of a reputable professional journal, that what you do has been judged a failure, written off. Maxine Hairston's "The Winds of Change: Thomas Kuhn and the Revolution in the Teaching of Writing" *(College Composition and Communication,* 33 [1982], 76-88) is an attempt to apply the notion of a "paradigm shift" to the field of composition teaching. In the course of doing so Professor Hairston catalogues, under the subheading "Signs of Change," what she calls "ad hoc" remedies to the writing "crisis":

> Following the pattern that Kuhn describes in his book, our first response to crisis has been to improvise ad hoc measures to try to patch the cracks and keep the system running. Among the first responses were the writing labs that sprang up about ten years ago to give first aid to students who seemed unable to function within the traditional paradigm. Those labs are still with us, but they're still only giving first aid and treating symptoms. They have not solved the problem. (p. 82)

What first struck me about this assessment—what probably strikes most people in the writing center business—is the mistaken history, the notion that writing labs "sprang up about ten years ago." The fact is, writing "labs," as Professor Hairston chooses to call them, have been around in one form or another since at least the 1930s when Carrie Stanley was already working with writers at the University of Iowa. Moreover, this limited conception of what such places can do—the fix-it shop image—has been around far longer that ten years, too. Robert Moore, in a 1950 *College English* article, "The Writing Clinic and the Writing Laboratory" (7 [1950], 388-393), writes that "writing clinics and writing laboratories are becoming increasingly popular among American universities and colleges as remedial agencies for removing students' deficiencies in composition" (p. 388).

Still, you might think that I ought to be happier with Professor Hairston's position than with, say, Professor Walvoord's. And to some extent I am: even if she mistakenly assumes that the skill and drill model represents all writing centers equally well, she at least recognizes its essential futility. Nevertheless—and this is what bothers me most about her position—her dismissal fails to lay the blame for these worst versions of writing centers on the right heads. According to her "sprang up" historical sketch, these places simply appeared—like so many mushrooms?—to do battle with illiteracy. "They" are still with "us," but "they" haven't solved the problem. What is missing here is a doer, an agent, a creator—someone to take responsibility. The implication is that "they" done it—"they" being, apparently, the places themselves.

But that won't wash. "They," to borrow from Walt Kelly, is *us*: members of English departments, teachers of writing. Consider, as evidence, the pattern of writing center origins as revealed in back issues of *The Writing Lab Newsletter:* the castoff, windowless classroom (or in some cases literally, closet), the battered desks, the old textbooks, a phone (maybe), no budget, and, almost inevitably, a director with limited status—an untenured or non-tenure track faculty member, a teaching assistant, an undergraduate, a "paraprofessional," etc. Now who do you suppose has determined what is to happen in that center? Not the director, surely; not the staff, if there is one. The mandate is clearly from the sponsoring body, usually an English department. And lest you think that things are better where space and money are not such serious problems, I urge you to visit a center where a good bit of what is usually grant money has been spent in the first year or two of the center's operation. Almost always, the money will have been used on materials: drills, texts, machines, tapes, carrels, headphones—the works. And then the director, hired on "soft" money, without political clout, is locked into an approach because she or he has to justify the expense by using the materials.

Clearly, then, where there is or has been misplaced emphasis on so-called basics or drill, where centers have been prohibited from dealing with the writing that students do for their classes—where, in short, writing centers have been of the kind that Professor Hairston is quite correctly prepared to write off—it is because the agency that created the center in the first place, too often an English department, has made it so. The grammar and drill center, the fix-it shop, the first aid station—these are neither the vestiges of some paradigm left behind nor pedagogical aberrations that have been overlooked in the confusion of the "revolution" in the teaching of writing, but that will soon enough be set on the right path, or done away with. They are, instead, the vital and authentic reflection of a way of thinking about writing and the teaching of writing that is alive and well and living in English departments everywhere.

But if my claims are correct—if this is not what writing centers are or, if it is what they are, it is not what they should be—then what are, what *should* they be? What *is* the idea of a writing center? By way of answer, let me return briefly to the family of metaphors by which my sources have characterized their idea of a writing center: Robert Moore's "removing students' deficiencies," Hairston's "first aid" and "treating symptoms," my colleague's "twenty-five errors per page," Hayward's punctuation and grammar referrers, and Walvoord's "carrying the ball for mechanics" (where, at least, writing centers are athletic and not surgical). All these imply essentially the same thing: that writing centers define their province in terms of a given curriculum, taking over those portions of it that "regular" teachers are willing to cede or, presumably, unable to handle. Over the past six years or so I have visited more than fifty centers, and read descriptions of hundreds of others, and I can assure you that there are indeed centers of this kind, centers that can trace their conceptual lineage back at least as far as Moore. But the "new" writing center has a somewhat shorter history. It is the result of a documentable resurgence, a renaissance if you will, that began in the early 1970s. In fact, the flurry of activity that caught Professor Hairston's attention, and which she mistook for the beginnings of the "old" center, marked instead the genesis of a center which defined its province in a radically different way. Though I have some serious reservations about Hairston's use of Kuhn's paradigm model to describe what happens in composition teaching, I will for the moment put things in her terms: the new writing center, far from marking the end of an era, is the embodiment, the epitome, of a new one. It represents the marriage of what are arguably the two most powerful contemporary perspectives on teaching writing: first, that writing is most usefully viewed as a process; and second, that writing curricula need to be student-centered. This new writing center, then, defines its province not in terms of some curriculum, but in terms of the writers it serves.

To say that writing centers are based on a view of writing as a process is, original good intentions notwithstanding, not to say very much anymore. The slogan—and I daresay that is what it has become—has been devalued, losing most of its impact and explanatory power. Let me use it, then, to make the one distinction of which it still seems capable: in a writing center the object is to make sure that writers, and not necessarily their texts, are what get changed by instruction. In axiom form it goes like this: our job is to produce better writers, not better writing. Any given project—a class assignment, a law school application letter, an encyclopedia entry, a dissertation proposal— is for the writer the prime, often the exclusive concern. That particular text, its success or failure, is what brings them to talk to us in the first place. In the center, though, we look beyond or through that particular project, that particular text, and see it as an occasion for addressing *our* primary concern, that process by which it is produced.

At this point, however, the writing-as-a-process slogan tends to lose its usefulness. That "process," after all, has been characterized as everything from the reception of divine inspiration to a set of nearly algorithmic rules for producing the five paragraph theme. In between are the more widely accepted and, for the moment, more respectable descriptions derived from composing aloud protocols, interviews, videotaping, and so on. None of those, in any case, represent the composing process we seek in a writing center. The version we want can only be found, in as yet unarticulated form, in the writer we are working with. I think probably the best way to describe a writing center tutor's relationship to composing is to say that a tutor is a holist devoted to a participant-observer methodology. This may seem at first glance, too passive—or, perhaps, too glamorous, legitimate, or trendy—a role in which to cast tutors. But consider this passage from Paul Diesing's *Patterns of Discovery in the Social Sciences* (Hawthorne, N.Y.: Aldine, 1971):

> Holism is not, in the participant-observer method, an a priori belief that everything is related to everything else. It is rather the methodological necessity of pushing on to new aspects and new kinds of evidence in order to make sense of what one has already observed and to test the validity of one's interpretations. A belief in the organic unity of living systems may also be present, but this belief by itself would not be sufficient to force a continual expansion of one's observations. It is rather one's inability to develop an intelligible and validated partial model that drives one on. (p. 167)

How does this definition relate to tutors and composing? Think of the writer writing as a kind of host setting. What we want to do in a writing center is fit into—observe and participate in—this ordinarily solo ritual of writing. To do this, we need to do what any participant-observer must do: see what happens during this "ritual," try to make sense of it, observe some more, revise our model, and so on indefinitely, all the time behaving in a way the host finds acceptable. For validation and correction of our model, we quite naturally rely on the writer, who is, in turn, a willing collaborator in—and, usually, beneficiary of—the entire process. This process precludes, obviously, a reliance on or a clinging to any predetermined models of "the" composing process, except as crude topographical guides to what the "territory" of composing processes might look like. The only composing process that matters in a writing center is "a" composing process, and it "belongs" to, is acted out by, only one given writer.

It follows quite naturally, then, that any curriculum—any plan of action the tutor follows—is going to be student-centered in the strictest sense of that term. That is, it will not derive from a generalized model of composing, or be based on where the student ought to be because she is a freshman or sophomore, but will begin from where the student is, and move where the student moves—an approach possible only if, as James Moffett suggests in *Teaching the Universe of Discourse* (Boston: Houghton Mifflin, 1968), the teacher (or tutor in this case) "shifts his gaze from the subject to the learner, for the subject is in the learner" (p. 67). The result is what might be called a pedagogy of direct intervention. Whereas in the "old" center instruction tends to take place after or apart from writing, and tends to focus on the correction of textual problems, in the "new" center the teaching takes place as much as possible during writing, during the activity being learned, and tends to focus on the activity itself.

I do not want to push the participant-observer analogy too far. Tutors are not, finally, researchers: they must measure their success not in terms of the constantly changing model they create, but in terms of changes in the writer. Rather than being fearful of disturbing the "ritual" of composing, they observe it and are charged to change it: to interfere, to get in the way, to participate in ways that will leave the "ritual" itself forever altered. The whole enterprise seems to me most natural. Nearly everyone who writes likes—and needs—to talk about his or her writing, preferably to someone who will really listen, who knows how to listen, and knows how to talk about writing too. Maybe in a perfect world, all writers would have their own ready auditor—a teacher, a classmate, a roommate, an editor—who would not only listen but draw them out, ask them questions they would not think to ask themselves. A writing center is an institutional response to this need. Clearly writing centers can never hope to satisfy this need themselves; on my campus alone, the student-to-tutor ratio would be about a thousand to one. Writing centers are simply one manifestation—polished and highly visible—of a dialogue about writing that is central to higher education.

As is clear from my citations in the first half of this essay, however, what seems perfectly natural to me is not so natural for everyone else. One part of the difficulty, it seems to me now, is not theoretical at all, but practical, a question of coordination or division of labor. It usually comes in the form of a question like this: "If I'm doing process-centered teaching in my class, why do I need a writing center? How can I use it?" For a long time I tried to soft-pedal my answers to this question. For instance, in my dissertation ("Writing Centers: A Source-book," Diss. SUNY at Albany, 1978) I talked about complementing or intensifying classroom instruction. Or, again, in our center we tried using, early on, what is a fairly common device among writing centers, a referral form; at one point it even had a sort of diagnostic taxonomy, a checklist, by which teachers could communicate to us their concerns about the writers they sent us.

But I have come with experience to take a harder, less conciliatory position. The answer to the question in all cases is that teachers, as teachers, do not need, and cannot use, a writing center: only writers need it, only writers can use it. You cannot parcel out some portion of a given student for us to deal with ("You take care of editing, I'll deal with invention"). Nor should you require that all of your students drop by with an early draft of a research paper to get a reading from a fresh audience. You should not scrawl, at the bottom of a failing paper, "Go to the Writing Center." Even those of you who, out of genuine concern, bring students to a writing center, almost by the hand, to make sure they know that we won't hurt them—even you are essentially out of line. Occasionally we manage to convert such writers from people who have to see us to people who want to, but most often they either come as if for a kind of detention, or they drift away. (It would be nice if in writing, as in so many things, people would do what we tell them because it's good for them, but they don't. If and when *they* are ready, we will be here.)

In short, we are not here to serve, supplement, back up, complement, reinforce, or otherwise be defined by any external curriculum. We are here to talk to writers. If they happen to come from your classes, you might take it as a compliment to your assignments, in that your writers are engaged in them enough to want to talk about their work. On the other hand, we do a fair amount of trade in people working on ambiguous or poorly designed assignments, and far too much work with writers whose writing has received caustic, hostile, or otherwise unconstructive commentary.

I suppose this declaration of independence sounds more like a declaration of war, and that is obviously not what I intend, especially since the primary casualties would be the students and writers we all aim to serve. And I see no reason that writing centers and classroom teachers cannot cooperate as well as coexist. For example, the first rule in our Writing Center is that we are professionals at what we do. While that does, as I have argued, give us the freedom of self-definition, it also carries with it a responsibility to respect our fellow professionals. Hence we never play student-advocates in teacher-student relationships. The guidelines are very clear. In all instances the student must understand that we support the teacher's position completely. (Or, to put it in less loaded terms—for we are not teacher advocates either—the instructor is simply part of the rhetorical context in which the writer is trying to operate. We cannot change that context: all we can do is help the writer learn how to operate in it and other contexts like it.) In practice, this rule means that we never evaluate or second-guess any teacher's syllabus, assignments, comments, or grades. If students are unclear about any of those, we send them back to the teacher to get clear. Even in those instances I mentioned above—where writers come in confused by what seem to be poorly designed assignments, or crushed by what appear to be unwarrantedly hostile comments—we pass no judgment, at least as far as the student is concerned. We simply try, every way we can, to help the writer make constructive sense of the situation.

In return, of course, we expect equal professional courtesy. We need, first of all, instructors' trust that our work with writers-in-progress on academic assignments is not plagiarism, any more than a conference with the teacher would be—that, to put it the way I most often hear it, we will not write students' papers for them. Second, instructors must grant us the same respect we grant them—that is, they must neither evaluate nor second-guess our work with writers. We are, of course, most willing to talk about that work. But we do not take kindly to the perverse kind of thinking represented in remarks like, "Well, I had a student hand in a paper that he took to the writing center, and it was *still* full of errors." The axiom, if you will recall, is that we aim to make better writers, not necessarily—or immediately—better texts.

Finally, we can always use classroom teachers' cooperation in helping us explain to students what we do. As a first step, of course, I am asking that they revise their thinking about what a writing center can do. Beyond that, in our center we find it best to go directly to the students ourselves. That is, rather than sending out a memo or announcement for the teachers to read to their classes, we simply send our staff, upon invitation, into classes to talk with students or, better yet, to do live tutorials. The standard presentation, a ten-minute affair, gives students a person, a name, and a face to remember the Center by. The live tutorials take longer, but we think they are worth it. We ask the instructor to help us find a writer willing to have a draft (or a set of notes or even just the assignment) reproduced for the whole class. Then the Writing Center person does, with the participation of the entire class, what we do in the Center: talk about writing with the writer. In our experience the instructors learn as much about the Center from these sessions as the students.

To argue that writing centers are not here to serve writing class curricula is not to say, however, that they are here to replace them. In our center, anyway, nearly every member of the full-time staff is or has been a classroom teacher of writing. Even our undergraduate tutors work part of their time in an introductory writing course. We all recognize and value the power of classroom teaching, and we take pride in ourselves as professionals in that setting too. But working in both situations makes us acutely aware of crucial differences between talking about wiring in the context of a class, and talking about it in the context of the Center. When we hold student conferences in our classes, we are the teacher, in the writers' minds especially, the assigner and evaluator of the writing in question. And for the most part we are pretty busy people, with conference appointments scheduled on the half hour, and a line forming outside the office. For efficiency the papers-in-progress are in some assigned form—an outline, a first draft, a statement of purpose with bibliography and note cards; and while the conference may lead to further composing, there is rarely the time or the atmosphere for composing to happen during the conference itself. Last but not least, the conference is likely to be a command performance, our idea, not the writer's.

When we are writing center tutors all of that changes. First of all, conferences are the writer's idea; he or she seeks us out. While we have an appointment book that offers half hour appointment slots, our typical session is fifty minutes, and we average between three and four per writer; we can afford to give a writer plenty of time. The work-in-progress is in whatever form the writer has managed to put it in, which may make tutoring less efficient, but which clearly makes it more student-centered, allowing us to begin where the writers are, not where we told them to be. This also means that in most cases the writers come prepared, even anxious to get on with their work, to begin or to keep on composing. Whereas going to keep a conference with a teacher is, almost by definition, a kind of goal or dead-line—a stopping place—going to talk in the writing center is a means of getting started, or a way to keep going. And finally—in a way subsuming all the rest—we are not the teacher. We did not assign the writing, and we will not grade it. However little that distinction might mean in our behaviors, it seems to mean plenty to the writers.

What these differences boil down to, in general pedagogical terms, are timing and motivation. The fact is, not everyone's interest in writing, their need or desire to write or learn to write, coincides with the fifteen or thirty weeks they spend in writing courses—especially when, as is currently the case at so many institutions, those weeks are required. When writing does become important, a writing center can be there in a way that our regular classes cannot. Charles Cooper, in an unpublished paper called "What College Writers Need to Know" (1979), puts it this way:

> The first thing college writers need to know is that they can improve as writers and the second is that they will never reach a point where they cannot improve further. One writing course, two courses, three courses may not be enough. If they're on a campus which takes writing seriously, they will be able to find the courses they need to feel reasonably confident they can fulfill the requests which will be made of them in their academic work.... Throughout their college years they should also be able to find on a drop-in, no-fee basis expert tutorial help with any writing problem they encounter in a paper. (p. 1)

A writing center's advantage in motivation is a function of the same phenomenon. Writers come looking for us because, more often than not, they are genuinely, deeply engaged with their material, anxious to wrestle it into the best form they can: they are motivated to write. If we agree that the biggest obstacle to overcome in teaching anything, writing included, is getting learners to decide that they want to learn, then what a writing center does is cash in on motivation that the writer provides. This teaching at the con-junction of timing and motivation is most strikingly evident when we work with writers doing "real world" tasks: application essays for law, medical, and graduate schools, newspaper and magazine articles, or poems and stories. Law school application writers are suddenly willing—sometimes overwhelmingly so—to concern themselves with audience, purpose, and persona, and to revise over and over again. But we see the same excitement in writers working on literature or history or philosophy papers, or preparing dissertation proposals, or getting ready to tackle comprehensive exams. Their primary concern is with their material, with some existential context where new ideas must merge with old, and suddenly writing is a vehicle, a means to an end, and not an end in itself. These opportunities to talk with excited writers at the height of their engagement with their work are the lifeblood of a writing center.

The essence of the writing center method, then, is this talking. If we conceive of writing as a relatively rhythmic and repeatable kind of behavior, then for a writer to improve that behavior, that rhythm, has to change—preferably, though not necessarily, under the writer's control. Such changes can be fostered, of course, by work outside of the act of composing itself—hence the success of the classical discipline of imitation, or more recent ones like sentence combining or the tagmemic heuristic, all of which, with practice, "merge" with and affect composing. And, indeed, depending on the writer, none of these tactics would be ruled out in a writing center. By and large, however, we find that the best breaker of old rhythms, the best creator of new ones, is our style of live intervention, our talk in all its forms.

The kind of writing does not substantially change the approach. We always want the writer to tell us about the rhetorical context—what the purpose of the writing is, who its audience is, how the writer hopes to present herself. We want to know about other constraints—deadlines, earlier experiences with the same audience or genre, research completed or not completed, and so on. In other ways, though, the variations on the kind of talk are endless. We can question, praise, cajole, criticize, acknowledge, badger, plead—even cry. We can read: silently, aloud, together, separately. We can play with options. We can both write—as, for example, in response to sample essay exam questions—and compare opening strategies. We can poke around in resources—comparing, perhaps, the manuscript conventions of the Modern Language Association with those of the American Psychological Association. We can ask writers to compose aloud while we listen, or we can compose aloud, and the writer can watch and listen.

In this essay, however, I will say no more about the nature of this talk. One reason is that most of what can be said for the moment, has been said in print already. There is, for example, my own "Training Tutors to Talk About Writing" (*CCC*, 33 [1982] 434-442), or Muriel Harris' "Modeling: A Process Method of Teaching" (*College English*, 45 [1983], 74-84). And there are several other sources, including a couple of essay collections, that provide some insights into the hows and whys of tutorial talk.[2]

A second reason, though, seems to me more substantive, and symptomatic of the kinds of misunderstanding I have tried to dispel here. We don't know very much, in other than a practitioner's anecdotal way, about the dynamics of the tutorial. The same can be said, of course, with regard to talk about writing in any setting—the classroom, the peer group, the workshop, the teacher-student conference, and so on. But while ignorance of the nature of talk in those settings does not threaten their existence, it may do precisely that in writing centers. That is, given the idea of the writing center I have set forth here, talk is everything. If the writing center is ever to prove its worth in other than quantitative terms—numbers of students seen, for example, or hours of

---

[2] See, for example, *Tutoring Writing: A Sourcebook for Writing Labs,* ed. Muriel Harris (Glenview, Ill: Scott-Foresman, 1982): and *New Directions for College Learning Assistance: Improving Writing Skills,* ed. Phyllis Brooks and Thom Hawkins (San Francisco: Jossey-Bass, 1981).

tutorials provided—it will have to do so by describing this talk: what characterizes it, what effects it has, how it can be enhanced.

Unfortunately, the same "proofreading-shop-in-the-basement" mentality that undermines the pedagogical efforts of the writing center hampers research as well. So far most of the people hired to run such places have neither the time, the training, nor the status to undertake any serious research. Moreover, the few of us lucky enough to even consider the possibility of research have found that there are other difficulties. One is that writing center work is often not considered fundable—that is, relevant to a wide enough audience—even though there are about a thousand such facilities in the country, a figure which suggests that there must be at least ten or fifteen thousand tutorials every school day, and even though research into any kind of talk about writing is relevant for the widest possible audience. Second, we have discovered that focusing our scholarly efforts on writing centers may be a professional liability. Even if we can publish our work (and that is by no means easy), there is no guarantee that it will be viewed favorably by tenure and promotion review committees. Composition itself is suspect enough; writing centers, a kind of obscure backwater, seem no place for a scholar.

These conditions may be changing. Manuscripts for *The Writing Center Journal*, for example, suggest that writing center folk generally are becoming more research-oriented; there were sessions scheduled at this year's meetings of the MLA and NCTE on research in or relevant to writing centers. In an even more tangible signal of change, the State University of New York has made funds available for our Albany center to develop an appropriate case study methodology for writing center tutorials. Whether this trend continues or not, my point remains the same. Writing centers, like any other portion of a college writing curriculum, need time and space for appropriate research and reflection if they are to more clearly understand what they do, and figure out how to do it better. The great danger is that the very misapprehensions that put them in basements to begin with may conspire to keep them there.

It is possible that I have presented here, at least by implication, too dismal a portrait of the current state of writing centers. One could, as a matter of fact, mount a pretty strong argument that things have never been better. There are, for example, several regional writing center associations that have annual meetings, and the number of such associations increases every year. Both *The Writing Lab Newsletter* and *The Writing Center Journal*, the two publications in the field, have solid circulations. This year at NCTE, for the first time, writing center people met as a recognized National Assembly, a major step up from their previous Special Interest Session status.

And on individual campuses all over the country, writing centers have begun to expand their institutional roles. So, for instance, some centers have established resource libraries for writing teachers. They sponsor readings or reading series by poets and fiction writers, and annual festivals to celebrate writing of all kinds. They serve as clearinghouses for information on where to publish, on writing programs, competitions, scholarships, and so on; and

they sponsor such competitions themselves, even putting out their own publications. They design and conduct workshops for groups with special needs—
essay exam takers, for example, or job application writers. They are involved
with, or have even taken over entirely, the task of training new teaching
assistants. They have played central roles in the creation of writing-across-the-
curriculum programs. And centers have extended themselves beyond their
own institutions, sending tutors to other schools (often high schools), or
helping other institutions set up their own facilities. In some cases, they have
made themselves available to the wider community, often opening a "Grammar Hotline" or "Grammaphone"—a service so popular at one institution, in
fact, that a major publishing company provided funding to keep it open over
the summer.

Finally, writing centers have gotten into the business of offering academic
credit. As a starting point they have trained their tutors in formal courses or,
in some instances, "paid" their tutors in credits rather than money. They have
set up independent study arrangements to sponsor both academic and nonacademic writing experiences. They have offered credit-bearing courses of
their own; in our center, for example, we are piloting an introductory writing
course that uses Writing Center staff members as small group leaders.

I would very much like to say that all this activity is a sure sign that the
idea of a writing center is here to stay, that the widespread misunderstandings
I described in this essay, especially those held so strongly in English departments, are dissolving. But in good conscience I cannot. Consider the activities
we are talking about. Some of them, of course, are either completely or
mostly public relations: a way of making people aware that a writing center
exists, and that (grammar hotlines aside) it deals in more than usage and
punctuation. Others—like the resource library, the clearinghouse, or the training of new teaching assistants—are more substantive, and may well belong in
a writing center, but most of them end up there in the first place because
nobody else wants to do them. As for the credit generating, that is simply
pragmatic. The bottom line in academic budget making is calculated in
student credit hours; when budgets are tight, as they will be for the fore-
seeable future, facilities that generate no credits are the first to be cut. Writing
centers—even really good writing centers—have proved no exception.

None of these efforts to promote writing centers suggest that there is any
changed understanding of the idea of a writing center. Indeed it is as though
what writing centers do that really matters—talking to writers—were not
enough. That being the case, enterprising directors stake out as large a claim
as they can in more visible or acceptable territory. All of these efforts—and, I
assure you, my center does its share—have about them an air of shrewdness,
or desperation, the trace of a survival instinct at work. I am not such a purist
as to suggest that these things are all bad. At the very least they can be good
for staff morale. Beyond that I think they may eventually help make writing
centers the centers of consciousness about writing on campuses, a kind of
physical locus for the ideas and ideals of college or university or high school
commitment to writing—a status to which they might well aspire and which,

judging by results on a few campuses already, they can achieve.

But not this way, not via the back door, not—like some marginal ball-player—by doing whatever it takes to stay on the team. If writing centers are going to finally be accepted, surely they must be accepted on their own terms, as places whose primary responsibility, whose only reason for being, is to talk to writers. That is their heritage, and it stretches back farther than the late 1960s or the early 1970s, or to Iowa in the 1930s—back, in fact, to Athens, where in a busy marketplace a tutor called Socrates set up the same kind of shop: open to all comers, no fees charged, offering, on whatever subject a visitor might propose, a continuous dialectic that is, finally, its own end.

Peer Tutoring and the "Conversation of Mankind"

by Kenneth A. Bruffee

The beginnings of peer tutoring lie in practice, not in theory. A decade or so ago, faculty and administrators in a few institutions around the country became aware that, increasingly, students entering college had difficulty doing as well in academic studies as their abilities suggested they should be able to do. Some of these students were in many ways poorly prepared academically. Many more of them, however, had on paper excellent secondary preparation. The common denominator among the poorly prepared and the apparently well prepared seemed to be that, for cultural reasons we may not yet fully understand, all these students had difficulty adapting to the traditional or "normal" conventions of the college classroom.

One symptom of the difficulty was that many of these students refused help when it was offered. Mainly, colleges offered ancillary programs staffed by professionals. Students avoided them in droves. Many solutions to this problem were suggested and tried, from mandated programs to sink-or-swim. One idea that seemed at the time among the most exotic and unlikely (that is, in the jargon of the Sixties, among the most "radical") turned out to work rather well. Some of us had guessed that students were refusing the help we were providing because it seemed to them merely an extension of the work, the expectations, and above all the social structure of traditional classroom learning. And it was traditional classroom learning that seemed to have left these students unprepared in the first place. What they needed, we had guessed, was help of a sort that was not an extension but an alternative to the traditional classroom.

To provide that alternative, we turned to peer tutoring. Through peer tutoring, we reasoned, teachers could reach students by organizing them to teach each other. Peer tutoring was a type of collaborative learning. It did not seem to change what people learned but, rather, the social context in which they learned it. Peer tutoring made learning a two-way street, since students' work tended to improve when they got help from peer tutors and tutors learned from the students they helped and from the activity of tutoring itself. Peer tutoring harnessed the powerful educative force of peer influence that had been—and largely still is—ignored and hence wasted by traditional forms of education.[1]

These are some of the insights we garnered through the practical experience of organizing peer tutoring to meet student needs. More recently, we have begun to learn that much of this practical experience and the insights it yielded have a conceptual rationale, a theoretical dimension, that had escaped us earlier as we muddled through, trying to solve practical problems in practical ways. The better we understand this conceptual rationale, however, the more it leads us to suspect that peer tutoring (and collaborative learning in general) has the potential to challenge the theory and practice of traditional classroom learning itself.

This essay will sketch what seems to me to be the most persuasive conceptual rationale for peer tutoring and will suggest what appear to be some of the larger implications of that rationale. The essay will begin by discussing the view of thought and knowledge that seems to underlie peer tutoring. Then it will suggest what this view implies about how peer tutoring works. Finally, the essay will suggest what this concept of knowledge may suggest for studying and teaching the humanities.

Conversation and the Origin of Thought

In an important essay on the place of literature in education published some twenty years ago, Michael Oakeshott argues that what distinguishes human beings from other animals is our ability to participate in unending conversation. "As civilized human beings," Oakeshott says,

> we are the inheritors, neither of an inquiry about ourselves and the world, nor of an accumulating body of information, but of a conversation, begun in the primeval forests and extended and made more articulate in the course of centuries. It is a conversation which goes on both in public and within each of ourselves.... Education, properly speaking, is an initiation into the skill and partnership of this conversation in which we learn to recognize the voices, to distinguish the proper occasions of utterance, and in which we acquire the intellectual and moral habits appropriate to conversation. And it is this conversation which, in the end, gives place and character to every human activity and utterance.[2]

Arguing that the human conversation takes place within us as well as among us and that conversation as it takes place within us is what we call reflective thought, Oakeshott makes the assumption that conversation and reflective thought are related in two ways: organically and formally. That is,

---

[1] The educative value of peer group influence is discussed in Nevitt Sanford, ed., *The American College* (New York: Wiley, 1962), and Theodore M. Newcomb and Everett K. Wilson, eds., *College Peer Groups* (Chicago: Aldine, 1966).

[2] Michael Oakeshott, "The Voice of Poetry in the Conversation of Mankind," in *Rationalism in Politics* (New York: Basic Books, 1962), 199.

as the work of Lev Vygotsky and others has shown,[3] reflective thought is public or social conversation internalized. We first experience and learn "the skill and partnership of this conversation" in the external arena of direct social exchange with other people. Only then do we learn to displace that "skill and partnership" by playing silently, in imagination, the parts of all the participants in the conversation ourselves. As Clifford Geertz has put it, "thinking as an overt, public act, involving the purposeful manipulation of objective materials, is probably fundamental to human beings; and thinking as a covert, private act, and without recourse to such materials, a derived, though not unuseful, capability."[4]

Since what we experience as reflective thought is organically related to social conversation, the two are also related functionally. That is, because thought originates in conversation, thought and conversation tend to work largely in the same way. Of course, in thought some of the limitations of conversation are absent. Logistics, for example, are no problem at all; I don't have to go anywhere or make an appointment to get together with myself for a talk. I don't even need to dial the phone, although I do sometimes need a trip to the coffeemaker. And in thought there are no differences among the participants in preparation, interest, native ability, or spoken vernacular. On the other hand, in thought some of the less fortunate limitations of conversation may hang on. Limitations imposed by my ethnocentrism, inexperience, personal anxiety, economic interest, and paradigmatic inflexibility can constrain my thinking just as they can constrain my conversation. If my talk is narrow, superficial, biased, and confined to cliches, my thinking is likely to be so, too. Still, it remains the case that many of the social forms and conventions of conversation, most of its language conventions and rhetorical structures, its impetus and goals, its excitement and drive, its potentially vast range and flexibility, and the issues it addresses are the sources of the forms and conventions, structures, impetus, range and flexibility, and the issues of reflective thought.

The formal and organic relationship I have been drawing here between conversation and thought illuminates, therefore, the source of the quality, depth, terms, character, and issues of thought. The assumptions underlying this argument differ considerably, however, from the assumptions we ordinarily make about the nature of thought. We ordinarily assume that thought is some sort of "essential attribute" of the human mind. The view that conversation and thought are fundamentally related assumes instead that thought is a social artifact. As Stanley Fish has put it, the thoughts we "can think and the mental operations [we] can perform have their source in some

---

[3] For example, L.S. Vygotsky, *Mind in Society* (Cambridge, Mass.: Harvard University Press, 1978).
[4] Clifford Geertz, "The Growth of Culture and the Evolution of Mind," in *The Interpretation of Cultures* (New York: Basic Books, 1973), 76-77. See also in the same volume "The Impact of the Concept of Culture on the Concept of Man" and "Ideology as a Cultural System," Parts IV and V.

or other interpretive community."[5] Reflective thinking is something we learn to do, and we learn to do it from and with other people. We learn to think reflectively as a result of learning to talk, and the ways we can think reflectively as adults depend on the ways we have learned to talk as we grew up. The range, complexity, and subtlety of our thought, its power, the practical and conceptual uses we can put it to, as well as the very issues we can address result in large measure (native aptitude, the gift of our genes, aside) directly from the degree to which we have been initiated into what Oakeshott calls the potential "skill and partnership" of human conversation in its public and social form.

To the extent that thought is internalized conversation, then, any effort to understand how we think requires us to understand the nature of conversation; and any effort to understand conversation requires us to understand the nature of community life that generates and maintains conversation. Furthermore, any effort to understand and cultivate in ourselves a particular kind of thinking requires us to understand and cultivate the community life that generates and maintains the conversation from which a particular kind of thinking originates. The first steps to learning to think better are to learn to converse better and to learn to create and maintain the sort of social contexts, the sorts of community life, that foster the kinds of conversations we value.

These relationships have broad applicability and implications far beyond those that may be immediately apparent. For example, Thomas Kuhn has argued that to understand scientific thought and knowledge, we must understand the nature of scientific communities.[6] Richard Rorty, carrying Kuhn's view and terminology further, argues that to understand any kind of knowledge, we must understand what Rorty calls the social justification of belief; that is, we must understand how knowledge is generated and maintained by communities of knowledgeable peers.[7] Stanley Fish completes the argument by positing that these "interpretive communities" are the source not only of our thought and the "meanings" we produce through the use and manipulation of symbolic structures, chiefly language; interpretive communities may also be in large measure the source of what we regard as our very selves.[8]

Conversation, Writing, and Peer Tutoring

The line of argument I have been pursuing has important implications for educators, especially those of us who teach composition. If thought is internalized public and social talk, then writing is internalized talk made

---

[5] Stanley Fish, *Is There a Text in This Class? The Authority of Interpretive Communities* (Cambridge, Mass.: Harvard University Press, 1980), 14. Fish develops his argument fully in Part 2, pages 303-71.

[6] Thomas Kuhn, *The Structure of Scientific Revolutions,* 2nd ed., International Encyclopedia of Unified Science, vol. 2, no. 2 (Chicago: University of Chicago Press, 1970).

[7] Richard Rorty, *Philosophy and the Mirror of Nature* (Princeton, N.J.: Princeton University Press, 1979). Some of the larger educational implications of Rorty's argument are explored in Kenneth A. Bruffee, "Liberal Education and the Social Justification of Belief," *Liberal Education* (Summer 1982): 8-20.

[8] Fish, 14.

public and social again. If thought is internalized conversation, then writing is internalized conversation re-externalized.[9]

Like thought, therefore, writing is temporally and functionally related to conversation. Writing is in fact a technologically displaced form of conversation. When we write, having already internalized the "skill and partnership" of conversation, we displace it once more onto the written page. But because thought is already one step away from conversation, the position of writing relative to conversation is more complex than even that of thought. Writing is at once both two steps away form conversation and a return to conversation. By writing, we re-immerse conversation in its social medium. Writing is two steps removed from conversation because, for example, my ability to write this essay depends on my ability to talk through with myself the issues I address here. And my ability to talk through an issue with myself derives largely from my ability to converse directly with other people in an immediate social situation.

The point is not that every time I write, what I say must necessarily be something I have talked over with other people first, although I may well often do just that. What I say can originate in thought. But since thought is conversation as I have learned to internalize it, the point is that writing always has its roots deep in the acquired ability to carry on the social symbolic exchange we call conversation. The inference writing tutors and teachers should make from this line of reasoning is that our task must involve engaging students in conversation at as many points in the writing process as possible and that we should contrive to ensure that that conversation is similar in as many ways as possible to the way we would like them eventually to write.

Peer Tutoring as Social Context

This practical inference returns us to peer tutoring. If we consider thought as internalized conversation and writing as re-externalized conversation, peer tutoring plays an important role in education for at least two reasons—both resulting from the fact that peer tutoring is a form of collaborative learning. First, peer tutoring provides a social context in which students can experience and practice the kinds of conversation that academics most value. The kind of conversation peer tutors engage in with their tutees can be emotionally involved, intellectually and substantively focused, and personally disinterested. There could be no better source of this than the sort of displaced conversation (i.e., writing) that academics value. Peer tutoring, like collaborative learning in general, makes students—both tutors and tutees—aware that writing is a social artifact, like the thought that produces it. However displaced writing may seem in time and space from the rest of a writer's community of readers and other writers, writing continues to be an act of conversational exchange.

---

[9] A case for this position is argued in Kenneth A. Bruffee, "Writing and Reading as Collaborative or Social Acts: The Argument from Kuhn and Vygotsky," in *The Writer's Mind* (Urbana, Ill.: NCTE, 1983).

Peer Tutoring as a Context for "Normal Discourse"

The second reason is somewhat more complex. Peer tutoring, again like collaborative learning in general, plays an important role in education because it provides a particular kind of social context for conversation, a particular kind of community: that of status equals, or peers. This means that students learn the "skill and partnership" of re-externalized conversation not only in a community that fosters the kind of conversation academics most value, but also in a community like the one most students must eventually write for in everyday life—in business, government, and the professions.

It is worthwhile digressing a moment to establish this last point. Ordinarily people write to inform and convince other people within the writer's own community, people whose status and assumptions approximate the writer's own.[10] That is, the sort of writing most people do most frequently in their everyday working lives is what Rorty calls "normal discourse." Normal discourse, a term of Rorty's coinage based on Kuhn's term "normal science," applies to conversation within a community of knowledgeable peers. A community of knowledgeable peers is a group of people who accept, and whose work is guided by, the same paradigms and the same code of values and assumptions. In normal discourse, as Rorty puts it, everyone agrees on the "set of conventions about what counts as a relevant contribution, what counts as a question, what counts as having a good argument for that answer or a good criticism of it." The product of normal discourse is "the sort of statement that can be agreed to be true by all participants whom the other participants count as 'rational.'"[11]

The essay I am writing here is an example of normal discourse in this sense. I am writing to members of my own community of knowledgeable peers. My readers and I (I suppose) are guided in our work by the same set of conventions about what counts as a relevant contribution, what counts as a question, what counts as an answer, what counts as a good argument in support of that answer or a good criticism of it. I judge my essay finished when I think it conforms to that set of conventions and values. And it is within that set of conventions and values that my readers will evaluate the essay, both in terms of its quality and in terms of whether or not it makes sense. Normal discourse is pointed, explanatory, and argumentative. Its purpose is to justify belief to the satisfaction of other people within the author's community of knowledgeable peers. Much of what we teach today— or should be teaching—in composition and speech courses is the normal

---

[10]Some writing in business, government, and the professions may of course be like the writing that students do in school for teachers, that is, for the sake of practice and evaluation. Certainly some writing in everyday working life is done purely as performance, for instance, to please superiors in the corporate or department hierarchy. So it may be true that learning to write to someone who is not a member of one's own status and knowledge community, that is, to a teacher, has some practical everyday value; but the value of writing of this type is hardly proportionate to the amount of time students normally spend on it.

[11]Rorty, 320.

discourse of most academic, professional, and business communities. The "rhetoric" taught in our composition textbooks comprises—or should comprise—the conventions of normal discourse of those communities.[12]

Teaching normal discourse in its written form is thus central to a college curriculum because the one thing college teachers in most fields commonly want students to acquire, and what teachers in most fields consistently reward students for, is the ability to carry on in speech and writing the normal discourse of the field in question. Normal discourse is what William Perry calls the fertile "wedding" of "bull" and "cow," of facts and their relevancies: discourse on the established contexts of knowledge in a field that makes effective reference to facts and ideas as defined within those contexts. In a student who can consummate this wedding, Perry says, "we recognize a colleague."[13] This is so because to be a conversant with the normal discourse in a field of study or endeavor is exactly what we mean by being knowledgeable—that is, knowledge*able*—in that field. Not to have mastered the normal discourse of a discipline, no matter how many "facts" or data one may know, is not to be knowledgeable in that discipline. Mastery of a "knowledge community's" normal discourse is the basic qualification for acceptance into that community.

The kind of writing we hope to teach students in college, therefore, is not only the kind of writing most appropriate to work in fields of business, government, and the professions; it is also writing most appropriate to gaining competence in most academic fields that students study in college. And what both kinds of writing have in common is that they are written within and addressed to a community of status equals: peers. They are both normal discourse.

This point having, I hope, been established, the second reason peer tutoring is important in education becomes clear. As a form of collaborative learning, peer tutoring is important because it provides the kind of social context in which normal discourse occurs: a community of knowledgeable peers. This is the main goal of peer tutoring.

Objections to Peer Tutoring

But to say this only raises another question: How can student peers, not themselves members of the knowledge communities they hope to enter, help other students enter those communities? This question is of course a variation of the question most often raised about all kinds of collaborative learning: isn't it the blind leading the blind?

---

[12] A textbook that acknowledges the normal discourse of academic disciplines and offers ways of learning it in a context of collaborative learning is Elaine Maimon, Gerald L. Belcher, Gail W. Hearn, Barbara F. Nodine, and Finbarr W. O'Connor, *Writing in the Arts and Sciences* (Cambridge, Mass.: Winthrop, 1981; distributed by Little, Brown). Another is Kenneth A. Bruffee, *A Short Course in Writing* (Cambridge, Mass.: Winthrop, 1980; distributed by Little, Brown).

[13] William G. Perry, Jr., "Examsmanship and the Liberal Arts," in *Examining in Harvard College: A Collection of Essays by Members of the Harvard Faculty* (Cambridge, Mass.: Harvard University Press, 1963); as reprinted in Bruffee, *Short Course,* 221.

One answer to this question is that while neither peer tutors nor their tutees may alone be masters of the normal discourse of a given knowledge community, by working together—pooling their resources—they are very likely to be able to master it if their conversation is structured indirectly by the task or problem that a member of that community (the teacher) provides.[14] The conversation between peer tutor and tutee, in composition or for that matter any other subject, is structured by the demands of the assignment and by the formal conventions of academic discourse and of standard written English. The tutee brings to the conversation knowledge of the subject to be written about and knowledge of the assignment. The tutor brings to the conversation knowledge of the conventions of discourse and knowledge of standard written English. If the tutee does not bring to the conversation knowledge of the subject and the assignment, the peer tutor's most important contribution is to begin at the beginning: help the tutee acquire the relevant knowledge of the subject and the assignment.

What peer tutor and tutee do together is not write or edit, or least of all proofread. What they do together is converse. They converse about the subject and about the assignment. They converse about, in an academic context, their own relationship and the relationships between student and teacher. Most of all they converse about and *pursuant to* writing.

Peer Tutoring and the Humanities

The place of conversation in learning, especially in the humanities, is the largest context in which we must see peer tutoring. To say that conversation has a place in learning should not of course seem peculiar to those of us who count ourselves humanists, a category that includes many if not most writing teachers. Most of us count "class discussion" one of the most effective ways of teaching. The truth, however, is that we tend to honor discussion more in the breach than in the observance. The person who does most of the "discussing" in most discussion classes is usually the teacher.

Our discussion classes have this fateful tendency to turn into monologues because underlying our enthusiasm for discussion is a fundamental distrust of it. The graduate training most of us have enjoyed—or endured—has taught us that collaboration and community activity is inappropriate and foreign to work in humanistic disciplines. Humanistic study, we have been led to believe, is a solitary life, and the vitality of the humanities lies in the talents and endeavors of each of us as individuals.[15] What we call discussion is more often than not an adversarial activity pitting individual against individual in an effort to assert what one literary critic has called "will to power over the text," if not

---

[14]For examples and an explanation of this process see Kenneth A. Bruffee, *Short Course,* and "CLTV: Collaborative Learning Television," *Educational Communication and Technology Journal* 30 (Spring 1982): 31ff.

[15]The individualistic bias of our current interpretation of the humanistic tradition is discussed further in Kenneth A. Bruffee, "The Structure of Knowledge and the Future of Liberal Education," *Liberal Education* (Fall 1981): 181-85.

over each other. If we look at what we do instead of what we say, we discover that we think of knowledge as something we acquire and wield relative to each other, not something we generate and maintain in company with and in dependency upon each other.

Two Models of Knowledge

Only recently have humanists of note, such as Stanley Fish in literary criticism and Richard Rorty in philosophy, begun to take effective steps toward exploring the force and implications of knowledge communities in the humanistic disciplines and toward redefining the nature of our knowledge as a social artifact. Much of this recent work follows a trail blazed a decade ago by Thomas Kuhn. The historical irony of this course of events lies in the fact that Kuhn developed his notion about the nature of scientific knowledge after first examining the way knowledge is generated and maintained in the humanities and social sciences. For us as humanists to discover in Kuhn and his followers the conceptual rationale of collaborative learning in general and peer tutoring in particular is to see our own chickens come home to roost.

Kuhn's position that even in the "hard" sciences knowledge is a social artifact emerged from his attempt to deal with the increasing indeterminacy of knowledge of all kinds in the twentieth century.[16] To say that knowledge is indeterminate is to say that there is no fixed and certain point of reference against which we can measure truth. If there is no such referent, then knowledge must be a made thing, an artifact. Kuhn argued that to call knowledge a social artifact is not to say that knowledge is merely relative, that knowledge is what any one of us says it is. Knowledge is generated by communities of knowledgeable peers. Rorty, following Kuhn, argues that communities of knowledgeable peers make knowledge by a process of socially justifying belief. Peer tutoring, as one kind of collaborative learning, models this process.

Here then is a second and more general answer to the objection most frequently raised to collaborative learning of any type: that it is a case of the blind leading the blind. It is of course exactly the blind leading the blind if we insist that knowledge is information impressed upon the individual mind by some outside source. But if we accept the premise that knowledge is an artifact created by a community of knowledgeable peers and that learning is a social process not an individual one, then learning is not assimilating information and improving our mental eyesight. Learning is an activity in which people work collaboratively to create knowledge among themselves by socially justifying belief. We create knowledge or justify belief collaboratively by cancelling each other's biases and presuppositions; by negotiating collectively toward new paradigms of perception, thought, feeling, and expression; and by joining larger, more experienced communities of knowledgeable peers

---

[16]The history of the growing indeterminacy of knowledge and its relevance to the humanities is traced briefly in Bruffee, "The Structure of Knowledge," 177-81.

through assenting to those communities' interests, values, language, and paradigms of perception and thought.

The Extension of Peer Tutoring

By accepting this concept of knowledge and learning even tentatively, it is possible to see peer tutoring as one basic model of the way that even the most sophisticated scientific knowledge is created and maintained. Knowledge is the product of human beings in a state of continual negotiation or conversation. Education is not a process of assimilating "the truth" but, as Rorty has put it, a process of learning to "take a hand in what is going on" by joining "the conversation of mankind." Peer tutoring is an arena in which students can enter into that conversation.

Because it gives students access to this "conversation of mankind," peer tutoring and especially the principles of collaborative learning that underlie it have an important role to play in studying and teaching the humanities. Peer tutoring is one way of introducing students to the process by which communities of knowledgeable peers create referential connections between symbolic structures and reality, that is, create knowledge, and by doing so maintain community growth and coherence. To study humanistic texts adequately, whether they be student themes or Shakespeare, is to study entire pedagogical attitudes and classroom practices. Such are the implications of integrating our understanding of social symbolic relationships into our teaching—not just into *what* we teach but also into *how* we teach. So long as we think of knowledge as a reflection and synthesis of information about the objective world, teaching *King Lear* seems to involve providing a correct text and rehearsing students in correct interpretations of it. But if we think of knowledge as socially justified belief, teaching *King Lear* involves creating contexts where students undergo a sort of cultural change in which they loosen ties to the knowledge community they currently belong to and join another. These two communities can be seen as having quite different sets of values, mores, and goals, and above all quite different languages. To speak in one of a person asking another to "undo this button" might be merely to tell a mercantile tale, or a prurient one, while in the other such a request could be both a gesture of profound human dignity and a metaphor of the dissolution of a world.

Similarly, so long as we think of learning as reflecting and synthesizing information about the objective world, teaching expository writing means providing examples, analysis, and exercises in the rhetorical modes—description, narration, comparison-contrast—or in the "basic skills" of writing and rehearsing students in their proper use. But if we think of learning as a social process, the process of socially justifying belief, teaching expository writing is a social symbolic process, not just part of it. Thus, to study and teach the humanities is to study and teach the social origin, nature, reference, and function of symbolic structures.

Humanistic study defined in this way requires, in turn, a reexamination of our premises as humanists and as teachers in light of the view that knowledge is a social artifact. Since to date very little work of this sort has been done, one can only guess what might come of it. But when we bring to mind for a moment a sampling of current theoretical thought in and allied to a single field of the humanities, for example, literary criticism, we are likely to find mostly bipolar forms: text and reader, text and writer, symbol and referent, signifier and signified. On the one hand, a critique of humanistic studies might involve examining how these theories would differ from their currently accepted form if they included the third term missing from most of them. How, for instance, would psychoanalytically oriented study of metaphor differ if it acknowledged that psychotherapy is fundamentally a kind of social relationship based on the mutual creation or recreation of symbolic structures by therapist and patient? How would semiotics differ if it acknowledged that connecting "code" and phenomenon are the complex social symbolic relations among the people who make up a semiotic community? How would rhetorical theory look if we assumed that writer and reader were partners in a common, community-based enterprise, partners rather than adversaries?

And having reexamined humanistic study in this way, we could suppose on the other hand that a critique of humanistic teaching might suggest changes in our demonstrating to students that they know something only when they can explain it in writing to the satisfaction of the community of their knowledgeable peers. To do this, in turn, seems to require us to engage students in collaborative work that does not just reinforce the values and skills they begin with but that promotes a sort of resocialization.[17] Peer tutoring is collaborative work of just this sort.

The Last Frontier of Collaborative Learning

The argument I have been making here assumes, of course, that peer tutors are well trained in a coherent course of study. The effectiveness of peer tutoring requires more than merely selecting "good students" and, giving them little or no guidance, throwing them together with their peers. To do that is to perpetuate, perhaps even aggravate, the many possible negative effects of peer group influence: conformity, anti-intellectualism, intimidation, and the leveling of quality. To avoid these pitfalls and marshal the powerful educational resource of peer group influence requires an effective peer tutor training course based on collaborative learning, one that maintains a demanding academic environment and makes tutoring a genuine part of the tutors' own educational development.

Given this one reservation, it remains to be said only that peer tutoring is not, after all, something new under the sun. However we may explore its conceptual ramifications, the fact is that people have always learned from their peers and doggedly persist in doing so, whether we professional teachers and educators take a hand in it or not. Thomas Wolfe's *Look Homeward,*

---

[17]Some possible curricular implications of the concept of knowledge as socially justified belief are explored in Bruffee, "Liberal Education and the Social Justification of Belief," *Liberal Education* (Summer 1982): 8-20.

Angel records how in grammar school Eugene learned to write (in this case, form words on a page) from his "comrade," learning from a peer what "all instruction failed" to teach him. In business and industry, furthermore, and in professions such as medicine, law, engineering, and architecture, where to work is to learn or fail, collaboration is the norm. All that is new in peer tutoring is the systematic application of collaborative principles to that last bastion of hierarchy and individualism, institutionalized education.

Writing as a Social Process:
A Theoretical Foundation for
Writing Centers?

by Lisa Ede

We all have stories that help us define who we are in our personal and professional lives. For those of us who work in writing centers, these stories are generally convoluted and circuitous. Few of us planned as graduate students to direct or work in writing centers, at least few graduate students of my generation (the early 70s) did. Yet most of us are now fully committed to our centers. The work that we do is demanding and undervalued—and we'd never consider changing jobs.

I would like to begin this essay by telling you the story of my own involvement with writing centers. Like many of you, I suspect, I began my graduate studies blissfully unaware of composition as a professional field. Sometime during my dissertation years my attitude toward composition changed. And sometime during my first job teaching at a SUNY college in upstate New York, my sense of my own professional identity changed: I defined myself as a teacher and researcher of composition studies.

I read research in composition studies; I began to write articles myself. And in 1980 I accepted a job at Oregon State University where, in addition to teaching composition, I became both the coordinator of the English department's writing program and the director of the Communication Skills Center, an independent support service with a Writing Lab and non-credit classes in reading and study skills. I will spare you the saga of my early years at the Communication Skills Center—my shocked recognition that I knew nothing about running a Writing Lab, the budget deficits, the frustration of hours spent making appointments, ordering supplies, and paying bills.

I survived these and other administrative traumas, thanks to an extraordinarily supportive staff and to English department colleagues. And thanks to my tutors (now called writing assistants, to avoid the remedial connotations of "tutor") I became educated about collaborative learning and peer tutoring as well. My writing assistants educated me by showing me what writing assistants can—and can't—do. With good humor and wisdom, they helped me understand collaborative learning as it occurs in actual peer conferences, not

Reprinted from *The Writing Center Journal* 9.2 (1989): 3-13. Used by permission.

in the pages of a book.

On my campus, I became an advocate of collaborative learning and of writing centers. I spoke with conviction of the unique nature and benefits of peer tutoring to colleagues, students, administrators—anyone who would give me ten minutes of their time. At first I fought for the Center's survival. Once we managed to get a still inadequate but permanent budget, I and my staff had the luxury of focusing on other issues.

These were satisfying years, but I was aware of a lingering sense of unease. For as I grew into my job as director—as my staff and the writing assistants continued to educate me—I recognized a troubling contradiction. Despite my convictions about the importance of our Writing Lab and the benefits of peer tutoring, I couldn't connect my pragmatic experience and understanding of the importance of this work with my more theoretical research in composition and rhetoric. Furthermore, the research that most interested me—research on classical and contemporary rhetorical theories—seemed to intersect little with my work in the Writing Lab.

I want to be as clear as possible about the nature of this contradiction and the reasons why it troubled me. In a sense, my awareness of this contradiction simply exacerbated a schizophrenic-like bifurcation already implicit in my situation. (I have two offices in two separate buildings, for instance, and until recently I reported to two different deans.) But my unease went deeper than that. I believe strongly in the interdependence of theory and practice, as do most in our profession. Theory without practice is likely to result in un-grounded, inapplicable speculation. Practice without theory, as we know, often leads to inconsistent, and sometimes even contradictory and wrong-headed, pedagogical methods.

Yet here I was, theorizing at nights and on weekends in ways that didn't seem to connect with my week-day work. I wondered if I was continuing the ghettoization of composition, only in a new form. The old version had literary critics theorizing while underpaid teaching assistants and instructors toiled in composition classes. Had I managed to internalize that opposition, so that the Writing Lab part of me couldn't find anything interesting or relevant to say to the weekend theorizer? If so, I gradually realized, I was implicitly contrib-uting to the general perception that writing centers are "extras," helpful additions to composition or writing across the curriculum programs that fall into the nice-to-have-if-you-can-get-it-but-not-essential category.

I have come to believe that my situation is not uncommon. For a variety of reasons, those of us who direct or work in writing centers have seldom been able to articulate theoretical support for our work that goes beyond the basic principles of collaborative learning. The most common reason for this failure, of course, is that we have been too busy working ourselves to death—running centers on inadequate or even nonexistent budgets, functioning as director, secretary, tutor, and public relations expert all at once—to take the time to theorize. Because we have in a sense been inventing ourselves as we started, developed, and defended our centers, we have naturally focused on the pragmatic.

WRITING AS A SOCIAL PROCESS: A THEORETICAL
FOUNDATION FOR WRITING CENTERS?

101

Anyone who has found a solution to a pressing problem by consulting a treasured collection of *Writing Lab Newsletters* knows how crucial the exchange of ideas and experiences is. We need to draw upon our shared experiences, to find out how others have solved problems that we face. But one consequence of our enforced pragmatism is that we have tended to talk mainly with one another. We have succeeded in creating a niche for ourselves in the larger world of composition studies, but we have not, I fear, convinced others in our field of our centrality. We are part of but not fully integrated into our own discipline.

In *Writing Centers: Theory and Administration*, Gary Olson observed that writing centers " . . . have always been diverse in their pedagogies, philosophies, and physical make-ups. But the writing center's period of chaotic adolescence is nearly over. Center directors are slowly articulating common goals, objectives, and methodologies; and writing centers are beginning to take on a common form to evolve into a recognizable species" (vii). Olson is right: our period of adolescence is nearly over. Part of our passage into professional adulthood, however, involves grounding this "common form" in fully articulated theory. For by so doing, we will not only clarify and justify the work we do, we will also connect in important ways with others in our field.

I believe that the time is right for those of us who direct or work in writing centers to place our work in a rich theoretical context. And we don't need to start from scratch. We can build not only on theories of collaborative learning, as articulated by Bruffee, Hawkins, and others, but on the work of those who have recently challenged us to view writing as a social, rather than a solitary and individual, process.

In this article, I would like to comment on several lines of research that either explicitly or implicitly place writing centers at the heart, rather than the periphery, of current theory in composition studies. I also hope to suggest some of the ways that those of us who work in writing centers can contribute to this intellectual dialogue. For we have an important contribution to make. Because of our experiences in writing centers, we know things that composition specialists who work only with graduate students—or even those who teach undergraduate writing classes—can't know. And our centers can provide unique opportunities for research.

Most of us are familiar with the research that stimulated current interest in collaborative learning—Thom Hawkins' *Group Inquiry Techniques for Teaching Writing* and Ken Bruffee's articles and textbook. Enough time has passed since this research was published—Bruffee's first article on collaborative learning appeared in 1972, while Hawkins' book was published in 1976—for us to gain distance from it. As John Trimbur explains in "Collaborative Learning and Teaching Writing," recent interest in collaborative learning grew out of a crisis, a rapid increase in student enrollment in the 70s, which drew many underprepared students who previously would not have attended college to our campuses. One response to this crisis was the establishment of writing centers, places where these and other students could get the help they needed. Those who directed these centers were pragmatists. To the degree that they grounded their work in theory—and few had time to do this—they looked primarily to such educational reformers as John Dewey, M. L. J. Abercrombie, Edwin Mason, and Paolo Friere. They emphasized the important role that social interaction played in learning, and they argued that students who participate in collaborative learning experiences learn more effectively—do better on exams, write more effective prose—than their peers.

Although this early research emphasized the importance of the social and cultural contexts of teaching and learning, it still tended to view both writing and thinking—the creation of knowledge—as inherently individual activities. In his early essays, for instance, Bruffee at times praises collaborative learning as a means of helping student writers escape the inevitable solitariness of writing, whose self-imposed isolation is often seen as particularly troubling for beginning writers. Cognitive-developmental research does suggest that basic writers find it difficult to move from the collaboration of conversation to the more independent creation of meaning that writing entails.

Bruffee's and others' claims for collaborative learning have potentially negative implications, however. For if writing is naturally and inevitably solitary, then collaborative learning is in a sense an unnatural and, for most writers, unnecessary interruption. Implicitly, then, such a view of writing suggests that only beginning or second-best writers would need the support and collaboration that in-class groups and writing centers provide. *Real writers*, experienced and professional writers, wouldn't need or seek out such concrete dialogue. Recognizing that writers naturally write alone and that, as Walter Ong states in a well-known article in PMLA, "the writer's audience is always a fiction," they would happily seclude themselves in their study or carrell.

I want to emphasize this point: as long as thinking and writing are regarded as inherently individual, solitary activities, writing centers can never be viewed as anything more than pedagogical fix-it shops to help those who, for whatever reason, are unable to think and write on their own. This understanding of thinking and writing not only places writing centers on the periphery of most colleges, where our second-class status is symbolized by our basement offices and inadequate staffs and budgets, it also places us on the periphery of our own field of composition studies. Think for a moment, for instance, of Flower and Hayes' cognitive-based research—research that has been particularly influential during the past decade. Where in the flow charts depicting task representation, audience analysis, and short-term and long-term memory is the box representing collaboration and conversation? As Marilyn Cooper says in "The Ecology of Writing":

> The ideal writer the cognitive process model projects is isolated from the social world. . . . The solitary author works alone, within the privacy of his own mind. He uses free writing exercises and heuristics to find out what he knows about a subject and to find something he wants to say to others; he uses his analytic skills to discover a

purpose, to imagine an audience, to decide on strategies, to organize content; and he simulates how his text will be read by reading it over himself, making the final revisions necessary to assure its success when he abandons it to the world of which he is not a part. The isolation of the solitary author from the social world leads him to see ideas and goals as originating primarily within himself and directed at an unknown and largely hostile other. *Writing becomes a form of parthenogenesis, the author producing propositional and pragmatic structures, Athena-like, full grown and complete, out of his brow.* (365-66; my emphasis.)

The assumption that writing is inherently a solitary cognitive activity is so deeply ingrained in western culture that it has, until recently, largely gone unexamined. Indeed, many people find it difficult to recognize that the term authorship refers not to the physical act of inscription, the process of writing texts, but to a concept. One of the best ways I've found to understand the concept of authorship is to take an historical perspective. I think you may be surprised, as I was when I first began this research, by what history tells us. In the Middle Ages, for instance, authors simply didn't exist: no distinction was made between the person who wrote a text and the person who copied it. In *The Friar as Critic: Literary Attitudes in the Middle Ages,* Judson Boyce Allen attempts to help scholars understand what it meant to be an author or reader in this period. Aware of the difficulty of his task, Allen comments that:

when we are faced with medieval authors . . . we are faced with a foreign, nonempirical sensibility. We are confronted by authors who are for the most part content to repeat inherited materials, making their own primary contribution . . . in the area of decoration, and often content to remain anonymous: if they name themselves, it is only in the later Middle Ages that they are not primarily doing so in order to solicit prayer. (59)

Or consider the Elizabethan period in England. When we think of this period, of course, we think of Shakespeare—now enthroned as one of the greatest authors in English literature. Surely Shakespeare typifies our contemporary notion of what it means to be an author? The fact is, however, that the conditions of the period precluded any such conception. During the Elizabethan period, for instance, only those playwrights who were also actors, and thus members of the company performing their work, could expect to receive any financial benefit other than a one-time payment. For, with a few exceptions, the actors, members of companies that functioned much like present-day cooperatives, owned the plays the company produced. Most plays, including Shakespeare's early plays, appeared without an author's name on the title page. Furthermore, once a company purchased a play, it felt free to make whatever alterations the actors wished. As Feuillerat notes in *The Composition of Shakespeare's Plays*, "A certain amount of reworking came naturally enough during the rehearsals, but far more important revisions of an author's text were frequent and often went so far as to change the very nature of the play" (7).

I wish that I could discuss the history of the concept of authorship more fully. Even a cursory historical examination indicates, however, that our modern concept of authorship, which might best be characterized as intellectual property rights (property rights that can, by their very nature, only be owned by a single person), is clearly an overdetermined concept. You can trace its development in literary history, from the tentative assertions of the claims of originality in the Renaissance to the Romantic's fully conceived argument for the primacy of the individual imagination. (In *Literary Theory: An Introduction,* Terry Eagleton notes that since the Romantics, literary theory has "assumed that, in the main, at the centre of the world is the contemplative individual self, bowed over its books, striving to gain touch with experience, truth, reality, history, or tradition" [196]. The impact of Cartesianism, which established epistemology as the central branch of philosophy, further supports the assumption that the individual thinking and writing in isolation is the source of all truth worth knowing.

It is also possible to trace the impact of technology on the concept of authorship, as Elizabeth Eisenstein does in *The Printing Press as an Agent of Change*. According to Eisenstein, "both the eponymous [or named] inventor and personal authorship appeared at the same time and as a consequence of the same process," the development of the printing press. "Scribal culture," she argues, "worked against the concept of intellectual property rights. It did not lend itself to preserving traces of personal idiosyncrasies, to the public airing of private thoughts, or to any of the forms of silent publicity that have shaped consciousness of self during the past four centuries" (229-230).

Still others have analyzed the way that copyright laws, which we take for granted but which were a bitter source of controversy in the eighteenth and nineteenth centuries, codified and extended authorship. It is startling indeed to read German intellectuals in the 1840s argue that writers can no more claim their texts as permanent property, theirs for a lifetime, than a cabinetmaker can expect to profit each time a chest that he has made is purchased. Once sold, both are gone forever; they are the property of the purchaser (Woodmansee). The inextricable link between writers and their ideas, one that undergirds our notions of both authorship and plagiarism, simply didn't exist.

I hope that this brief historical excursion doesn't strike you as a digression, a curiosity. Recognizing that authorship is a concept, not a physical activity, and then tracing how that concept developed can help us understand why collaborative learning, and our writing centers, have always been resisted, marginalized. For although we may be unaware of it, our effort to encourage collaboration and dialogue is inherently subversive—not just of our traditional educational institutions (we have always known that), but of one of the most important, because most hidden and commonsensical, assumptions of our culture: that writing and thinking are inherently individual, solitary activities.

This historical excursion also clarifies what has always, for me at least, been a puzzling and frustrating mystery: the fact that those who most resist or misunderstand the kind of collaborative learning that occurs in writing centers are often our own colleagues in departments of English. Their immersion in our Romantic and Post-Romantic literary tradition, as well as their experience as students and teachers, has reinforced their often unconscious allegiance to the image of the solitary writer working silently in a garrett. Though they often want—and try—to support us, their acceptance of writing as a solitary act prevents them from fully doing so.

I indicated previously that the time is right for those of us who are committed to collaborative learning and writing centers to locate our work in a rich theoretical context—one that places us at the center of current theory. A number of researchers are endeavoring to articulate a theory of writing that recognizes, as Marilyn Cooper notes, that "language and texts are not simply the means by which individuals discover and communicate information, but are essentially social activities, dependent on social structures and processes not only in their interpretive but also in their constructive phases" (367). These researchers—Marilyn Cooper, Anne Gere, Patricia Bizzell, Kenneth Bruffee, Karen LeFevre, Jim Reither, Linda Brodkey, and others—are attempting to enrich the cognitive approach to writing with what Cooper calls "an ecological model of writing, whose fundamental tenet is that writing is an activity through which a person is continually engaged with a variety of socially constructed systems" (36).

If you aren't familiar with this research, you may be surprised to discover the diverse range of disciplines upon which these writers draw. Kenneth Bruffee's later essays, which attempt to lay the framework for a social constructivist epistemology, cite studies in philosophy, education, sociology, anthropology, psychology, and literary criticism. Such a display of learning may seem pretentious—the unnecessary piling up of sources—but I don't think that's the case. What we're witnessing is a fundamental epistemological shift, one that both draws on and will influence a broad range of disciplines, including our own.

I don't want to mislead you, however. Not all these discussions of writing as a social process are as scholarly as Bruffee's. Some, such as Min-Zhan Lu's recent essay "From Silence to Words: Writing as Struggle," are surprisingly personal. We're not used to reading essays whose authors ground their theoretical observations in personal experience, as Min-Zhan Lu does when she discusses the conflicts she experienced growing up in China during the Cultural Revolution. For despite our adherence to an individualist and subjectivist ideology, as scholars, at least, we have insisted, in Eagleton's words, on "abstracting personal values and qualities from the whole concrete context . . . in which they are embedded" ("The Subject of Literature," 103). We have granted AUTHORity—and I hope that by now you see the "author" in authority—only to those who establish their claims by referring to other texts. A number of those who advocate a social view of writing resist such restrictions, choosing instead to place themselves in a particular, contextualized scene of writing and reading (as I have tried to do in this essay).

We've got a lot at stake, I've been arguing, in the research on writing as a social process that I've been describing here, for such research implicitly argues for the centrality of what we do in our writing centers. We've also, I believe just as strongly, got a lot to contribute. A recent critique of Bruffee's work by Greg Myers, for instance, charges Bruffee and other advocates of collaborative learning with naively refusing to recognize the role that ideology (which Myers defines as "the thoughts that structure our thinking so deeply that we take them for granted" [156]) plays in collaborative learning. Bruffee and others talk, Myers charges, as though the social construction of reality is inevitably positive and beneficial to our students, presenting an idealized view of writing that has little resemblance to actual group dynamics.

I think that Greg Myers is at least partly right, and that those of us who work in writing centers are just the right folks to help keep theoreticians like Bruffee honest. We can do case studies, or even more detailed ethnographic analyses, for instance, of what actually happens when two or more peers collaborate. And we can learn something about the role that power and ideology play in our writing classrooms by comparing our experiences as teachers and as participants in the culture of writing centers. Last year, for instance, I kept a reading journal during a quarter when I taught a section of my university's freshman composition class and read the journals and essays written by students working as writing assistants in our lab. I was shocked to discover that my experience of reading my freshmen's essays and writing assistants' journals differed so fundamentally that I could hardly call both experiences reading. I am still considering the implications of this recognition for my teaching and for my work with students in the Writing Lab.

These examples suggest, I hope, that it is hardly necessary to master the philosophical tradition before one can contribute to the ongoing conversation about writing as a social process—though an understanding of the degree to which this movement constitutes a genuine epistemological revolution is certainly helpful. *Those of us who work in writing centers need to be part of this conversation.* This means that many of us will first have to fight for the time we need to do such thinking and writing. We will have to convince our deans or vice-presidents that our job requires us to do more than hire and train tutors, balance budgets, and promote our centers. We will, in other words, have to argue for a revised definition of our positions. But then, precisely because of our work in writing centers, we have known for quite some time that, as Min-Zhan Lu notes, writing is struggle.

I'd like to close this essay with a quotation from Bakhtin that I think applies both to us and to our students. Language, Bakhtin says, "lies on the borderline between oneself and the other. The word in language is half someone else's. It becomes 'one's own' only when the speaker populates it with his own intentions, his own accent, when he appropriates the word, adapting it to his own semantic and expressive intention. Prior to this moment of appropriation, the word does not exist in a neutral and personal language . . . but rather it exists in other people's mouths, in other people's contexts, serving other people's intentions: it is from there that one must take the word, and make it one's own" (cited in Gates, 1). It is time for us to take the word and make a real place for ourselves in the world of composition studies, and of the academy.

Works Cited

Abercrombie, M. L. J. *Aims and Techniques for Group Teaching.* Guildford: U of Guildford, 1970.

Allen, Judson Boyce. *The Friar as Critic: Literary Attitudes in the Middle Ages.* Nashville: Vanderbilt UP, 1971.

Bakhtin, Mikhail. "Discourse in the Novel." Cited in Henry Louis Gates, Jr., Ed. *Race, Writing, and Difference.* Chicago: U of Chicago P, 1986.

Bizzell, Patricia. "Foundationalism and Anti-Foundationalism in Composition Studies." *Pre/Text* 7 (1986): 37-56.

Brodkey, Linda. *Academic Writing as Social Practice.* Philadelphia: Temple UP, 1987.

____. "Modernism and the Scene(s) of Writing." *College English* 49 (1987): 396-418.

Bruffee, Kenneth. "The Brooklyn Plan: Attaining Intellectual Growth Through Peer-Group Tutoring." *Liberal Education* 64 (1978): 447-68.

____. "Collaborative Learning and the 'Conversation of Mankind.'" *College English* 46 (1984): 635-52.

____. "Collaborative Learning: Some Practical Models." *College English* 34 (1973): 579-86.

____. *A Short Course in Writing,* 2nd ed. Cambridge, Ma.: Winthrop, 1980.

____. "Social Construction, Language, and the Authority of Knowledge: A Bibliographic Essay." *College English* 48 (1986): 773-90.

____. "The Structure of Knowledge and the Future of Liberal Education." *Liberal Education* 67 (1981): 177-86.

____. "The Way Out." *College English* 33 (1972): 457-70.

Cooper, Marilyn. "The Ecology of Writing." *College English* 48 (1986): 364-75.

Dewey, John. *Experience and Education.* 1938. New York: Collier, 1963.

____. *The Public and Its Problems.* Denver: Alan Swallow, 1927.

Eagleton, Terry. *Literary Theory: An Introduction.* Minneapolis: U of Minnesota P, 1983.

____. "The Subject of Literature.: *Cultural Critique* 2 (1985-86): 95-104.

Eisenstein, Elizabeth. *The Printing Press as an Agent of Change.* Cambridge: Cambridge UP, 1979.

Feuillerat, Albert. *The Composition of Shakespeare's Plays.* New Haven: Yale UP, 1953.

Freire, Paolo. *Pedagogy of the Oppressed.* New York: Leabury, 1968.

Gere, Ann Ruggles. *Writing Groups: History, Theory, and Implications.* Carbondale, Il.: SIUP, 1987.

Hawkins, Thom. *Group Inquiry Techniques for Teaching Writing.* Urbana, Il.: NCTE, 1976.

Mason, Edwin. *Collaborative Learning.* London: WardLock Educational, 1970.

Myers, Greg. "Reality, Consensus, and Reform in the Rhetoric of Composition Teaching." *College English* 48 (1986): 154-74.

Olson, Gary. *Writing Centers: Theory and Administration.* Urbana, Il.: NCTE, 1984.

Ong, Walter J. "The Writer's Audience Is Always a Fiction." *PMLA* 90 (1975): 9-21.

Reither, James A. "Writing and Knowing: Toward Redefining the Writing Process." *College English* 47 (1985): 620-28.

Trimbur, John. "Collaborative Learning and Teaching Writing," *Perspectives on Research and Scholarship in Composition.* Ben W. McClelland and Timothy Donovan, Eds. New York: MLA, 1985.

Woodmansee, Martha. "The Genius and the Copyright: Economic and Legal Conditions of the Emergence of the 'Author'." *Eighteenth-Century Studies* 17 (1984): 425-448.

Collaboration, Control, and the Idea of a Writing Center

by Andrea Lunsford

The triple focus of my title reflects some problems I've been concentrating on as I thought about and prepared for the opportunity to speak last week at the Midwest Writing Centers Association meeting in St. Cloud, and here at the Pacific Coast/Inland Northwest Writing Centers meeting in Le Grande. I'll try as I go along to illuminate—or at least to complicate—each of these foci, and I'll conclude by sketching in what I see as a particularly compelling idea of a writing center, one informed by collaboration and, I hope, attuned to diversity.

As some of you may know, I've recently written a book on collaboration, *in* collaboration with my dearest friend and co-author, Lisa Ede. *Singular Texts/Plural Authors: Perspectives in Collaborative Writing* was six years in the research and writing, so I would naturally gravitate to principles of collaboration in this or any other address.

Yet it's interesting to me to note that when Lisa and I began our research (see "Why Write . . . Together?"), we didn't even use the term "collaboration"; we identified our subjects as "co- and group-writing." And when we presented our first paper on the subject at the 1985 CCCC meeting, ours was the only such paper at the conference, ours the only presentation with "collaboration" in the title. Now, as you know, the word is everywhere, in every journal, every conference program, on the tip of every scholarly tongue. So—collaboration, yes. But why control? Because as the latest pedagogical bandwagon, collaboration often masquerades as democracy when it in fact practices the same old authoritarian control. It thus stands open to abuse and can, in fact, lead to poor teaching and poor learning. And it can lead—as many of you know—to disastrous results in the writing center. So amidst the rush to embrace collaboration, I see a need for careful interrogation and some caution.

We might begin by asking where the collaboration bandwagon got rolling. Why has it gathered such steam? Because, I believe, collaboration both in theory and practice reflects a broad-based epistemological shift, a shift in the way we view knowledge. The shift involves a move from viewing knowledge and reality as things exterior to or outside of us, as immediately accessible,

Reprinted from *The Writing Center Journal* 12.1 (1991): 3-10. Used by permission.

individually knowable, measurable, and shareable—to viewing knowledge and reality as mediated by or constructed through language in social use, as socially constructed, contextualized, as, in short, the product of *collaboration.*

I'd like to suggest that collaboration as an embodiment of this theory of knowledge poses a distinct threat to one particular idea of a writing center. This idea of a writing center, what I'll call "The Center as Storehouse," holds to the earlier view of knowledge just described—knowledge as exterior to us and as directly accessible. The Center as Storehouse operates as information stations or storehouses, prescribing and handing out skills and strategies to individual learners. They often use "modules" or other kinds of individualized learning materials. They tend to view knowledge as individually derived and held, and they are not particularly amenable to collaboration, sometimes actively hostile to it. I visit lots of Storehouse Centers, and in fact I set up such a center myself, shortly after I had finished an M.A. degree and a thesis on William Faulkner.

Since Storehouse Centers do a lot of good work and since I worked very hard to set up one of them, I was loathe to complicate or critique such a center. Even after Lisa and I started studying collaboration in earnest, and in spite of the avalanche of data we gathered in support of the premise that collaboration is the norm in most professions (American Consulting Engineers Council, American Institute of Chemists, American Psychological Institute, Modern Language Association, Professional Services Management Association, International City Management Association, Society for Technical Communication), I was still a very reluctant convert.

Why? Because, I believe, collaboration posed another threat to my way of teaching, a way that informs another idea of a writing center, which I'll call "The Center as Garret." Garret Centers are informed by a deep-seated belief in individual "genius," in the Romantic sense of the term. (I need hardly point out that this belief also informs much of the humanities and, in particular, English studies.) These Centers are also informed by a deep-seated attachment to the American brand of individualism, a term coined by Alexis de Toqueville as he sought to describe the defining characteristics of this Republic.

Unlike Storehouse Centers, Garret Centers don't view knowledge as exterior, as information to be sought out or passed on mechanically. Rather they see knowledge as interior, as inside the student, and the writing center's job as helping students get in touch with this knowledge, as a way to find their unique voices, their individual and unique powers. This idea has been articulated by many, including Ken Macrorie, Peter Elbow, and Don Murray, and the idea usually gets acted out in Murray-like conferences, those in which the tutor or teacher listens, voices encouragement, and essentially serves as a validation of the students' "I-search." Obviously, collaboration problematizes Garret Centers as well, for they also view knowledge as interiorized, solitary, individually derived, individually held.

As I've indicated, I held on pretty fiercely to this idea as well as to the first one. I was still resistant to collaboration. So I took the natural path for an academic faced with this dilemma: I decided to do more research. I did a *lot* of it. And, to my chagrin, I found more and more evidence to challenge my ideas, to challenge both the idea of Centers as Storehouses or as Garrets. Not incidentally, the data I amassed mirrored what my students had been telling me for years: not the research they carried out, not their dogged writing of essays, not *me* even, but their work in groups, their *collaboration*, was the most important and helpful part of their school experience. Briefly, the data I found all support the following claims:

1. Collaboration aids in problem finding as well as problem solving.
2. Collaboration aids in learning abstractions.
3. Collaboration aids in transfer and assimilation; it fosters interdisciplinary thinking.
4. Collaboration leads not only to sharper, more critical thinking (students must explain, defend, adapt), but to deeper understanding of *others*.
5. Collaboration leads to higher achievement in general. I might mention here the Johnson and Johnson analysis of 122 studies from 1924-1981, which included every North American study that considered achievement or performance data in competitive, co-operative/collaborative, or individualistic classrooms. Some 60% showed that collaboration promoted higher achievement, while only 6% showed the reverse. Among studies comparing the effects of collaboration and independent work, the results are even more strongly in favor of collaboration.

   Moreover, the superiority of collaboration held for all subject areas and all age groups. See "How to Succeed Without Even Vying," *Psychology Today*, September 1986.
6. Collaboration promotes excellence. In this regard, I am fond of quoting Hannah Arendt: "For excellence, the presence of others is always required."
7. Collaboration engages the whole student and encourages active learning; it combines reading, talking, writing, thinking; it provides practice in both synthetic and analytic skills.

Given these research findings, why am I still urging caution in using collaboration as our key term, in using collaboration as the idea of the kind of writing center I now advocate?

First, because creating a collaborative environment and truly collaborative tasks is damnably difficult. Collaborative environments and tasks must *demand* collaboration. Students, tutors, teachers must really need one another to carry out common goals. As an aside, let me note that studies of collaboration in the workplace identify three kinds of tasks that seem to call consistently for collaboration: high-order problem defining and solving; division of labor tasks, in which the job is simply too big for any one person; and division of expertise tasks. Such tasks are often difficult to come by in writing centers, particularly those based on the Storehouse or Garret models.

A collaborative environment must also be one in which goals are clearly defined and in which the jobs at hand engage everyone fairly equally, from the student clients to work-study students to peer tutors and professional staff. In other words, such an environment rejects traditional hierarchies. In addition, the kind of collaborative environment I want to encourage calls for careful and ongoing monitoring and evaluating of the collaboration or group process, again on the part of all involved. In practice, such monitoring calls on each person involved in the collaboration to build a *theory* of collaboration, a theory of group dynamics.

Building such a collaborative environment is also hard because getting groups of any kind going is hard. The students', tutors', and teachers' prior experiences may work against it (they probably held or still hold to Storehouse or Garret ideas); the school day and term work against it; and the drop-in nature of many centers, including my own, works against it. Against these odds, we have to figure out how to constitute groups in our centers; how to allow for evaluation and monitoring; how to teach, model, and learn about careful listening, leadership, goal setting, and negotiation—all of which are necessary to effective collaboration.

We must also recognize that collaboration is hardly a monolith. Instead, it comes in a dizzying variety of modes about which we know almost nothing. In our books, Lisa and I identify and describe two such modes, the hierarchical and the dialogic, both of which our centers need to be well versed at using. But it stands to reason that these two modes perch only at the tip of the collaborative iceberg.

As I argued earlier, I think we must be cautious in rushing to embrace collaboration because collaboration can also be used to reproduce the status quo; the rigid hierarchy of teacher-centered classrooms is replicated in the tutor-centered writing center in which the tutor is still the seat of all authority but is simply pretending it isn't so. Such a pretense of democracy sends badly mixed messages. It can also lead to the kind of homogeneity that squelches diversity, that waters down ideas to the lowest common denominator, that erases rather than values difference. This tendency is particularly troubling given our growing awareness of the roles gender and ethnicity play in all learning. So regression toward the mean is not a goal I seek in an idea of a writing center based on collaboration.

The issue of control surfaces most powerfully in this concern over a collaborative center. In the writing center ideas I put forward earlier, where is that focus of control? In Storehouse Centers, it seems to me control resides in the tutor or center staff, the possessors of information, the currency of the Academy. Garret Centers, on the other hand, seem to invest power and control in the individual student knower, though I would argue that such control is often appropriated by the tutor/teacher, as I have often seen happen during Murray or Elbow style conferences. Any center based on collaboration will need to address the issue of control explicitly, and doing so will not be easy.

It won't be easy because what I think of as successful collaboration (which I'll call Burkean Parlor Centers), collaboration that is attuned to diversity, goes deeply against the grain of education in America. To illustrate,

I need offer only a few representative examples:

1. Mina Shaughnessy, welcoming a supervisor to her classroom in which students were busily collaborating, was told, "Oh . . . I'll come back when you're teaching."
2. A prominent and very distinguished feminist scholar has been refused an endowed chair because most of her work had been written collaboratively.
3. A prestigious college poetry prize was withdrawn after the winning poem turned out to be written by three student collaborators.
4. A faculty member working in a writing center was threatened with dismissal for "encouraging" group-produced documents.

I have a number of such examples, all of which suggest that—used unreflectively or *un*cautiously—collaboration may harm professionally those who seek to use it and may as a result further reify a model of education as the top-down transfer of information (back to The Storehouse) or a private search for Truth (back to The Garret). As I also hope I've suggested, collaboration can easily degenerate into busy work or what Jim Corder calls "fading into the tribe."

So I am very, very serious about the cautions I've been raising, about our need to examine carefully what we mean by collaboration and to explore how those definitions locate control. And yet I still advocate—with growing and deepening conviction—the move to collaboration in both classrooms and centers. In short, I am advocating a third, alternative idea of a writing center, one I know many of you have already brought into being. In spite of the very real risks involved, we need to embrace the idea of writing centers as Burkean Parlors, as centers for collaboration. Only in doing so can we, I believe, enable a student body and citizenry to meet the demands of the twenty-first century. A recent Labor Department report tells us, for instance, that by the mid-1990s workers will need to read at the 11th grade level for even low-paying jobs; that workers will need to be able not so much to solve pre-packaged problems but to identify problems amidst a welter of information or data; that they will need to reason from complex symbol systems rather than from simple observation; most of all that they will need to be able to work with others who are different from them and to learn to negotiate power and control (Heath).

The idea of a center I want to advocate speaks directly to these needs, for its theory of knowledge is based not on positivistic principles (that's The Storehouse again), not on Platonic or absolutist ideas (that's The Garret), but on the notion of knowledge as always contextually bound, as always socially constructed. Such a center might well have as its motto Arendt's statement: "For Excellence, the presence of others is always required." Such a center would place control, power, and authority not in the tutor or staff, not in the individual student, but in the negotiating group. It would engage students not only in solving problems set by teachers but in identifying problems for themselves; not only in working as a group but in monitoring, evaluating, and building a theory of how groups work; not only in understanding and valuing collaboration but in confronting squarely the issues of control that successful collaboration inevitably raises; not only in reaching consensus but in valuing dissensus and diversity.

The idea of a center informed by a theory of knowledge as socially constructed, of power and control as constantly negotiated and shared, and of collaboration as its first principle presents quite a challenge. It challenges our ways of organizing our centers, of training our staff and tutors, of working with teachers. It even challenges our sense of where we "fit" in this idea. More importantly, however, such a center presents a challenge to the institution of higher education, an institution that insists on rigidly controlled individual performance, on evaluation as punishment, on isolation, on the kinds of values that took that poetry prize away from three young people or that accused Mina Shaughnessy of "not teaching."

This alternative, this third idea of a writing center, poses a threat as well as a challenge to the status quo in higher education. This threat is one powerful and largely invisible reason, I would argue, for the way in which many writing centers have been consistently marginalized, consistently silenced. But organizations like this one are gaining a voice, are finding ways to imagine into being centers as Burkean Parlors for collaboration, writing centers, I believe, which can lead the way in changing the face of higher education.

So, as if you didn't already know it, you're a subversive group, and I'm delighted to have been invited to participate in this collaboration. But I've been talking far too long by myself now, so I'd like to close by giving the floor to two of my student collaborators. The first—like I was—was a reluctant convert to the kind of collaboration I've been describing tonight. But here's what she wrote to me some time ago:

> Dr. Lunsford: I don't know exactly what to say here, but I want to say something. So here goes. When this Writing Center class first began, I didn't know what in the hell you meant by collaboration. I thought —hey! yo!—you're the teacher and you know a lot of stuff. And you better tell it to me. Then I can tell it to the other guys. Now I know that you know even more than I thought. I even found out I know a lot. But that's not important. What's important is knowing that knowing doesn't just happen all by itself, like the cartoons show with a little light bulb going off in a bubble over a character's head. Knowing happens with other people, figuring things out, trying to explain, talking through things. What I know is that we are all making and remaking our knowing and ourselves with each other every day—you just as much as me and the other guys, Dr. Lunsford. We're all— all of us together—collaborative recreations in process. So—well—just wish me luck.

And here's a note I received just as I got on the plane, from another student/ collaborator:

I had believed that Ohio State had nothing more to offer me in the way of improving my writing. Happily, I was mistaken. I have great expectations for our Writing Center Seminar class. I look forward to every one of our classes and to every session with my 110W students [2 groups of 3 undergraduates he is tutoring]. I sometimes feel that they have more to offer me than I to them. They say the same thing, though, so I guess we're about even, all learning together. (P.S. This class and the Center have made me certain I want to attend graduate school.)

These students embody the kind of center I'm advocating, and I'm honored to join them in conversation about it, conversation we can continue together now.

Works Cited

Corder, Jim W. "Hunting for Ethos Where They Say It Can't Be Found." *Rhetoric Review.* 7 (Spring 1989): 299-316.

Ede, Lisa S., and Andrea A. Lunsford. "Why Write...Together?" *Rhetoric Review.* 1 (Jan 1983): 150-58.

____. *Singular Texts/Plural Authors: Perspectives on Collaborative Writing.* Carbondale, IL: Southern Illinois UP, 1990.

Heath, Shirley Brice. "The Fourth Vision: Literate Language at Work." *The Right to Literacy.* Eds. Andrea A. Lunsford, Helen Moglen, and James Slevin. New York: Modern Language Association, 1990.

Kohn, Alfie. "How to Succeed Without Even Vying." *Psychology Today.* (Sept 1986): 22-28.

Writing Centers In Context: Responding To Current Educational Theory

by Christina Murphy

Having come into prominence in the last forty years as an important aspect of supplemental instruction, writing centers are essentially constructs of the postmodern world. As such, they reflect the educational philosophies and socio-political currents shaping American society and contending for paramountcy in the second half of the twentieth century.

In *Education Under Siege,* Stanley Aronowitz and Henry A. Giroux describe this conflux of competing ideologies as "the conservative, liberal and radical debate over schooling" (iii). The conservative perspective envisions a schooling system in which "the mastery of techniques is equivalent to progress" (2). The model that underlies the conservative perspective is that of education as a type of regimented and highly authoritarian training for future roles within society.

The liberal vision is of schooling "as a broad preparation for life, as an effective means to reproduce the kind of society and individual consistent with western humanist traditions" (5). The paradigm that guides this view is that of liberation, the vast capacity education possesses for freeing—through intrapersonal enrichment—the varied capacities individuals are endowed with as pre-actualized potentials.

The radical view conceptualizes the process of education as a microcosm of the power relations and oppositional politics that exist in any society and any historical era. Educators, thus, "are, perhaps unwittingly, clerks not only of the state, but also of the class that dominates it," and they exemplify the Marxist view that "the ruling ideas of any society are the ideas of the ruling class" (6). Like the liberal view, the radical paradigm envisions education as liberatory but adds a broader dimension to this concept by emphasizing that schools should "promote ongoing forms of critique and a struggle against objective forces of oppression" (Giroux xviii).

The contemporary concept of the writing center has emerged from the matrix of these conflicting ideologies and the responses to educational issues

Reprinted from *The Writing Center: New Directions*, ed. Ray Wallace and Jeanne Simpson (New York: Garland, 1991), pp. 276-88. Used by permission.

favored by each. Initially, in the 1940's and 50's, writing centers were established to address the instructional problems of weaker students by strengthening their writing and critical thinking skills and thus better preparing them for the academic experience (North 436). Since the early writing centers were extensions of English departments, they emerged from the humanities as their root discipline and embodied the liberal concept of developing students' potentials and facilitating their intellectual growth.

Interestingly, though, the writing centers formulated upon this basis also served to foster the conservative agenda of having task-oriented students working to achieve the "markers," or measurable objectives by which both intellectual progress and mastery of the techniques of literacy could be measured. The result of this inadvertent merging of objectives was a difficult, if not uneasy, alliance that has affected the design and axiological underpinnings of writing centers ever since.

From the conservative perspective, writing centers are effective when they advance a student's mastery of skills—specifically, grammar, mechanics, vocabulary, and sentence complexity and variety. The energy of the conservative view pushes writing centers in the direction of becoming remediation centers to rectify deficiencies in the language arts training students are expected to have received in high schools. Writing centers should serve, too, the ancillary purpose of diagnostic assessment of students to detect weaknesses and to offer supplemental, corrective instruction, often of a drill/review nature. Philosophically, there is an "overwhelming emphasis on immediate, empirically measurable objectives" and "a tendency to consider such short-term prespecified outcomes (behavioral objectives, skill acquisition, grade equivalency achievement) as conceptually adequate to guide research and development" (de Castell, Luke, MacLennan 4).

From the liberal perspective—in which literacy education is the catalyst for the empowerment of intellectual abilities—the conservative model of the writing center (and of literacy education) is anathematic. It represents reductionism by asserting that a complex intellectual task like writing can be understood in terms of a mechanistic model of parts being put together to make a whole. The concomitant focus upon learning these separate parts as "skills" narrows the time and attention given to higher-level cognitive processes—specifically those involved in the formulation and evaluation of ideas—and de-emphasizes their value. Equally reductive is the role of the tutor, who functions as a quasi-technician in diagnosing skill levels and designing appropriate models for remediation that will produce the highest number of measurable results for the largest number of students in the shortest time frame.

Within the liberal model, recognition is given to the nature of the bond established between tutor and student that facilitates learning through individual attention and instructional approaches. Students learn how to develop their analytical and critical thinking skills through dialogic exchanges with the tutor. The paradigm for this method is apprenticeship learning in which the craft of writing is learned by an apprentice writer from a more experienced and knowledgeable writer, the tutor, who is also able to articulate aspects of his or her craft. The tutor is, in essence, an additional instructor who supplements and enhances the learning processes initiated by the classroom teacher, and the tutor's teaching skills and capacity to guide students in their learning processes are highly valued. Obviously, this factor is considerably more difficult to measure than the factors that can be quantified under the conservative model.

As writing center practice sought to address the changes in education that occurred in the 1960's and 70's, the tension that had existed in attempting to balance the philosophical and methodological oppositions inherent in the conservative and liberal models was intensified by three factors: the shift in pedagogical emphasis in writing instruction from product to process; increased enrollments in writing classes and the emergence of radical challenges to the value of the educational process as traditionally structured.

With the shift in pedagogical emphasis in writing instruction from the written product—which focused upon the formal aspects of writing (such as grammar and mechanics)—to the writing process—which emphasized the cognitive acts involved in composition—it became clear that writing and the teaching of writing were much more complex acts than originally imagined (Moffett 195). This focus upon the writing process of each individual writer contributed to a backlash against the conservative philosophy with its strong emphasis upon normative standards of instruction and assessment and a concomitant "rediscovery" of the liberal emphasis upon the uniqueness of each student as a learner.

To many writing theorists and instructors, writing centers seemed to be an important medium for addressing both the formal and cognitive aspects of writing instruction by providing students access to training in the fundamentals of written expression as well as tutoring in the heuristics involved in conceptualizing the writing process as a whole. In addition, the emphasis writing centers placed upon tutorial conferences reinforced the uniqueness of the student as a learner whose intelligence, talents, and writing processes could not effectively be addressed by the unitary practices of the conservative model.

Increases in college and university enrollments during the 1960's and 70's and proportional increases in the number of students assigned to writing classes greatly accelerated the use of writing centers as a form of supplemental instruction. Writing instructors who had from two to four classes of twenty-five students or more often found they simply could not focus the amount of time and attention necessary to help each student develop ideas dialectically and to mature in his or her writing skills. If, for example, a teacher were to meet individually for a half hour with 100 students in a single week, that teacher would be conferencing for 50 hours—a gargantuan, if not impossible task, given that teacher's additional academic duties. Thus, the writing center, with its emphasis upon providing tutoring to students and complementary instructional assistance to the writing teacher, seemed a practical, effective, and pedagogically sound medium for providing an institutional response to important needs in writing instruction.

How this institutional response was to be shaped, however, brought writing centers into conflict once more with the opposing philosophies of the conservative and the liberal models. The liberal response is perhaps best exemplified by Stephen M. North in "The Idea of a Writing Center":

> Maybe in a perfect world, all writers would have their own ready auditor—a teacher, a classmate, a roommate, an editor—who would not only listen but draw them out, ask them questions they would not think to ask themselves. A writing center is an institutional response to this need.... Writing centers are simply one manifestation— polished and highly visible—of a dialogue about writing that is central to higher education. (439)

The conservative response to this same situation of increased enrollments and larger class sizes in writing courses, coupled with the expansion of the educational process in the 1960's and 70's to admit a wider range of differently prepared students, was to focus upon the writing center as an institutionally sanctioned medium for recodifying educational processes of instruction and assessment. The call was for writing centers to exemplify a return to instruction in the basics and to work toward a hegemonic sense of the educational enterprise.

Ironically, the strength of this demand was intensified in the 60's and 70's by the emergence of the computer as a technological tool for writing instruction. The inclusion of computers and software for literacy instruction in the educational process represented a significant philosophical statement, for, as Harry Braverman indicates in *Labor and Monopoly Capital*, technology embodies social relations, and the computer is value-laden. Aronowitz and Giroux phrase this position even more compellingly:

> We would argue that the introduction of computer mediated learning, often presented entirely in its technological mode, is only part of a larger shift in the ideology of schools, proposed by conservatives and rapidly becoming hegemonic in all discussions of the [literacy] "crisis." This larger shift proposes that school ambience no longer conform to the surrogate family metaphor, but more or less self- consciously adopt a market orientation in the learning process itself. (190-91)

Walter J. Ong voices the liberal objection to this view by arguing that "deep familiarity with complex technologies encourages taking machines as models for everything; ultimately it encourages thinking of consciousness itself as simply a technology and even of the human being as kind of machine" (190).

While the conservative philosophy encouraged writing centers to embrace a hegemony of educational standards and objectives, the radical perspective argued for the ideal of counterhegemony. In the radical view, writing centers should serve as advocates for literacy by respecting and encouraging multiple literacies rather than by enforcing only one definition of literacy—or literacy with a capital L.

As the conservative pressures intensified for the type of competency testing that emphasized one definitive standard for assessing cognitive skills and writing abilities in our culture, feminist and Marxist critics found an ally in writing centers that emphasized a multiplicity of approaches to writing instruction and assessment. Writing centers, with their focus upon individual tutorials and one-on-one assessments of students' writing skills as well as their avowed and actual function of serving a myriad of student populations with different language skills and belief systems, could serve as an alternative to competency tests that emphasized normative rather than individual concerns. Proponents of feminist and Marxist rhetorical theory argued that focusing upon ways that writing centers could emphasize multiple views of writing instruction and assessment and could incorporate these perspectives into university-wide writing programs provided one of the richest and most challenging opportunities for change within the university.

While the conservative, liberal and radical views of how education is to be conducted represent socio-political formulations and develop from historical influences, these opposing positions also represent differing philosophies of the function of knowledge within a culture. Certainly, within the conservative model there is an effort to incorporate into writing instruction the objectivity traditionally associated with the sciences and to reconceptualize the process of literacy education as a social science rather than as a branch of the humanities.

In contrast, the liberal and radical perspectives reject the false scientism of the conservative model and propose, instead, an interpretive or hermeneutic approach that embraces ambiguity and denies the relevance of positivist goals to literacy education. Louis A. Sass in "Humanism, Hermeneutics, and the Concept of the Human Subject," for example, argues that

> ... both humanists and hermeneuticists are heirs to the intellectual tradition of Romanticism, itself largely a reaction against the Enlightenment tradition of objectivism.... Indeed, both these groups can be called *humanistic* in a broad sense—if by this we mean committed to developing an approach respectful of the special characteristics of human experience and action, and free of the positivism, mechanism, and reductionism of 19th-century physical sciences and the social sciences modeled on them. (222)

Philosopher Jurgen Habermas conceptualizes the conflict between these two positions of scientism and humanism as a struggle between differing "cognitive interests," which, in turn, generate their own rhetorics and epistemologies. Scientific rhetoric is "empirical-analytic" discourse underlain by a technical interest in interpreting and controlling natural phenomena. Humanistic interests involve a "historical-hermeneutic" discourse in which there is an emphasis upon understanding meanings rather than upon interpreting data objectively (*Knowledge* 197). Jerome D. Frank argues that "the fundamental problem may be that traditional scientific methods have been devised to discover relationships between facts, that is, objectively definable, measurable, repeatable phenomena. Facts can be confirmed or disconfirmed by the objective criteria of the scientific method; meanings cannot" (298).

Frank's focus on meanings and Habermas' assertion that the rhetoric of each discipline or "cognitive interest" represents a meaning-making activity that structures an epistemology raise interesting questions over what role writing centers are to play in present and future debates about literacy education. All theorists, for example, whether conservative, liberal, or radical, tend clearly to perceive literacy "as a source of autonomous behavior, and illiteracy is presumed to contribute to powerlessness; literacy is mind-expanding and a source of freedom; illiteracy is a cause of enslavement" (Stevens 7). The debate, thus, is not over the value of literacy, but over the means by which literacy is to be valorized and implemented as a societal objective. Paulo Freire, for example, in *Pedagogy of the Oppressed*, argues that definitions of what shall constitute literacy and who shall possess this knowledge are intimately connected with the power relationships that structure historical eras, and W. Ross Winterowd states in *The Culture and Politics of Literacy* that "defining literacy is not idle semantic debate or academic hair-splitting but is almost always a consequential political act"(4).

At present, writing centers seem caught up in the debate between the conservative emphasis upon empiricism and the "technicization" of writing instruction and assessment and the liberal and radical goal of "conscienti-zation" described by Freire in *The Politics of Education: Culture, Power, and Liberation*:

> The starting point for such an analysis must be a critical compre-hension of man as a being who exists *in* and *with* the world. Since the basic condition for conscientization is that its agent must be a subject (i.e., a conscious being), conscientization, like education, is specif-ically and exclusively a human process. It is as conscious beings that men are not only *in* the world but *with* the world, together with other men. Only men, as "open" beings, are able to achieve the complex operation of simultaneously transforming the world by their action and grasping and expressing the world's reality in their creative language. (68)

One response to the dilemma created by the two different epistemological views of literacy that John Wilson calls the "society-oriented or utilitarian purposes" and the "purposes benefitting the individual human being as such, not as a role filler in a particular society at a particular time" (30) resides in Habermas' description of a third sphere of intellectual activity, or "cognitive interest," which he defines as the "empirical-critical." Using Marxism and Freudian psychoanalysis as examples, Habermas contends that empirical-critical intellectual activity is characterized by an emancipatory interest combined with a capacity to reflect critically upon the fundamental premises of one's own epistemology and ideology. As Habermas states, "The critiques which Marx developed as a theory of society and Freud as metapsychology are distinguished precisely by incorporating in their consciousness an interest which directs knowledge, an interest in emancipation going beyond the technical and the practical interest of knowledge" (*Theory*).

Since it is apparent that contemporary writing centers are involved with both dimensions of knowledge as Habermas defines them, the emancipatory and the technical/practical, they offer potentials for what Freirean critics describe as the capacity for transcendence. As Henry Giroux explains in his introduction to Freire's *The Politics of Education*, "As a referent for change, education represents a form of action that emerges from a joining of the languages of critique and possibility" (xiii). Salvatore R. Maddi, in an interesting essay titled "On the Problem of Accepting Facticity and Pursuing Possibility," discusses the potentials for possibility in this fashion:

> It is clear that, according to existentialism, the best thrust of human functioning is toward possibility. Minimizing facticity leaves one's options open for personal growth through new experiences. This way lies freedom, renewal, richness, sensitivity, deepening understanding, sophistication in the best sense. But facticity cannot be avoided completely. It is inherent in our experience, not only in our own limitations, but also in what we have become, even if in that becoming we have pursued possibility vigorously. Hence, our sense of what is possible is intertwined with what we perceive as given, and the dynamic balance between the two gives our lives its particular flavor. (183)

Both Giroux and Maddi focus on a "sense of what is possible" within the given constraints of facticity. Ironically, for writing centers, the "dynamic balance" between possibility and facticity is more difficult to attain than for other components of the educational system, largely because writing centers are administrative constructs of the present century and are not a discipline in the traditional sense of the arts, humanities, natural sciences, and social sciences. As a result, writing centers come into being to address specific needs on specific campuses, and the pragmatic truth or "facticity" is that writing centers reflect and serve the "social context" of which they are a part. Winterowd states that "literacy is always grounded in a social context" (11), and so, too, is the significance of any writing center.

On most college and university campuses, writing centers are instructional hybrids composed of a balance between administrative aims and the traditional practices of writing instruction that reflect writing centers' early alliance with English departments directly and indirectly with the humanities. From different perspectives, this hybridism represents, at once, the limitations of writing centers in educational settings and their transformative possibilities. Essentially, the dispute centers upon whether writing centers will serve instructional aims of self-efficacy and self-enrichment or administrative aims of the quantitative assessment of identifiable literacy skills.

This dispute, however, is not so easily dichotomized, for what also needs to be considered is the enormous power writing centers possess, by virtue of their hybridism, to bridge administrative and instructional aims through what Toby Fulwiler describes as a "comprehensive long-term program to develop more fully all the interrelated learning and communication skills of the whole campus community" (124). Thom Hawkins states that "the growth of writing centers is but one part of a search for new vitality in the humanities" (xi), indicating that a major aspect of a writing center's ability to generate a new vitality in the humanities is the writing center's capacity to bridge disciplines in a common search for the most effective long-term methods to instruct students and encourage their intellectual growth. In this regard, a writing center can serve as a true "center" for an outreach amongst disciplines, and even for a community and regional outreach that offers the type of transformative and liberatory educational experiences described by Freire in which philosophy and practice join for social transformation. Hawkins also focuses upon the important outreach role writing centers play in assisting faculty with writing instruction and in drawing faculty from a range of disciplines into the structuring of writing curricula:

> If writing centers are to continue making substantial contributions to classroom practices and curricula, if they are to reach a productive and long-lasting maturity, they must do more than patch together fragments of successful practices. To begin with, writing centers can ally themselves with faculty who are redefining what it means to teach writing. Writing centers are not alone in meeting the challenge of teaching the new constituency of nontraditional students and the new methodologies of collaborative learning. Faculty from various departments look to the writing center for knowledge and expertise in these areas, but also for a place to share experiences, to compare notes. . . . In years to come there will be an increasing demand on writing centers to participate in campuswide efforts to improve the teaching of writing. (xiii)

The potential writing centers have to transform the rhetorical communities of college and university campuses by extending and redefining the dialogue on literacy education represents their most significant power and makes them agencies for change within academics. In composition studies' efforts to define a metatheory and metamethod to address such questions as "what topics and problems should a field address? What relations hold among theories? What grounds would justify choosing one over another?" as Louise Wetherbee Phelps suggests in *Composition as a Human Science* (183), clearly writing centers can play an important role—precisely because they are hybrids of the two most pervasive and influential conflicts of interpretation operating in American society today, "between positivist or objectivist modes of inquiry and interpretive ones, more relativistic and subjective" (Phelps 184).

Developing out of and exemplifying both traditions of theory and method, writing centers manifest the potential inherent in the bridging of different discourse communities. Defining toward what ends this potential will be used represents one of the more significant and challenging issues affecting literacy education today. Since each of the philosophies of education, the conservative, liberal, and radical, makes legitimate claims on what the character and identity of a writing center should be within the educational system, determining whether writing centers will be humanistic or technopragmatic; hegemonic or counterhegemonic; liberatory or objectivist; multi-disciplinary in outreach or centripetal in focus; remedial or multi-based are all important challenges that will need to be addressed as writing center practice moves forward into the next century.

Works Cited

Aronowitz, Stanley and Henry A. Giroux. *Education Under Siege*. South Hadley: Bergin & Garvey, 1985.

Braverman, Harry. *Labor and Monopoly Capital*. New York: Monthly Review Press, 1974.

de Castell, Suzanne, Allan Luke, and David MacLennan. "On Defining Literacy." *Literacy, Society, and Schooling: A Reader*. Ed. Suzanne de Castell, Allan Luke, and David MacLennan. Cambridge: Cambridge UP, 1986. 3-14.

Frank, Jerome D. "Psychotherapy, Rhetoric, and Hermeneutics: Implications for Practice and Research. *Psychotherapy* 24 (1987): 293-302.

Freire, Paulo. *Pedagogy of the Oppressed*. New York: Seabury, 1973.

____. *The Politics of Education: Culture, Power, and Liberation*. South Hadley: Bergin & Garvey, 1985.

Fulwiler, Toby. "How Well Does Writing Across the Curriculum Work?" *College English* 46.2 (1984): 115-25.

Giroux, Henry A. Introduction. *The Politics of Education: Culture, Power, and Liberation*. By Paulo Freire. South Hadley: Bergin & Garvey, 1985. xi-xxv.

Habermas, Jurgen. *Knowledge and Human Interests*. Boston: Beacon, 1970.

____. *Theory and Practice*. Boston, Beacon, 1973.

Hawkins, Thom. Introduction. *Writing Centers: Theory and Administration*. Ed. Gary A. Olson. Urbana: NCTE, 1984. xi-xiv.

Maddi, Salvatore R. "On the Problem of Accepting Facticity and Pursuing Possibility." *Hermeneutics and Psychological Theory: Interpretive Perspectives on Personality, Psychotherapy and Psychopathology*. Ed. Stanley B. Messer, Louis A. Sass, and Robert L. Woolfolk. New Brunswick: Rutgers UP, 1988. 182-209.

Moffett, James. *Teaching the Universe of Discourse*. Boston: Houghton Mifflin, 1968.

North, Stephen M. "The Idea of a Writing Center." *College English*. 46.5 (1984): 433-46.

Ong, Walter J. "Reading, Technology, and Human Consciousness." *Literacy as a Human Problem*. Ed. James C. Raymond. University: U of Alabama P, 1982. 170-201.

Phelps, Louise Wetherbee. *Composition as a Human Science: Contributions to the Self-Understanding of a Discipline*. New York: Oxford U P, 1988.

Sass, Louis A. "Humanism, Hermeneutics, and the Concept of the Human Subject." Messer, Sass, Woolfolk 222-271.

Stevens, Edward W., Jr. *Literacy, Law, and Social Order*. DeKalb: Northern Illinois U P, 1988.

Wilson, John. "The Properties, Purposes, and Promotions of Literacy." *Literacy, Society, and Schooling; A Reader*. Ed. Suzanne de Castell, Allan Luke, and David MacLennan. Cambridge: Cambridge U P, 1986. 27-36.

Winterowd, Ross W. *The Culture and Politics of Literacy*. New York: Oxford UP, 1989.

Writing Center Ecology:
A Bakhtinian Perspective

by Alice M. Gillam

Like a fertile, overgrown garden, the writing center breeds conversations between writer and tutor which grow and spread in directions neither consciously intends. Voices of others—past and current teachers, friends, parents, other texts—intrude, and boundaries between the language of the writer, reader, and text blur. Like fussy gardeners, those of us charged with tending to this environment try to keep things under control by pruning back the conversation and staking out borders: "Let the writer set the agenda"; "Don't let the writer use your words"; "Keep the ownership of the paper with the writer."

These efforts, while well intended and even necessary, fail to accomplish their goal of offering clearcut guidelines and a coherent philosophy. As Tilly Eggers suggests, "Things fall apart ... pretty regularly in a Writing Center... [and] when things do not fall apart, the Center is too fixed" (33). From a Bakhtinian perspective, this state of affairs is neither surprising nor unsettling; rather, it is a natural result of the multi-vocality and contradictions inherent in language. In this essay, I argue that reading our writing center past and present through the work of critical theorist Mikhail Bakhtin offers new perspectives on writing center ecology.

Re-reading the Past

I was first introduced to peer tutoring in the mid-1960s when I was assigned as an undergraduate to help problem writers at my university. Like many of its era, my university's writing center acted as a "normalizing" agent, the guardian of what Bakhtin calls the "centripetal forces" in language which serve to centralize, unify, and stabilize language (*Dialogic Imagination* 271). In the university, these forces operate through grammatical rules, discourse conventions, and textbook prescriptions. As a tutor, my job was to offer a crash course in these matters, a Berlitz course in the "authoritative discourse" of the academy which Bakhtin describes as "prior discourse ... a given [which] demands our unconditional allegiance ... the word of the fathers" (342).

Reprinted from *The Writing Center Journal* 11.2 (1991): 3-12. Used by permission.

What this concept of the writing center failed to account for were the "centrifugal forces" of language with which centripetal forces continually contend. According to Bakhtin, centrifugal forces, which he calls *heteroglossia,* perpetually destabilize language through multiple meanings, varying contexts, and the free play of dialects (271). As an untrained novice tutor, I was keenly aware of destabilizing forces which constantly undermined my attempts to diagnose problems and prescribe solutions. But since I had no name for them, I assumed that the failures were my fault—"if I only knew more about grammar and the rules of good writing."

Years later, in the late seventies, I came to another university's writing center, this time as a graduate student in composition and rhetoric. Although the university at large still expected writing centers to act as normalizing agents, writing center practitioners increasingly viewed themselves as liberating agents, working to free students from the oppressive, centripetal forces of academic discourse. I embraced this radically revised version of the writing center with enthusiasm. In this scenario, I need not pretend to be an expert. In good conscience, I could train other tutors to be good listeners who reflected back the writer's emerging ideas and facilitated the writer's self-expression.

While the conception of the writing center as liberatory is appealing, certainly more appealing than the one it replaced, I now see it as mistaken in theory and practice. Again, the ideas of Bakhtin—or more precisely of Volosinov, Bakhtin's other self or collaborator—explain why. In its own way, this view of tutoring was also "monological," only this time the writer's voice prevailed. Undergirded by romantic theories of language, the liberatory approach imagined writers as possessing innate, pure ideas which yearned for expression. Although the tutor might act as amanuensis, it was important that the tutor not influence the writer's voice which would contaminate its purity of insight and expression.

Bakhtin/Volosinov argues that there is no such thing as unique, innate ideas or experience outside of language: "It is not experience that organizes expression, but the other way around—*expression organizes experience*" (*Marxism and the Philosophy of Language* 85). Further, our language and construction of meaning occur through social interaction:

> The word is a *two-sided act.* It is determined equally by whose word it is and for whom it is meant. . . . A word is a bridge thrown between myself and another. If one end of the bridge depends on me, then the other depends on my addressee. A word is territory shared by both addresser and addressee, by the speaker and his interlocutor. (86)

By privileging the writer's voice and restraining the tutor's, the liberatory center stunted the growth of conversation, the writing center's richest resource.

Re-reading the Present

I recount this personal and shared history because the concepts of the writing center as normalizing agent and liberating agent are still operative. Though I would like to characterize our center at the University of Wisconsin-Milwaukee as a dialogizing agent, we inevitably enfold these other two identities into our agency, making us a double or actually a triple agent. Like Bakhtin, we wish to foreground the centrifugal forces of language—the writer's accent which may be nonstandard, foreign, or idiosyncratic, and the writer's perspective which may be unconventional in form or style. Yet we must also address the centripetal forces at work in our student's writing and academic lives—the proficiency test which they must pass to achieve junior standing, the knowledge of discourse conventions they need to remain in school and to pursue professional goals.

From a Bakhtinian perspective, these tensions in language and this multiple agency can serve positive, creative ends. The tensions which seem so indigenous to writing center life, the competing ideologies and mixed loyalties which collide and contend on a daily, even hourly basis, can be re-read as positive, as providing fertile ground for writing and talk about writing.

However, pronouncing these conflicts positive does not take us very far in terms of actual practice. Here again, Bakhtin comes to my aid. Specifically, I would like to suggest that his notions of *dialogism, addressivity,* and *answerability* offer lenses through which we might re-conceptualize current practice. To illustrate this re-conceptualization, I will use an excerpt from a recent tutoring case study as a point of reference.

In this tutoring case study, Belinda, a novice peer tutor, comments on her semester-long work with Mary, a returning adult basic writer:

> As I listen I feel a sense of loss, knowing that Mary has stripped this story to its skeleton to please her instructor and me. Almost all the vivid details are gone. This semester, like a Zen master in a cheap Kung Fu movie, I've exhorted Mary to focus.

Belinda, herself an aspiring fiction writer, feels pulled between Mary's mesmerizing narrative voice and the teacher's expectation for focus and unity of theme. However, given Mary's desire to succeed, Belinda feels she has no choice but to encourage Mary to "normalize" her voice so that it can be heard and found acceptable in the academy. Reading this all-too-familiar case, I, too, feel a sense of loss. But what were Belinda's alternatives, I wonder? How might a Bakhtinian perspective have enabled Belinda to respond differently?

Continuing her description of this tutoring encounter, Belinda writes:

> Mary's essay was to be on her reading habits. What she shared with me was an explosion of experience, barely contained on the four pages she presented me. The explosion opened with the sentence, "Reading is an essential tool of which individuals can gain information." It went on to discuss her early years living with alcoholic parents, the grades she received in math in second grade, the semester she had in college studying nursing, a humorous anecdote about finding (or in this case not finding) the meaning of words through

context clues, several biblical quotations, and a section describing her current goals.

After she read it, I remember asking her to read it once again while the word "focus" lit up in my mind as though it were neon. I asked her for the assignment directions and read them several times before asking her, "What is the main thing you're trying to say?"

In Belinda's mind, the battle is between the externally imposed centripetal force of the teacher's demand for focus and the centrifugal forces embedded in Mary's essay—the loosely connected anecdotes, the multivocal intonations, the mixed emotions about her reading past. But what would happen if Belinda had been able to see these opposing forces as an opportunity to explore options rather than as a battleground in which one side had to win and one side had to lose?

Bakhtin would suggest that in apparent disunity there are always forces working toward unity and in unity always forces working toward disunity. Mary's first sentence—"Reading is an essential tool of which individuals can be informed"—suggests a centralizing force both in its dissonant tone and conventional message. The unidiomatic phrasing, as well as the sentiment, sound like someone else's words which Mary has borrowed but not yet "populated with [her] own intention, [her] own accent" (*Dialogic Imagination* 293). What if this "truism" about the value of reading were re-accented in Mary's voice and then deployed as a repeated litany against which Mary's experiences could reverberate? Playing with various options, Belinda might ask Mary what would be gained or lost in rendering this experience in standard essay form with a clear, unproblematic thesis statement like "Reading is important, but it is hard for me"? Or alternatively, what would be gained or lost in using a less conventional structure in which the social injunction were interspersed with disparate bits of narrative?

The central question, perhaps, is whether the univocal conventional wisdom about reading ought to organize Mary's interpretation of her experience or whether her experiences ought to reorganize or complicate conventional wisdom. After all, Mary is in college despite a high school teacher's prediction that she would never go beyond high school given her eighth-grade reading level. And although she has been described by her academic counselor as a "non-reader," she reads the Bible on a daily basis.

I am suggesting, in other words, that opening or dialogizing this text through the play of oppositions might enable Mary to see ways of satisfying her teacher's demand for focus without sacrificing richness of voice and detail. Indeed, the richness of voice and detail may hold the key to focus. Rather than stripping her "story" to the bone in order to impose a focus, perhaps Mary needs to flesh out the contradictions embedded in the text and puzzle over the off-key shifts in voice as a way of discovering focus. Once discovered, the focus, which need not be univocal nor simple, might then suggest ways of managing and rearranging the text. In short, a Bakhtinian perspective might have allowed Belinda to help Mary see the dissonances in voice and narrative as opportunities to dialogize and clarify meaning rather than as the enemies of focus, as forces to be subdued and "normalized."

For this to occur, however, Belinda would have to enlist Mary's full participation. Although the seeds for opening or dialogizing Mary's text are already present in her draft, Belinda can do no more than set the process in motion by asking questions and conversing about options. If the text is to become dialogized, it must be Mary who invokes and engages the multiple voices implicit in the text.

And this is where Bakhtin's concept of *addressivity* offers a useful perspective on the tutorial conversation. *Addressivity* goes beyond traditional notions of audience to include the writer's "inner audience," the topic or "hero" of the discourse, and other discourses or utterances about that subject. According to Bakhtin/Volosinov, "each person's inner world and thought has its stabilized [inner] *social audience* that comprises the environment in which reason, motives, values, and so on are fashioned" (*Marxism* 86). Consequently, inner audience as well as outer audience participates in the construction of meaning. Further, any piece of writing addresses other utterances, spoken and written: "The work is a link in a chain . . . Like a rejoinder in a dialogue it is related to other utterances: both those to which it responds and those that respond to it" (*Speech Genres and Other Late Essays* 76). In short, *addressivity* incorporates "the otherness of language in general and of given dialogic partners in particular" (Clark and Holquist 217).

The tutorial conversation enacts this rich sense of *addressivity,* "this quality of turning to another," (*Speech Genres* 99) in a variety of ways. Most obviously, the tutor is a literal addressee who can offer immediate response. Ideally, the tutor offers multiple responses, some the tutor's own, some those of other addressees. Although Belinda acted in at least two responsive roles, as "captivated," appreciative listener and as critical surrogate teacher, she represented these responses to Mary as irreconcilable. But what if Belinda were to dramatize her responses in dialogical terms, looking for points of intersection? The lover of stories might encourage, "Tell me about how you felt about your grades in second grade math; tell me about your favorite passages in the Bible; tell me more about the semester you studied nursing." The critic, on the other hand, might challenge, "What do your grades in second grade math have to do with your reading? If reading is difficult for you, why do you read the Bible so consistently? How did your semester of pre-nursing courses affect you as a reader?" Perhaps the critical response would still have drowned out the appreciative one, but perhaps Mary could have used both to gain a new perspective on her text.

Through the tutor's responses, the writer begins to see the text through the eyes of the tutor and this alters the meaning of the text. Once this happens, once one has received a response or "rejoinder," one's utterances are altered and take on a double life; that is, one's utterances live in a "combined context made up of one's own words and the words of another" (*Dialogic Imagination* 284). As Belinda is all too aware, the tutor's responses inevitably affect subsequent writing. Even if the writer dismisses the tutor's responses, those responses affect the writer's attitude and conception of the piece.

The tutorial conversation also enacts the concept of *addressivity* in that the writer herself becomes an addressee as she reads the text aloud. Hearing the intonations or emotional coloration in the text, the writer becomes a listener and a reader of her own text. In addition, this oral performance of the text encourages a separation between writer and text which can in turn enable the writer to see the distinction between what Mary Louise Buley-Meissner calls "the self writing and the self which is written." From this perspective the writer can begin to engage in a dialogue with her text. For Mary's part I suspect that her ear was as keen as her voice was strong, and with a little encouragement, she might have been able to detect the discordant notes and to hear the shifts from anger to determination, from pride to shame. Such a perspective would then set the stage for rewriting her experience.

Finally, the tutor can introduce into the conversation other aspects of *addressivity*. "To what other texts does this text respond?" Belinda might ask. In Mary's case, such texts might include stories of adults who have overcome reading difficulties, articles about the importance of reading to children, biblical injunctions about the need for perseverance in the face of adversity. Or the tutor might ask, "To what inner audiences is this writing addressed?" Mary's inner audiences, I imagine, might include former teachers who labeled her a "poor reader," her alcoholic parents who never read to her, and a society which is willing to dismiss her as unintelligent because she has difficulty reading.

Related to the concept of *addressivity* is the concept of *answerability*. In addressing others, we participate in communal life which Bakhtin sees as a moral imperative. The idea of *answerability*, in other words, adds an ethical dimension to *addressivity*. According to Clark and Holquist, Bakhtin's critical biographers, Bakhtin develops the idea of *answerability* in an untranslated, untitled text which they call *The Architectonics of Answerability*. In this text, Bakhtin claims we are answerable "for our unique place in existence" and for "the means by which we relate that uniqueness to the rest of the world which is other to it.... We must be responsible, or answerable, for ourselves" (64). And it is through activity, through performances of all kinds , that we answer "other selves and the world from the unique place and time [we] occupy in existence" (64).

The Bakhtinian self who "answers" is at once socially created and unique: socially created in that it "exists only dialogically," only in relation to others and that which is other (65-66); unique in that its "locus of apperception," its place in time and space, is singular (69). Our "answers," then, whether they be words or deeds, are simultaneously the means by which we participate communally and the means by which we announce our difference. Through our "answers" we "author" or continually shape our selves in response to others and the world. And although these "answers" are populated with others' voices and intentions, they are nonetheless our unique contribution to what Michael Oakeshott calls the "conversation of mankind."

Although this is an oversimplified rendering of a complex concept, the idea of *answerability* offers ethical grounds for the dilemmas we frequently face in writing center work. In his recently published *Dialogue, Dialectic, and Conversation,* Gregory Clark refers to this Bakhtinian ethic by saying, "Because the language we use makes us, unavoidably, participants in a meaning-making dialogue, we must hold ourselves responsible for the meaning we help to make" (9).

Participants in the tutorial conversation are jointly as well as separately "answerable" for the meaning created through this conversation. This joint responsibility is implicit in the root word for *conversation, to converse* which means to "turn together" (Singley and Boucher 11). No matter who said what or how much each talked, conversation creates and alters meaning, and for that meaning both participants are responsible. On the other had, tutor and writer are "answerable" in ways that are not co-extensive. Since the tutor's response intervenes in the writer's process and alters the writer's "answer," the tutor is responsible by role and training to make that response as enabling as possible. This means, in part, that the tutor bears a responsibility to be the kind of addressee who enables the writer to "answer" or accept responsibility for the text. At the same time, the tutor can never fully anticipate the writer's response to the tutor's intervention; therefore, the tutor can only act according to her best judgment in the given circumstance while continuing to assess and revise that judgment in light of the writer's response.

In the case of Belinda and Mary, Belinda's answerability would entail careful reading of Mary's responses to her invitations to reconsider the text. Had Belinda undertaken the dialogic responses suggested earlier, such responses may or may not have enabled Mary to reconceptualize her text in productive ways. Indeed, such responses might have "disabled" or confused her. The tutor's answerability, then, is not a matter of set responses, but rather a readiness to alter her approach in response to the writer's reactions and ideas. Plainly, Belinda feels responsible, perhaps too responsible, for "stripping" away the richness of voice and detail in Mary's text; but in another sense, Belinda is enacting her answerability in her willingness to question her intervention and to consider options for responding differently.

Most importantly, the tutor's answerability entails a recognition of the limits of her ability to answer for the text and the need to allow the writer to be fully answerable. After all, the tutor's response is useful to the writer precisely because it is other than, not identical to, the writer's answer. It is Mary not Belinda who must answer for and to the paper she submits; it is Mary not Belinda who must continually answer for and to her reading past.

The writer's answerability in Bakhtinian terms goes beyond simply being the one who is held accountable, the one who receives the grade. For Bakhtin, writing is the author's "answer" to others and to the world; the writer is responsible for the answer that is the text. Moreover, the writer is responsible for the responses set in motion by her "answer." To be answerable is to be continually turning, continually engaged in a conversation that has no end.

And it is in this sense that the writing center, too, is answerable. For we who participate in the writing center are responsible for authoring a social discourse that remains perpetually open, continually turning; a social discourse that addresses and answers to many divergent audiences—each other, our own inner audiences, the writers we serve, the faculty, university administrators, and the community at large—and that recognizes the dialogical relationship between the centripetal and centrifugal forces in language. Like our tutors, we who direct writing centers must offer advice, make policies, and act according to our best judgement while at the same time recognizing the absence of fixed answers, predictable outcomes, and determinate meanings. And like our tutors, our answerability entails observant reading of the local scene and constant assessment and revision of our judgments.

For Bakhtin, the fact that we, individually or collectively, can never arrive at certain answers nor establish a final, "unitary identity" is "not to be lamented," but rather to be celebrated (Clark and Holquist 66). In this spirit, then, we may act as "merry" gardeners who cultivate the writing center as fertile ground for the play of language, knowing that things will inevitably grow out of control and that borders will need to be continually restaked but also that our labors will often yield fruitful rewards.

Works Cited

Bakhtin, Mikhail. *The Dialogic Imagination.* Trans. Caryl Emerson and Michael Holquist. Ed. Michael Holquist. Austin: U of Texas P, 1981.

____. *Speech Genres and Other Late Essays.* Trans. Vern W. McGee. Ed. Caryl Emerson and Michael Holquist. Austin: U of Texas P, 1986.

Buley-Meissner, Mary Louise. "Rhetorics of the Self." *Balancing Acts: Essays on the Teaching of Writing.* Ed. Virginia Chappell, Mary Louise Buley-Meissner, and Chris Anderson. Carbondale and Edwardsville: Southern Illinois UP, in press.

Clark, Gregory. *Dialogue, Dialectic, and Conversation: A Social Perspective on the Function of Writing.* Carbondale and Edwardsville: Southern Illinois UP, 1990.

Clark, Katerina, and Michael Holquist. *Mikhail Bakhtin.* Cambridge: Belknap P of Harvard UP, 1984.

Eggers, Tilly. "Things Fall Apart: The Writing Center Will Hold." *The Writing Center Journal* 1.2 (1981): 33-40.

Oakeshott, Michael. "The Voice of Poetry in the Conversation of Mankind." *Rationalism in Politics.* New York: Basic Books, 1962. 197-247.

Singley, Carol J., and Holly W. Boucher. "Dialogue in Tutor Training: Creating the Essential Space for Learning." *The Writing Center Journal* 8.2 (1988): 11-22.

Volosinov, V. V. *Marxism and the Philosophy of Language.* Trans. Ladislav Matejka and I. R. Titunik. 1973. Cambridge: Harvard UP, 1986.

Really Useful Knowledge:
A Cultural Studies Agenda
for Writing Centers

by Marilyn M. Cooper

People—not just my students—often tell me that as a writing teacher, I am "different" (if they're being polite) or "crazy" or "bizarre" (if they're being frank). I believe students should be intellectually challenged in their writing classes, that they need to be engaged in a struggle over complex ideas that matter to them. I give them hard books to read, I ask them hard questions, I ask them to make up their own assignments. I believe that college students are completely capable of reading hard books and writing in interesting ways. I also know that they often don't believe that, and that they have faced a variety of obstacles that have taught them that they are "bad" or "nonstandard" or (what is sometimes worse) "good" writers. Changing their attitude toward writing and their understanding of what it means to write well is a long and difficult task, not to be achieved in one or two classes or by a single teacher. So as a writing teacher I see writing centers as essential places where students can go to continue the conversations about ideas begun in class and in electronic conferences, to find people they can complain to, to work out solutions to the problems they face in their writing, to find a friend and a colleague and an advocate—all of those things I cannot really be for them. But because I have also worked with the writing center research group at MTU and am now directing dissertations by a number of graduate students who are doing research in the writing center, I also see writing centers as a site of great deal of exciting research, a site where we can really begin to see what goes on with students' writing and what keeps them from writing.

The question I have already begun to answer—what is the function of writing centers? or, as it is alternatively framed, what is the role of the writing center tutor or coach or consultant in teaching writing?—is, I would venture to say, the central concern of recent discussions of writing centers. In fact, the ongoing discussion over what to call writing center tutors is a good demonstration of the centrality of this concern. I want to align myself with certain answers to this question: that writing centers are in a good position to serve as a site of critique of the institutionalized structure of writing instruction in

Reprinted from *The Writing Center Journal* 14.2 (1994): 97-111. Used by permission.

college, and that, as a consequence of this, the role of the tutor should be to create useful knowledge about writing in college and to empower students as writers who also understand what writing involves and who act as agents in their writing—these two goals being closely intertwined. Since I know that writing centers vary a lot from site to site, I should say at the outset that I am thinking primarily about writing centers that are staffed by undergraduate students and that allow students to work over a period of time with a single tutor, although I believe that all types of writing centers and all kinds of tutors can have the function and role I describe. I should also say that my ideas about these questions have been most heavily influenced by Nancy Grimm, who directs the writing center at Michigan Tech and who has written very directly about a critical role for writing centers. Nancy says, "Writing centers are places where students struggle to connect their public and private lives, and where they learn that success in the academy depends on uncovering and understanding tacit differences in value systems and expectations" (5). In this struggle, students and their tutors come to know a lot about the real situation of college writing.

What I want to do here is to develop a rationale for thinking of writing centers as having the essential function of critiquing institutions and creating knowledge about writing, a rationale that will make clear the politics of such a belief and that will connect the goal of inquiry with the daily practice of writing center tutors. This rationale also will have clear implications for what tutors should know and how they should be trained. But I'd like to start by suggesting why it is useful to think of writing centers in this way by looking closely at some advice on tutoring offered by Jeff Brooks in his article on minimalist tutoring that came out in 1991 in the *Writing Lab Newsletter.*

I chose Brooks' article because it has been widely admired and because it enunciates very clearly some oft-heard advice for tutors. I also like a great deal of what he suggests, particularly his emphasis on tutors' responsiveness to students and on students as active writers. He argues that tutors should not be in the business of "fixing" students papers but rather should focus on students as writers, offering them strategies and support and encouraging them to fix their own papers; he says, "The student, not the tutor, should 'own' the paper and take full responsibility for it. The tutor should take on a secondary role, serving mainly to keep the student focused on his own writing" (2). He goes on to suggest how this principle can be implemented, pointing out that "The primary value of the writing center tutor to the student is as a living human body who is willing to sit patiently and help the student spend time with her paper" (2). He offers a list of "ways we can put theory into practice" (3) and concludes, "If, at the end of the session, a paper is improved, it should be because the student did all the work" (4).

Perhaps because I am "outside" the writing center culture, I did also find a couple of things odd in Brooks' suggestions. For one thing, almost all of his specific suggestions involve tactics designed to distance tutors from students' papers in order to "establish the student as sole owner of the paper and [the tutor] as merely an interested outsider" (4). I worry about the notion of students' owning papers, and this worry connects with the other thing I find odd in Brooks' suggestions: the focus on improving individual student papers. Brooks repeatedly asserts that in writing center sessions tutors are not to focus on papers but instead on students and on their writing. But students are still expected to focus on their papers, and thus their individual papers remain the focus of writing center sessions.

Now, of course, in some ways this is not odd: students overwhelmingly show up at writing centers to get help with particular papers and particular assignments, and it would be incredibly perverse for writing center tutors simply to refuse to respond to this very real need. At the same time, it is not obvious to me—even though classroom teachers often believe this—that helping students fix papers is or should be the central purpose of writing centers and I expect many of you agree with me on this. But I also think that it is this assumption that writing center sessions must focus on improving individual papers that leads to the trap Brooks describes, the trap of tutors serving as editors of student papers, and that leads to his emphasizing negative tactics that help tutors to refuse that role.

When writing center sessions remain resolutely focused on how a student can fix a paper, it is difficult for tutors to focus instead on what students know and need to know about writing. In such sessions, tutors can find little to do other than directly fix papers, indirectly show students how to fix papers, or simply abdicate all responsibility for mistakes in papers. Though Brooks asserts that "we forget that students write to learn, not to make perfect papers," he remains fixated on the notion of perfection in student texts: "student writing ... has no real goal beyond getting it on the page," he says, and, "Most students simply do not have the skill, experience, or talent to write the perfect paper" (3). Given these assumptions, it is not at all surprising that, as Brooks says, "writing papers is a dull and unrewarding activity for most students" (2). Nor do I think that, in this situation, simply insisting that students take responsibility for their papers and treat them as valuable will either change their attitude toward writing in college or help them learn much about writing.

In order to make my point, I've emphasized how Brooks' suggestions lead to a focus on fixing student papers. But clearly, other things besides editing for effectiveness and correctness go on in the kind of writing center sessions he is talking about. Tutors help students learn processes of writing by helping them figure out what an assignment asks them to do or by helping them brainstorm in response to assignments. By asking students, "What do you mean by this?" tutors help students learn that readers often need more information or explanation in order to understand what writers had in mind. By asking students, "What's your reason for putting Q before N?" and similar questions, tutors help students learn to think about the decisions they make in writing as reasonable rather than simply a matter of following rules. By asking students to read final drafts aloud in order to find mistakes, tutors help students learn that they can correct many of their own mistakes. As long as students understand that it is what they are learning about writing in these activities that is important, not that their papers are being improved, these are useful thing to do.

This, of course, is the position advocated by Stephen North in the axiom which has become a writing center mantra: "Our job is to produce better writers, not better writing." North explains,

> Any given project—a class assignment, a law school application, an encyclopedia entry, a dissertation proposal—is for the writer the prime, often the exclusive concern. That particular text, its success or failure, is what brings them to talk to us in the first place. In the center, though, we look beyond or through that particular project, that particular text, and see it as an occasion for addressing *our* primary concern, the process by which it is produced. (438).

In other words, tutors can use the situation of students writing particular papers to focus on what students know and need to know abut college writing. Brooks certainly has activities like this in mind when he suggests that tutors have better things to do with their time than to edit student papers, when he says that "we sit down with imperfect papers, but our job is to improve their writers" (2). But North's formulation of this position also makes clear how the goals of students and tutors can conflict: students come for help in making their document perfect (for very good reasons, like getting into law school, getting their dissertation proposal approved, passing the course and getting their degree) and are confronted with tutors who have their own primary concern, a concern with the process of writing. In this situation I think that tutors must not only make clear what their concern in tutoring sessions is but also explain why they think this concern should be primary for students as well, and they must negotiate a common goal in their sessions, one that does not simply ignore the students' concerns. If tutors are not up front about their concerns, they risk losing track of them as they strive to help students or frustrating and confusing students with their uncooperativeness—both of these reactions seem inevitable in the kind of minimalist tutoring Brooks describes.

At the same time, in spite of the problems I see in Brooks' suggestions for minimalist tutoring, I think he is reaching for a purpose for writing centers beyond that enunciated by North. Brooks wants students to get more from writing center sessions than just instruction in how to write well. In his insistence that "we need to make the student the primary agent in the writing center session" (2) and that "ideally the student should be the only active agent in improving the paper" (4), I hear the desire to empower students as agents that has characterized many recent calls for reforms in writing pedagogy. It is a desire I heartily endorse, but also one that has turned out to be decidedly difficult to enact. One of the difficulties in implementing this goal arises, as Lester Faigley has pointed out, from the strong rationalist and expressivist traditions in composition studies that encourage us to see agency in writing as Brooks does in his article, in terms of owning or taking responsibility for a text. These are the same traditions Andrea Lunsford sees operating to produce the notions of the writing center as a storehouse of positivist knowledge or as a garret where individual students get in touch with their genius.

As Lunsford points out, both traditions "tend to view knowledge as individually derived" (4), and, as Faigley points out, both traditions deny "the role of language in constructing selves" (128). For both rationalists and expressivists, knowledge and writing are dependent on a preexisting coherent and rational self. Given this assumption, agency in writing becomes a matter of subduing the text to the self by achieving personal control over it, either by creating in it a rational and coherent point of view on the topic addressed, a point of view that is dependent on the rational and coherent self of the writer, or by expressing one's personal vision or true self in it—often referred to as achieving an authentic voice. Unfortunately, as the modern world taught us that selves (or, as we learned to call them, subject positions) are constantly in the process of construction and that one of the activities that contributes most to the construction of subject positions is language use (including writing), we came to understand that writers cannot and do not achieve agency in writing by subduing language to their selves but rather by using language to construct subject positions. Agency in writing depends not on owning or taking responsibility for a text but on understanding how to construct subject positions in texts. From Brooks' point of view, it is ironic, then, that what this comes down to is that tutors can best help students become agents of their own writing by helping them understand how and the extent to which they are *not* owners of their texts and *not* responsible for the shape of their texts, by helping them understand, in short, how various institutional forces impinge on how and what they write and how they can negotiate a place for their own goals and needs when faced with these forces.

Students know that they don't own their texts only too well, and tutors know it too, but the overwhelming discourse in textbooks, classroom advice, training materials for teachers and tutors, and in much of the scholarship and research in composition studies on the importance of individual control in producing writing works to obscure this fact and to keep both students and tutors from realizing what they know. In her *Writing Center Journal* article, Nancy Welch observes,

> my work in the writing center at a large public university has also introduced me to students who arrive at the center already aware, sometimes painfully so, that their meanings are contested and that their words are populated with competing, contradictory voices. ... Even alone, these students write with and against a cacophony of voices, collaborating not with another person but with the Otherness of their words. (4)

Students and tutors who are outside mainstream culture are usually more aware of the way language coerces them, but all students and tutors know how institutions coerce them in writing classes. They know that students in writing classes are offered and can exercise little or no control over such things as the topic or genre of their papers, the argument structure or organization of their papers, the length of their papers, and the style or register of language in their papers. Students know that in order to get a good grade they must carefully follow assignments that specify these things, and tutors are advised explicitly not to criticize or in any way try to subvert teachers' assignments. Students and tutors respond—quite rationally—by trying to make the papers match as perfectly as possible the specifications of assignments while at the same time—quite irrationally—trying to believe that in doing this students are asserting ownership over their texts and learning to write. Meg Woolbright says, "In thinking one thing and saying another, the tutor is subverting the conflict she feels" (23); she is not being honest, and thus she subverts her chances of establishing egalitarian conversations with her students and alienates both herself and them (28-9).

But if tutors need to help students—and themselves—realize that what they know about institutional constraints is true and important, they also need to help students understand that if they are to achieve agency in writing, they must learn how to challenge these constraints productively in the service of their own goals and needs. Agency in writing is not a matter of simply taking up the subject positions offered by assignments but of actively constructing subject positions that negotiate between institutional demands and individual needs. In his discussion of what cultural studies offers to teachers of writing, John Trimbur explains that "one of the central tasks that [cultural studies] sets for radical intellectuals is to point out the relatively autonomous areas of public and private life where human agency can mediate between the material conditions of the dominant order and the lived experience and aspirations of the popular masses" (9). Because writing assignments, no matter how tightly specified, require the active participation of human agents, they offer relatively autonomous spaces in which the institutional constraints on writing imposed by the dominant order can be made to respond to the lived experience and aspirations of students.

If tutors want to help students develop agency in writing, they need to cast themselves as radical intellectuals who help students find and negotiate these spaces. Such tutors cannot, as Stephen North advises them to do, simply help students operate within the existing context without trying to change it. And, yes, I *am* thinking about undergraduate tutors, whose cogent critiques of assignments often leak out in writing center sessions even when they don't make them explicit. Furthermore, in helping students become agents of their own writing, tutors also become agents of change in writing pedagogy, helping teachers create better assignments, letting teachers know what students are having trouble with. As intellectuals, tutors contribute both to the endeavor of helping students learn about writing and to the endeavor of creating useful knowledge about writing. Speaking of what tutors can learn and how they can affect writing pedagogy, Nancy Grimm says,

> Our excursions into students' heads, like our excursions into films and
> novels, change the way we see and the way we act and the way we

think and the way we teach. Our promise to support the teachers'
position completely prevents us from sharing these altered perspectives that can in turn change the rhetorical context of teaching. In
a writing center, one discovers how smart students are and how
arbitrary and limiting linguistic conventions and educational hierarchies can be. (6)

And, I want to argue, it is in a writing center that one discovers how the goal
of empowering students as agents of their writing can actually be achieved,
for writing center tutors, by virtue of their constant contact with institutional
constraints *and* with student's lived experiences, are best positioned to serve
as what Trimbur calls radical intellectuals, or what Gramsci calls organic
intellectuals.

In order for you to better understand why I believe that the goal of
empowering students can best be achieved in a writing center and why tutors
are more likely to be organic intellectuals than are classroom teachers of
writing, I now want to explain the rationale that underlies my argument. To
do so, I will draw on some theories that are connected with work in cultural
studies and especially on the ideas of a theorist who has arguably had the
most influence on cultural studies, Antonio Gramsci. Gramsci's work has also
heavily influenced Paulo Freire, and recently we have begun to see some
direct influences of Gramsci in composition studies. As a member of the
Communist Party in Italy, Gramsci was arrested by Mussolini in 1924. In his
trial, the prosecutor claimed, "We must stop this brain working for twenty
years!" But, during the eight years he spent in prison, Gramsci wrote 2,848
pages in thirty-two notebooks, working out his theories of how social groups
gain legitimacy and power, how political change comes about, and most
importantly for us as writing teachers, what role intellectuals and education
play in this process.

Gramsci argues that the function of education in a democratic society is
to produce intellectuals, for "democracy, by definition, cannot mean merely
that an unskilled worker can become skilled. It must mean that every 'citizen'
can 'govern' and that society places him, even if only abstractly, in a general
condition to achieve this" (40). According to Gramsci, everyone is on some
level and potentially an intellectual:

each man . . . carries on some form of intellectual activity, that is, he
is a "philosopher," an artist, a man of taste, he participates in a particular conception of the world, has a conscious line of moral conduct,
and therefore contributes to sustain a conception of the world or to
modify it, that is, to bring into being new modes of thought. (9)

Thus, intellectuals are produced not by "introducing from scratch a scientific
form of thought into everyone's individual life, but [by] renovating and
making 'critical' an already existing activity" (330-31). According to Gramsci,
intellectuals become intellectuals not by virtue of any inherent qualifications
but by virtue of their efforts to elaborate critically and systematically the

philosophy of their social group.

When a social group becomes well established and dominant, its intellectuals often come to see what they do as valuable in and of itself and see themselves as somehow specially qualified for intellectual activities; they lose sight of how their activities function primarily to further the goals of their particular social group. These intellectuals are what Gramsci calls traditional intellectuals, intellectuals who because of their tenure as the intellectuals of a successful and powerful social group come to see themselves as "autonomous and independent of the dominant social group" (7). A second characteristic of traditional intellectuals is that they are the apologists for a dominant group whose vision is failing, whose ideas are no longer productive in a changing society. In his recent article on Gramsci in *Pre/Text,* Victor Villanueva offers E. D. Hirsch as a good example of an American traditional intellectual, an apologist for the status quo whose recommendations for instilling cultural literacy in all students, though well intentioned, are neither disinterested nor progressive but rather serve the interest of an established but increasingly discredited elite.

Traditional intellectuals are no longer agents of change in a society for these two reasons: they have lost contact with the purposes and goals of the group whose philosophy they represent, and they serve, although often unknowingly, the status quo. Organic intellectuals, in contrast, are those intellectuals who understand that their function as intellectuals derives from their involvement in the work and the purposes of their social group. Furthermore, they are the intellectuals of an emergent social group, one which is not yet dominant but whose vision is more directly responsive to the current historical conditions of the society than that of the dominant group, whose vision developed out of past historical conditions. Organic intellectuals exemplify the basic marxist postulate of the unity of theory and practice. Gramsci calls them "the whalebone in the corset," "*elites . . .* of a new type which arise directly out of the masses, but remain in contact with them" (340).

Organic intellectuals are agents of change because they develop through their fusion of theory and practice and through critique of the common sense of their group the philosophy of an emergent social group. Both contact with everyday practice and critique are important in this process. Contact with everyday practice ensures that the philosophy of the group more accurately represents the real historical situation; critique of the commonsense knowledge of the group frees it from the influence of the views and beliefs of the dominant social group, who have achieved power in large part because of their success in persuading all groups in a society that their world view is true and useful. Organic intellectuals must work to achieve critical understanding of the current situation of a society; they must sort through the various arguments and perspectives that are represented in the common sense of their group in order to produce what Richard Johnson has called really useful knowledge, knowledge that arises out of everyday practice and that is purified of contradictory beliefs left over from the world view of the dominant group. In Johnson's terms, critique is always an ongoing process that resists closure

and is antithetical to the procedures of academic codification and disciplin-
arity, for critique offers "procedures by which other traditions are approached
both for what they may yield and for what they inhibit" (38). Ongoing critique ensures that organic intellectuals do not turn into traditional intellectuals,
that really useful knowledge is not turned into disciplinary knowledge, that
knowledge is continually produced in the contact of theory and practice.
Really useful knowledge, Johnson argues, demands that the priority always be
"to become more 'popular' rather than more academic" (40).

To return now from the realms of theory to the situation of students
writing in college, I want to argue that composition studies and its scholars
and researchers and classroom teachers function for the most part as
traditional intellectuals of the dominant social group, intellectuals who have
lost sight of how their beliefs and practices are dependent on the world view
of the white middle class of America and whose everyday experience is quite
separate from and foreign to the life experiences of most students in college
writing classes. Some scholars and teachers, it is true, struggle to remain in
contact with the everyday experience of students in writing classes and struggle to define their problems and practices on the basis of this contact, but
neither scholars nor classroom teachers of writing are favorably positioned to
succeed in this effort. Whether scholars or teachers, whether regular faculty,
part-time teachers, or graduate students, their position in the writing
classroom is guaranteed by the institutional structures of the dominant social
group: they are responsible to standards developed by this group in service to
its purposes; they are subject to education and training that has developed
within the perspective of the dominant group; they are in daily contact with
the discourse of other traditional intellectuals; and, finally, they are usually
expected to separate theory from practice. In the case of faculty and graduate
students they are admonished that their own work should have priority over
teaching, and, in the case of part-time teachers, they are subjected to work
loads that preclude efforts at reflection and critique and theory building. It is
thus not surprising that it is difficult for classroom writing teachers to empower students as agents of their own writing, for the main prerequisite of
such an endeavor is, as Freire has long pointed out, having some idea of what
students' purposes and experiences are.

In contrast, tutors in writing centers who are in close contact with
students and their everyday writing concerns, who reflect on their practices as
tutors, and who study and critique theories of writing and language in light of
their practice are better positioned to be organic intellectuals, who, along with
their students, develop really useful knowledge of writing practices and of
ways of teaching writing that help students achieve agency. Because writing
centers are marginalized in relation to the central institutional structures of
writing pedagogy and because writing center tutors are not generally expected
to perform the function of intellectuals, the pressure on them to promulgate
beliefs and practices that serve the purposes of the dominant group is less
organized and less direct, although it is certainly not absent. North details
some of the informal attempts of faculty to bring writing center practice into

line with the authorized knowledge about writing, and his widely followed stricture that tutors are to support the classroom teacher's position completely is clear evidence of how writing centers do not escape domination. Yet one of the benefits of being excluded from the dominant group is that in this position one has less to protect and less to lose. Undergraduate students who serve as tutors have little investment in disciplinary beliefs and practices, and they are thus less responsive to its standards and expectations than they are to the needs and experiences of their peers. And, even for classroom teachers and graduate students, the continuous contact with the needs and experiences of writing students moves tutors to critique, to observe both what the traditional practices of writing instruction yield and what they inhibit.

I could continue to argue in support of my contention that tutors should and can serve as agents of change who empower students and who produce really useful knowledge, but I suspect that I can win your agreement better in another way. I want to conclude by recounting examples of how this is already happening in writing centers across the country. Following are five examples of practices of tutors and writing center administrators that seem to me to exemplify how writing centers can serve as a site of critique and how tutors can function as organic intellectuals.

1. Alice Gillam draws on Bakhtin to suggest a dialogic approach to tutoring that encourages students to negotiate between the demands of an assignment and their own interests in writing. She asks "whether the univocal conventional wisdom about reading ought to organize [a particular student's] interpretation of her [reading] experience or whether [the student's] experiences ought to reorganize or complicate conventional wisdom" (6), and she suggests that

> opening or dialogizing this text through the play of oppositions might enable Mary to see ways of satisfying her teacher's demand for focus without sacrificing [her own] richness of voice and detail. . . . Rather than stripping her "story" to the bone in order to impose a focus, perhaps Mary needs to flesh out the contradictions embedded in the text and puzzle over the off-key shifts in voice as a way of discovering focus. . . . In short, a Bakhtinian perspective might have allowed [Mary's tutor] to help Mary see the dissonances in voice and narrative as opportunities to dialogize and clarify meaning rather than as the enemies of focus, as forces to be subdued and "normalized." (7)

2. Lucy Chang demonstrates how through conversation with a Chinese student she "came to understand the cultural reasoning" that dictated the shape of the student's paper, which she describes as "a chaotic dance of ten letter words" (17). She found out that

> First, in China a scholar's intellectual power is measured by the number of Chinese characters he or she knows, not by how coherently words are arranged as this particular assignment demanded. Second, the words she knew in English translated into something else, a dis-

tant relative of her initial thought. She believed that with one English word she could express everything she was feeling as she could with one Chinese character. Third, she believed that good writing was the kind that is found in textbooks, language that is condensed and lacking in emotion. The confusion and conflict began here. Last, her deficiency in English grammar was a huge insecurity. As a result, she took no responsibility for her writing, as a means of protecting herself from the shame of her grammatical mistakes. (17-18)

Chang concludes, "From this collective understanding, I believe that I was better equipped to facilitate her writing process" (18). Chang's experience contrasts strikingly with the experience of the tutor described by Anne DiPardo, whose ignorance of her Native American student's culture and experiences with writing frustrated all her persistent and well-intentioned efforts to help the student succeed.

3. Kate Latterell, in exploring the actual practices of student-centered tutoring, discovers that, for the two tutors she interviewed,

being student-centered . . . does not seem to mean being passive, for they both stressed the importance of developing personal relationships with students as being a big factor. . . . Suzanne . . . suggests that "the more effective teaching that I've seen happens in places like this . . . where there's personal interaction and personal factors that are helping out." And Dave seems to suggest the same thing, saying, "I really believe very strongly in the powerful influences of individual and personal relationships" in making learning meaningful. (10)

Dave also refers to the importance of active engagement between tutor and student when he tells Kate that his idea of what tutoring involves has changed " 'from believing that this is totally undirected stuff' to thinking that his role is to provide a focus for the session by 'keying in on' what the student needs to talk about" (9).

4. Drawing on Julia Kristeva's notion of exile as the creation of a space in which writers can question received knowledge and social norms and in the process transform them, Nancy Welch elaborates a style of tutoring that enables both tutors and students to achieve critical distance. She recounts her work with Margie, who is engaged in writing about her experience of sexual harassment for a panel discussion during the university's annual Women's Week. Welch notes how, early in the process, she has "already constructed a template of what [Margie] should eventually write for the Women's Week panel" and is "disturbed by the gap between that 'Ideal Text' (to borrow Knoblauch and Brannon's term) and the actual text [Margie] reads to" her and how, when she resists "the pressure of perfection," Margie "displaces that template text I had formed and encourages me to listen to her emerging text instead" (9-10). At the end of a prolonged series of sessions when Margie is about to write a draft of the actual presentation, Welch offers her only one suggestion, that she remind herself to describe what happened to her. Welch

recounts Margie's reaction: "Margie grins. 'Sure, I get it,' she replies. 'I still tend to avoid that. Yeah. The monster needs a description. *I* can do that. *I* know what the monster looks like'" (16).

5. Tom Fox describes the tutor training program at Chico in which tutors are asked "to reflect critically on how social and educational inequalities affect writing and learning" and how he explores with tutors "how the institution around us is shot through with actual hierarchies and habits of hierarchies and how we more easily fall into these habits than into a truly democratic writing center, no matter whether the tables are round or square" (21). His tutors read theory—"Paulo Freire on how all education is political, Dale Spender, Richard Ohmann, Geneva Smitherman-Donaldson, and John Ogbu on how gender, class, and race affect language use, and . . . Mike Rose on how institutional history and politics shape our conceptions of writing, especially remedial writing" (22-23)—and they reflect on their own practices and educational histories. Fox concludes,

> When tutors reflect on and define their own role in a multi-cultural writing center and explore the relationship between a progressive writing center and a conservative university, they gain a sense of control over the interpretation of their experience. This control can lead to action both within and without the writing center. (23)

In these practices I see the beginnings of a vision of a writing center as a site of inquiry and critique, where tutors not only are helping students learn how to improve their writing but also are developing better practices of teaching writing and really useful knowledge about the experiences of students writing in college and in our society. Rather than "always focusing on the paper at hand" (Brooks 2), tutors build personal relationships with their students and come to understand how their students' lives and experiences shape their writing practices. Rather than insisting that students are the only ones responsible for their texts, tutors help students understand how their words and their texts are inhabited by multiple and often alien voices that they must learn to deal with. Rather than "supporting the teacher's position completely" (North 441), tutors help students negotiate a place within the confines of writing assignments for interests and abilities that arise out of their experiences. Rather than lamenting the inability of students to produce perfect papers, tutors celebrate students' ability to develop new "templates" for texts. Rather than learning to sit across from the student and not write on their papers, tutors learn to critique the social and institutional setting of writing pedagogy and to reflect on their practices in light of theories of writing and language.

I think we can push this vision further. I would like, for example, to see writing center sessions sometimes focus on the critical reading of the syllabuses and assignments that students are given to work with so that tutors could help students see what subject positions are being offered to them in these texts and what spaces are left open in which they can construct different subject positions. Classroom teachers occasionally try to get their students to engage in such critical readings, but the teachers' investment in the subjectivities they have imagined for their students fairly regularly defeats their efforts. In critical reading sessions in writing centers, tutors could also help students figure out why their teachers' ideas of what they need to learn sometimes conflict with what they think they need to learn and how recognizing these conflicts can lead to change as well as to accommodation.

I would also like to see tutor training seminars begin to blend with research groups, so that faculty, writing center administrators, and/or graduate students work together with undergraduate tutors and with the students who come to writing centers to develop systematic inquiries into the nature of writing in college and the value of different methods of teaching writing. I know that this is happening in some writing centers, and I think that in such research we can begin to bridge the chasm that often separates writing center workers from classroom teachers and theorists of writing. Writing centers are and can be at the heart of our joint inquiry into the functions of literacy in our society. We need to make better use of these "border" spaces within our institutions, spaces where the lines of power blur and the demands of discipline and evaluation weaken in ways that allow us to create together better ways of writing and of teaching writing.

Part 3:
Writing Center Praxis

War, Peace, and Writing Center Administration

by Jeanne Simpson, Steve Braye, Beth Boquet

At the 1993 Conference on College Composition and Communication, part of a pre-convention workshop on writing centers addressed the issue of communicating successfully with administration. Joyce Kinkead and I (Jeanne Simpson) offered a few techniques based upon our experiences as writing center directors and administrators.

During this segment, Steve Braye raised the question of apparent conflicts between the goals and loyalties of a writing center and those of the larger institution. I answered his question briefly but felt dissatisfied, knowing that it was an inadequate answer, constrained by time, to a big, important question. So I found Steve later and told him my thoughts. We agreed to conduct an e-mail conversation on the subject.

Of course, we could have perched on bar stools in the Sheraton, hashed through it all, and that would have been that. However, both of us felt that the issues were important to other people as well and that e-mail offered us a way of keeping the spontaneity and energy of a one-to-one discussion, while creating a written record to share. The result is here.

What issues? The big one, repeatedly on the WCENTER list, is the institutional status of writing centers. The word "marginalized" crops up again and again in these discussions; the concept was implicit in Steve's original question. This single issue influences all the others: budget, staffing, mission, methodology, space, and so on. As our e-mail conversation developed, the importance of institutional status for writing center personnel became clear.

Beth Boquet entered the conversation through a WCENTER post in which she alluded to her dissertation research on this very subject. We invited her to join us, wanting the third perspective she could provide.

Our purpose here is to offer a preliminary exploration of the subject. We hope it will encourage thought, research, and vigorous debate. And we hope that this model will alert others to the possibilities of e-mail; this conversation could never have happened in any other format.

* * *

Reprinted from *Composition Studies/Freshman English News* 22.1 (1994): 65-95. Used by permission.

Steve,

Well, I'm as "un-buried" as I'm likely to be. So, let's get this dialogue started.

In the workshop, you raised the question of "selling out," of abandoning the student (and faculty?) orientation of writing center work for the institution orientation (or management orientation?) of administration. My response at the time ... what WAS my response? Something about remembering that writing center directors are part of the institution too, and that it is defined by the people present at any one time.

But I also recall thinking that my response was simplistic, though necessarily in that context. I thought there was more to this issue. We know that writing center directors apparently regard themselves as 1) still "outsiders" (meaning what?), as 2) subversive of uninformed institutional notions of writing pedagogy, and 3) frustrated by the lack of financial and other support for their efforts on the part of administration. And is developing information to meet the needs of an administrative audience a form of pandering? Is administration an enemy? Obviously I don't think so, but I am biased.

So, here's a start.

                                                            Jeanne

- — - — - — - — - — -

Jeanne:

It seems to me that writing centers exist because there was no place in the institution, or in the spaces sanctioned by the institution, to do what centers attempt. I don't know whether this is because colleges and universities don't want to admit to teaching some of the things we do (I'm always amazed at how little faculty sometimes know about the ability level of a first year student) or that such problems seem outside what we want the curriculum to include. But this means that centers, at some level, were (are?) beating against the institutional current. Many centers were likely funded to do things other than what they really accomplished. I can imagine some centers were created to "eradicate" the campus of writing problems. Those in charge likely knew better from the start. But they used the opening to secure a place for helping such students.

If centers have been successful, I would think they are breaking down this institutional view. Their popularity makes me believe that centers are doing their job (whatever this may be or however they may be perceived). Today centers are considered, I think, a positive addition to campuses. Our admissions people, for example, always include the center on campus tours and mention it prominently in slide shows, etc.

Here's where my fears arise. I do still think of myself as an outsider when I think of the campus as a whole. While my discipline is as old, if not older, than any in the institution, I feel our treatment by the institution and the variety of ideas generated by the figures in our field makes me a subversive force (to use your term) on the campus. I see tradition in a significantly different way. I am more open to radical notions, hold traditional ideas like canons less precious than my peers, and look to other disciplines for ideas to shake up the way I see my own field (which means I always try to recognize the limited vision of my own field). This does not mean I want to bring the institution to its knees. In the same way that I want to change the way my students see the world (I call it education), I want the institution to revise its mission, to see what it can accomplish.

Obviously, this cannot be done from the "outside." But I worry about how quickly I identify myself with the "tradition." When administration gives me a budget, does that free me to bring about more changes? Or does it weigh me down with institutional values and priorities? All the talk, for a while, at San Diego was on how to become a member of the institution. But I don't necessarily want to do that. It isn't because I see administration as the enemy. But I think institutions have a power of their own (Foucault discusses this) no matter who is in certain administrative positions. At the same time, I feel people like yourself, in administrative positions, who are cognizant of how to use their position to manipulate or change the goals of the institution, can be powerful forces of change in education.

So let me finish by asking a few questions of you.

1. Should writing centers remain on the outside? I'm still not sure what that means, but I think it is important as we consider what the role of centers will be in the next century (heck, in this decade).

2. How do we walk that tightrope between our own goals, often contrary to the institution, and the goals of our schools, which we must serve in some way in order to have any effectiveness or power?

3. Should centers be permanently on the "cutting edge?" Should we be disappointed if they ever become places where you can only find given, traditional knowledge? Should we always maintain our subversive roots?

I hope this isn't too much. I do think as centers age the relationship between the centers and their schools becomes more complex and important to understand.

                                                            Steve

                        - — - — - — - — -

Steve:

Well, yes and no to your vision of how centers emerge. While of course there is a certain filling in of interstices, there still exists a basic shared vision: the need to help students. There is a recognition, sometimes badly stated or oversimplified, that classroom instruction in writing is not enough. Now the need to help students may be motivated by genuine altruism, but it is motivated also by the institutional need to survive via student retention. Especially these days.

You are right about the naiveté of faculty, re: students' ability levels, preparation, maturity, etc. I would argue that our entire higher education system is responsible for that: we don't prepare college teachers, by and large; we prepare scholars who, oh by the way, will also teach.

The success of writing centers is based entirely too much on perception and not enough on hard documentation. And, probably, on relief: "we've got this center to address these messy problems so we look responsible without most of us actually having to deal with them." I certainly share your alarm about this.

Being open to radical notions is, one hopes, the result of a good education. Otherwise, we'd all belong to the Flat Earth Society. But one of the paradoxes of our institutions is that, while their expressed purpose in a free society is to protect the exchange of ideas and to encourage fresh thought, they are in fact most conservative. Conservative both in its political and its literal senses. I don't think this tension is resolvable. I am not sure resolution should be attempted. Rather, I think the tension is one of the most important facts of American higher education, perhaps one of the things that makes it so powerful and attractive.

I confess to not having read Foucault. But herewith my own observations.

Institutions retain a power of their own because people perceive power and acknowledge it. Knowing, probably, that institutions that project power are a cohesive force, an order-imposing force. Anarchy, after all, is frightening. And institutions that serve a multiplicity of functions are that much more powerful, such as universities. Even so, while the basic perception of the institution may not change significantly over a long period, the actual thing will change, simply because of the presence of different people operating within it over time.

Am I belaboring the obvious? Well, consider it thinking onscreen, ok? I am very old-fashioned; the essays I think of for this instance are those of Tolstoy, the interim chapters in "War and Peace" in which he struggles with the problem of the effect of the individual (Pierre or Napoleon) on history as opposed to the effects of large forces beyond human control.

I guess, Steve, that you see a polarity between yourself and the institution, between the individual and the university. Whereas I see a pair of circles of activity which overlap to some extent and yet also cover separate areas.

Tolstoy's problems, ultimately, were addressed by the Annalist historians in France, who argued that EVERYTHING influences the events of history— geography, economics, climate, individual personalities, technological developments, etc. Exactly right, to my mind. Likewise, institutions. It is hubris to imagine that we may, alone and separate, influence an institution's course. Yet we can contribute to its change, understanding that others will change our changes and the result will not necessarily be as we expect. The courage to try anyway, believing that one must, is important.

Should writing centers remain on the outside? Of what? If they exist, sanctioned by budgets, within the institution, they are not outside of it. On the outside of traditional English depts.? Yes. And if they (centers) become separate, discrete entities within the institution, will they change? Oh, a little. They will, I think, expand services, create little empires that will need defending, grab space that others want, etc. The thing is, it is impossible to sustain revolution. Marx was dead wrong about that or Mao or whomever.

Eventually, the revolutionaries become the establishment until a new gang of revolutionaries comes along to trash the joint. Jefferson understood that, embraced it. He was right.

I still wonder why you perceive your goals as being contrary to the goal of the institution. Most institutions have the goal of survival. The rest—educating young people, etc.—are part of that matter: "we want to survive because we like this life; the way to do it is to perform, well enough to get continued approval, the functions required of us." Your goal in the center is 1) survive and 2) do the function as well as possible. You have considerable latitude in defining that, don't you? Where is the real dispute? With central administration or lower down? My bet is that it is lower down. In which case, your goals and some other group's goals may conflict. I seem to be a Darwinist, don't I?

Question 3. Writing centers can try to remain cutting edge, perhaps, but we will delude ourselves. Hmm. Centers can indeed be on the cutting edge, in part because they don't generate credit hours or employ faculty in the same way courses/curricula do. Permanently? I guess theoretically that is possible.

Can a writing center director remain cutting edge? No. No human being is that strong, Steve. The best service we can do for Centers is to know when to leave them to someone else with more energy, fresher vision, etc. We need humility as well as courage and fighting spirit. And knowing that and acting on it is, ironically, a way of "maintaining our subversive roots," is it not? Jefferson again. Not sustained revolution but periodic ones. I like being forced to think carefully about this. I knew when you asked your original question that the question was complicated and so was any answer likely to be. Only the circumstance of the moment led me to respond as if it were otherwise. I'll be interested to read responses.

Jeanne

- — - — - — - — - -

Steve:

Just what you want after I send you the e-mail equivalent of *War & Peace*. But I've been gnawing on the questions you asked me.

Do you find divergence between your personal goals and the institution's announced goals? Of course that problem exists in all employment where you work for somebody else. If the two sets of goals have too little overlap, then would you be happier elsewhere (happier defined as coming closer to reaching your goals without conflict with the employer?) I'm serious. It is always a struggle to decide if you are compromising personal principles to an intolerable extent. That is one reason I am here instead of the writing center. My frustration with being regarded as marginal was very high. The perception of marginality belonged to others, not to me. So I moved on.

Some people achieve more or feel better about themselves if they conduct their work in the matrix of conflict. Lawyers come to mind immediately. I am not wired that way, though I certainly seem to have a tolerance for other people's conflicts. Again, this is not judgement, but observation. Will you do a better job of making the writing center operate if you perceive your work as subversion, even if others don't perceive it that way at all? Maybe so. This begins to become a hall of mirrors, and my pragmatic soul cringes.

I have come close to flaming on WCENTER (a temptation I have really resisted, believing that WCENTER's tone is part of its great strength) over what sounds like pious victim-hood. It is NOT a blessed state. It is merely a common one. That we should attempt to make it less common is appropriate. We need not make it holy. For writing centers to fret about marginalization and/or victimization is to waste time. Define the specific problem and find a solution is my response. And the problem should be defined in terms of service to students or the whole thing is a sham.

I sound as if something is wrong with you. Please don't take it that way. The thoughts here are exploratory, presented as a sounding board.

Jeanne

- — - — - — - — - — -

Jeanne:

It seems a bit obvious that I am torn between two positions here. The reason I as attracted to the San Diego workshop was my recognition that I need to be more successful in accomplishing the changes I would like to help generate. And that workshop did help me see how to act in more acceptable (?), hence successful, ways. I don't mean that comment to be negative. I think all center staff need to be cognizant of our place in the bigger picture in order to keep the center viable.

Your comments about victim-hood mirror the comments our Dean made after he was hooked to the WPA network for a few months. He commented on the negative tone of many comments and how people feel that the world is against them. I want to fight against such a mode. We are only victims if we allow ourselves to be so, or, even worse, if we present ourselves as such. I know the institution means well. That is what drew me to it. Its resistance to change is positive. It keeps us in touch with our past and with our mission.

I agree, too, that we don't want to resolve the tension; it is necessary for a successful educational system. But this tension seems to settle often in writing programs and centers. It feels like we are in a touchy field, where any motion spurs some type of reaction. My department is sensitive, to say the least, to issues concerning writing and the center, even though they have little or no background in writing theory. Sometimes I think this makes me overly conscious of the tension and how to deal with it.

Steve

- — - — - — - — - — -

Steve:

Aha! NOW we're to the nitty-gritty. It isn't the institution that is making you grind your teeth, it's the DEPARTMENT. No surprise there.

Let's talk about that. First, the dept's position on something is not necessarily the college's official position on the same issue. I am familiar with one English dept. that is significantly out of step with its institution's views on several things, such as ESL and freshman retention programs. The inclination of many depts. is to assume a "don't tread on me" posture—"leave us alone to deconstruct texts, write articles and poems and what not. And, oh yes, we'll grudgingly teach freshman comp for you because obviously it needs to be done (the riff-raff you let in this place can't write for beans) and obviously no one else is qualified to do it, so don't push it, buddy." English depts are notoriously uncooperative about WAC programs, too, because of the implication that other people CAN teach writing.

Eng Depts have a vested interest in keeping writing (sections = faculty positions = power) and a vested interest in keeping writing 2nd class (use it to create a hierarchy for young faculty to navigate and to provide incentive, in the form of upper division lit. classes, for them to publish, etc.) Also, if most depts. admitted that teaching writing is a bit more complicated than falling off a log and just knowing a smidgen of grammar, then they'd admit that they've employed people who were unqualified to teach writing and who regularly botched the job.

The assumption that writing centers have a natural affiliation with English depts. needs to be questioned. Given the institutional posture of many Eng. Depts. vis-a-vis writing, the more natural thing to do is to get away from an English dept. as fast as possible and get a larger, institutional profile. Most of us who direct(ed) WC's came out of English depts. and are comfortable with the career development notions they represent. We blend our experience with our aspirations. But to our peril.

Your willingness to rebel would be a real asset in the "breakout of English" scenario. As long as you understand that the "rebel" label need not (should not?) be permanent. My guess is that you might find support for this further up the line if you can make a case for 1) saving money and 2) meeting mission. And, if you can find some small bone for administration to throw toward English, so much the better.

Jeanne

- — - — - — - — - -

Jeanne:

You comment that writing center success is "based entirely too much on perception and not enough on hard documentation." How do we prove we are successful? Is it clear what we are established to do? I can set goals for my center and strive to meet them. But I worry about the subtext. What does a writing center do to achieve institutional success (if there is such a thing!)? I know that the college and the center are both striving to educate our students. But success can be nebulous. And I'm interested, especially from your perspective as a Dean, what hard documentation might be. Visitations? Student evaluations?

This leads to a bigger concern. What are the foundational principles of writing centers which should be adhered to in order to maintain integrity? I don't want the center to be a remedial center, or a place for proofreading, but what does that make us? It is more the perception of "selling out" and the historical weight that carries in my life that makes me anxious. But I'm also not sure what makes us what we are. What makes a center good? How do we keep in touch with the principles which generated us? Should we maintain touch with these principles? What makes us a valuable part of the university? I know these probably seem like simple questions. But I received a fine education without a writing center. Does this writing center make the institution better? Does it change the pedagogy on the campus? The ethos? I want to make sure that as we evolve, we don't transform into something inconsistent with who we want to be. I know the way I'm saying this it seems like there is some force out there pushing us in the wrong direction. I don't mean that. I'm not sure what I mean.

I don't like the victim mode, though. I work in the center by choice. I could be teaching literature. But I understand the value in writing, teaching, and the center. That seems to contradict what I said earlier. I think I am confused.

You are right when you point out there is no dichotomy between myself and the institution. If my goals and the institution's are antithetical, I need to find another line of work. I also agree that we can inspire change, though that change is not necessarily what we will expect. But not everyone in the institution is pursuing change. Many want merely to preserve the status quo.

If I "walk the walk and talk the talk," do I risk losing my own identity? If the center is great at playing the game, do we forget at some point that it is a game? If the center becomes integrated into the various aspects of the institution (budget lines, etc.), are we more or less likely to inspire change? Does this better equip us to reach our goals? Much of this may revolve around the fact that I am not easily satisfied. Something makes me want to push beyond established bounds. Writing centers have done just that. They have developed new pedagogies, new approaches to dealing with writing problems, and new ways of viewing education. Do we lose this capacity if we become just another budget line? Or, as you suggest, perhaps we are already one.

I don't think so, though. We are on the outside, though I'm not sure on the outside of what. Writing center directors are often treated differently than other professors. Some are purely administrative. Some are denied tenure lines. Many are paid differently. Recent WCENTER discussions have shown this. We have a center but no budget line. I have no money for workshops, etc. I am given 2/9 release time to run, staff, advertise, and supervise the center. The Honors program is not run like this. In fact, no other program is run like the center. Can we forget we are different if we are constantly treated as such? Writing courses, on our campus, are the only courses taught by people who are required to teach in a field of study beyond their own (i.e., literature specialists). We have the usual resentment for this. Does that not contribute to keeping us on the outside?

When you suggest that we leave centers at some point in time, are you suggesting that the centers should stay on the edge, pushing at the boundaries, even though individuals cannot sustain this? So the center could be a continuing revolution, though the individuals leading the revolution periodically change?

Your second response hits a nerve. If the institution and writing centers both exist to serve students, why were you marginalized? Why was/is writing? Or writing centers? Who was doing this and to what end? What were these people trying to accomplish and why? It makes me feel that WCS proposed goals that differed from those within the institution. Otherwise, we would always have been treated as equals. Or am I oversimplifying? This brings me back to our roots. Was there something in our creation, in the way we were originally considered by the institution, that caused this split? A friend of mine occasionally reminds English Department members that literature and literary criticism is an offshoot of rhetoric. She says she doesn't want us to forget where we came from (history again!). I guess I'm having trouble "defining the specific problem." And I want to be cautious about how we accomplish our goals.

Steve

- - - — - — - — - — -

Steve:

Um, I'm not a dean; my title is long and clunky: assistant vice president for academic affairs. I don't consider that better or worse than a dean. However, the office of academic affairs perforce takes an institution-wide point of view; deans are still territorial. Ferociously so, in my experience. That doesn't answer your question, though it reminds me to suggest that a university/college is often seen by faculty as a democracy. Well, there are democratic elements in it, but most institutions are more feudal than democratic.

How to prove success? Let's define success two ways. First, we can agree that assisting students to become more adept at communicating with writing is success for writing centers. It is our primary reason for existence. Tough to prove—no one who's ever worked with centers thinks this proof is easy to get. It is maddeningly elusive. But you can try. Must try.

Second, writing centers do things that assist institutions and that don't get talked about or proved sufficiently. E.g., tutor training is a fine form of education. Here, it strengthens a good but small master's program; our placement rate for graduates is very high, in part because their WCENTER experience makes them very marketable. The WCENTER confirms the institution's stance as "student friendly." "Support" is a friend-implying word, even as it also suggests marginality. The WCENTER is a place where research can be conducted, experimentation, and pilot programs. We certainly tried to involve the center in practical matters for other disciplines, including secondary education and student personnel services. The reports that came out of these documented success for students and also success in the budgetary sense: the university was getting a lot of bang for its buck.

Integrity by what definition, Steve? Again, personal integrity and institutional integrity certainly overlap but are not a perfect match. While I agree that a solely remedial WCENTER is missing the boat, I don't think a center should avoid remedial activities entirely. A student in need is a student in need. The real problem is determining who decides the center's mission. That is negotiated between the director and the institutional leadership. Over and over, I might add. Oh, and students, too. They sometimes define mission without knowing it. Really, every time student and tutor sit down together, this negotiation occurs.

Of course you run into the unpersuadable and unconvinced. That's that tension we discussed yesterday. All I can say is, don't butt your head uselessly against the immovable. Obstacles can be walked around as well as pushed over, and with less effort. Aim your efforts at the persuadable and forget about the ones who won't ever come around. Every institution has them. So what? They resist everything and still the place changes.

The goal of inspiring change is a bit different from the goal of changing. Writing centers can change. They can participate in change. Inspiring change? Who do you want to inspire? How? To do what? Do you want to inspire other English teachers? Fat chance. But the director of a center who has sent improved writers back to X dept. will very likely have the ears of chair and faculty in X dept. when it comes time to suggest new ideas. Inspiration is more like Chinese water torture than it is like a biblical epiphany—you keep plugging and eventually somebody's lightbulb switches on. How's that for a Waring blender of a metaphor?

What's wrong with being "another budget line?" It beats the alternative.

Yes, yes, yes, resentment of writing keeps us "on the outside." Of course it does. But it is not necessarily administration that inflicts that situation. The locus for this thinking is the DEPARTMENT.

My experience is that when you indicate to administration that something as huge as teaching writing can be done better AND more cheaply (an issue that cannot be avoided; nor should it be), they'll ask you to present a model and explain it all. They will listen. They may not act immediately or as you wish, but remember that change on that scale is dangerous politically. They generally prefer a gentler approach.

How did the Honors program get better treatment? Did the Honors director agitate for it up in central admin? You gotta ASK. And keep ASKing (water torture, like I said.) And don't ask the English dept. They'll always say no, for the reasons I mentioned yesterday.

To whom would you be selling out? What would you be selling? What would the cost actually be? In what form do you require respect to be demonstrated? A budget line is the ultimate form of respect in most universities. Do you mean more released time? Rank? All those are, in the end, forms of money. What form do you want it in?

Should centers stay on the cutting edge (an awful metaphor!)? I think that is exactly what I mean. But I'll cogitate further and see if I find holes in that thinking.

I was marginalized (to an extent) because I fell for all the English dept. rhetoric and stupidly stayed there. Now, I'm agitating like hell to get centers moved out.

Later. I hope you enjoy this as much as I.

Jeanne

- — - — - — - — - -

Steve:

Been thinking briefly (just got out of a 2-½ hour meeting and my butt is numb, so my thinking may be also) about my description of univ. as a feudal structure. Sort of. But let's explore the analogy to feudalism a bit.

What ultimately destroyed feudalism was the rise of separate economic structures, like towns, and the enterprise of people outside the feudal structure—merchants and bankers, guilds and other such groups. And of course superior technologies that left the mounted knight behind in the dust. Now as long as a writing center operates within the feudal hierarchy, it is going to be subject to both the advantages and the constraints imposed by the hierarchy. Advantage: clear definition of place. Constraints: money and power have to trickle (the right word for it!) down from way up above. And not much gets through. You have to work really hard and carry a big burden for not much reward. Always the lot of a serf. If you leave the feudal hierarchy, you become more exposed in a way, but also you have more opportunity for enterprise. Kings protected towns and the merchants therein, but did not handle them the same way as they handled armed, castle-dwelling vassals. They had a vested interest in encouraging their prosperity, right?

The analogy isn't perfect but it offers some possibilities for understanding.

LUNCH!

Jeanne

- — - — - — - — - -

Jeanne:

I want to come back to a question you asked at the beginning and lies at the basis of centers and their current role on any campus. You said you were marginalized, and I know I often feel this way. Why is this? If we were created to serve an important institutional need, like honors programs are, why would we have ever been marginalized? Why would the Eng. dept., or any other, want us to be outside the group (whatever this group is)?

It makes me feel that our discussions of marginalization and exclusion have some basis in fact. Isn't removing the center from the English department avoiding the problem? Is it a form of victimhood to say that our problems originate in the Eng. dept? Are we marginalized because of something we do, our purpose, our goals, our theories of teaching? Could the Eng. dept have some view of writing that is significantly different than the rest of the campus? (Especially since most of our colleagues developed their views of writing in Eng. depts?) It seems to me that while I often feel marginalized by the institution, you focus more directly on the Eng. department. I'm interested to know why that is.

I see the writing center as an experimental site on our campus. No, we don't have to go counter to the institution. But can we deny we are different, and we want this difference respected? Doesn't the fact that we value student voice send us in a slightly different direction than most others who use writing on the campus? Yes, we try to educate others (does that sound parental or what?) but it seems like we are out there all alone, trying new ideas as if we are some type of faculty development forum. I think we parallel feminist theory. Feminists are not saying that history should be destroyed or rejected. But our current ways of seeing the world are limited and exclusionary. Feminist theory opens us up to new ways of looking and valuing the world. Many faculty use writing well. But we seem to be the leaders, providing new ways of looking and understanding.

I also see this difference in the make-up of our center. The design and spirit of the center is different from any other "classroom" on campus. Our center is used exclusively for tutorials. Students comment on the tables and comfortable chairs that make this room unlike any other classroom they've ever known. It's not that we have soft chairs or anything. It just doesn't look like a traditional classroom. Almost all the activity is student centered, whether this means center sessions or students playing hangman. So again, being different, or being perceived as different, gives the center flexibility that allows it to do what it does.

This does relate to your feudalism analogy. I am apprehensive as to whether it is best for the center to join the given economic structure, to be subject to the many rules of the hierarchy, or whether we retain more control and power by maintaining an identity outside the given structure. I know we are already a part of the structure. But I don't see us as accepted members. It's almost like we are on probation. If we learn how to play by the rules, we will be more fully integrated into the system. I know if I "dressed for success," which I don't, I might get more money for the center sooner. But would I compromise the identity of the center, which revels in its lack of institutional identification? Our tutors have commented that they like how they control what occurs in the center, how the center gives them a place unlike others on campus. How much do I need to be loyal to this spirit, to protect this environment from the feudal system? I know I have to keep it alive and I do this with yearly reports, etc. But I'm not sure I want to become just another program. I remember Eric Hobson, at the San Diego cccc pre-convention workshop, talking about how he gets around much of the institutional garbage by being outside departments. I wonder whether you see this as a positive or negative direction for centers. In fact, when you see centers leaving the Eng. dept, where do you see them in the feudal system? Would such a move marginalize us further in the eyes of our peers or would it empower us to bring about more change, or both? I do think it is important to remember, too, that serfs never achieved their rights under the feudal system. The system ultimately had to be destroyed in order for the serfs to achieve some respect and independence.

Steve

— — · — · — · — · — -

Steve:

The marginalization is not a figment of your imagination nor mine. There are, I think, two different kinds of marginalization. One involves English depts. and the whole traditional approach to the teaching of writing. Writing Centers ARE different from other classrooms, as you so eloquently describe. Traditionalism in English Depts. has no way to address WCENTERS except in the most traditional/surface way: grammar fixit shops. Some depts. are more accommodating, but in the end the English dept. has a vested interest in keeping writing in a secondary position (as long as the dept. is dominated by literature specialists, that is). Which is why I think WCENTERS need to occupy the position of merchants and guilds, outside the usual vassalage of the feudal structure. Eric Hobson's point, in other terms.

The second source of marginalization is harder to deal with. In the competition for resources, one measure of who deserves resources and who does not is student credit hour production (which is another way of calculating tuition income). Writing centers do not produce credit hours, at least not many. It is, by tough economic definition, a support service and therefore secondary to the central mission of any institution. That it is a site for some excellent, efficient teaching may be true, but this definition of credit hour production dominates most institutions, right or wrong. That's why I've argued that the best way to defend a writing center is to connect it to retention. Retention means tuition. It is a step removed from credit hour production but operating within the same economic system.

My own experience was primarily with the Eng. Dept. (no change, either; their latest version of the major includes little attention to composition theory). My institution has been very supportive of the center and willing to let it define its own mission, by and large. It serves many outside the English dept., but its budget is still IN the dept. making it perpetually vulnerable.

And there is the problem of personal professional advancement for WCENTER directors, especially if they are officially faculty in the Eng. dept. As long as directors are tap dancing between the need to satisfy a dept's standards for promotion and tenure and at the same time the need to lead a center forward, they will face these problems. Yet directors who are not faculty lose some credibility as campus leaders. It is a dilemma, and I don't pretend to have answers. However, I think the approach likeliest to produce good results at this time is to 1) move the center out of a dept. and make it report as high and as directly as possible and 2) have faculty rank for directors so they have credibility. That requires a tough bit of diplomacy for directors.

My consistent theme through all this involves the hard economics of institutions. I am not addressing the intrinsic value of writing centers. They have value, obviously. We all KNOW that. But being on the side of the angels simply is not enough. Everybody in an institution believes the same thing about their particular causes. And when times are hard, as they are and are going to be for a long time, when no institution has the wherewithal to do everything everyone there wants done, there will be brutal competition for resources, based on criteria not necessarily related to educational worth.

Jeanne

- — - — - — - — - — -

Jeanne:

Your point about credit hours and retention is one we deal with too little in writing center discussions.

So let's role play a little.

We agree that the institution is credit hour driven and that WCENTERS will never generate credit hours (though this latter may not be true). How does this hard-working, well-meaning angel (boy, am I dreaming) compete with the other needy, important interest groups?

My center is one of the most important parts of the institution. (I can't believe you would classify us merely as a support service.) We have an impact on every department on campus. We reach students galore. It is almost impossible to measure our importance to the institution (which is part of the problem.)

The center serves over one-third of the student body. Over 80% of the students rate the WCENTER as excellent in exit evaluations. We had students visit from 60% of the faculty on campus, so the center has helped in almost every class. We've provided comment sheets to faculty, who consistently claim that such sheets have helped them deal with their students better. I have written responses from faculty in a variety of disciplines who thank us for helping them improve the writing in their classes. The tutors constantly write about how much the center has helped them and how much they enjoy it. Our director of English Education has written that the center has produced quality writing teachers and that this will help them to get jobs.

Yet my budget is only work study money to pay tutors. Any other money I receive comes from the writing program, which is woefully underfunded, or the English department, which often has other interests from mine. I have asked for years for a budget which allows the center to grow. But you, as Dean, won't fund my budget. You say no money is available, though other people are getting money for new projects. What am I doing wrong? What do I need to do that I'm not? Do I not recognize what I must do in order to be successful? I would rather blame you and your own shortsightedness. But how can I show you that a strong center means money for the college?

I'm thinking that I might have to play the game better to gain the autonomy I value the most. Perhaps, though, those of us who run centers come from a way of thinking that is quite unlike administrative concerns. Perhaps we don't understand. But will providing more statistics be the answer? What might you suggest that we do, from an administrative standpoint, that will help us accomplish our goals?

Time for lunch.

Steve

- — - — - — - — - -

Steve:

"We have an impact on every department on campus." But you are not a department. You don't have majors. See, implicit in that statement—to the average non-writing center person—is the notion that writing is a thing that serves disciplines. The idea that writing itself is a discipline is still not widely known or accepted, in or out of English depts.

Mind, I am not saying this is how things should be, just that it is how they are, most places, most of the time. Change is happening in some places. Now there are writing departments separated from lit departments; how that might change the politics of writing centers isn't clear to me, but it seems likely that it is a major opportunity for writing centers to redefine their places in institutions. Won't happen fast, but seems to be happening over the whole country, here and there, both large and small institutions: U. of Illinois, U of Texas, U of Arkansas Little Rock, for example.

This is the terrible dilemma: you are doing a great job with meager resources. And since you've proved that you can do that, there is no incentive for the dean/provost to give you more resources. You need to do a great job and also prove that you are about to collapse. Or define other goals that cannot be met without more resources.

I'd like to work on this issue more, later, Steve. Gotta go—going to be meeting-ed to death today. Have a good one!

Jeanne

- — - — - — - — -

Steve:

Been re-reading your message to the Dean. I note your $$ comes through the English dept. See, if the dean gives $$ to you, it has to go through the dept. the way things are structured now. So if he gives YOU money, the rest of his college sees it as giving $$ to English, which is probably one of the largest units on campus and therefore a target for envy.

It is also not clear what the role of your chair is here. Is your chair supportive of your work? And what's the attitude of English faculty? Are you perceived as empire-building? Chairs and deans worry a lot about perception as well as reality; they spend a remarkable amount of time listening to people bitch about stuff and it's an awful drag doing that. So, if they can alleviate some of the bitching, they do.

Having a good case is NOT enough. It isn't always even relevant, unfortunately. Just as in state legislatures and in Congress, the goodness of a cause is often quite lost in the political hurly-burly.

I'm sure your dean thinks you do a great job. And I'm sure you do. The problem is that you've given the dean a wonderful example to point to: here's a program that really works and look how little we have to spend on it.

What to do? Point to a problem and how you can solve it and give clear budget projections (don't ask for the moon, however) on what it would cost. R-E-T-E-N-T-I-O-N. D-I-V-E-R-S-I-T-Y. A-S-S-E-S-S-M-E-N-T. All these are matters at which institutions are throwing money these days. Can you pilot in techniques for accommodating disabled students—using computers, etc.? Or portfolio assessment? Or workshops on diversity as it connects to teaching writing/ WAC? Keep doing a good job, but attach your budget needs to something with a little glamour. This seems cynical, doesn't it? But retention and diversity and assessment are also good things, and if some students get help that otherwise would not, have you really compromised your basic principles?

Well, back to my local wars, which are currently bloodier than usual. Feeling more than a little cynical. Battle weary, even. Later,

                                                        Jeanne

- — - — - — - — - -

Jeanne:

A short message since I too have to get "meetinged" today.

Your response is quite intriguing. If I hear you right, you are suggesting that WCENTERS may not be integrated, supported, etc. like other college services until writing is accepted as a discipline, an action that seems quite beyond the realm of most writing centers. Are you suggesting that disciplinary status, with majors, minors, etc., will help us achieve recognition and esteem?

Also, this tightrope you present makes me even less certain how I should deal with you. (Again, I think much of our discussion involves WCENTER folks understanding and appreciating the decision-making process of administration.) I should make clear that we are doing an excellent, important job. Then I should either make clear that this support could disappear because I'm killing myself and others to make it happen or that we are only scratching the surface and that with money we could assist the campus in a variety of ways (i.e., retention, etc.). Should I also provide some very subtle threats, that certain things cannot continue to be done at the current level of funding?

Your perspective seems so important here. Most center people I know are always looking for rave reviews. You seem to suggest that we need to temper our year end reports with economic reality. How do I convince you that while the center may be the best thing going, it could disappear in a wink of an eye?

Wow. And I thought the negotiations in Eastern Europe were tough.

                                                        Steve

- — - — - — - — - -

Steve:

As long as current, traditional constructs exist, yes, that is what I am saying. Now, it may not be necessary for writing centers to enter the same realm as, say, math departments. But the perception of a hierarchy will exist.

Meanwhile, however, we have to decide if that is a fight worth fighting. Maybe, maybe not. Is it a WRITING CENTER fight? I think not. A writing center can be very useful, dead center in curriculum matters, etc., and still, ultimately, be a support service and still get lots of $$$. We just have to accept that being a support service carries with it permanent vulnerability. The same is true of food services, residence halls, and so on. Some institutions could ditch them. Likewise advisement centers. But the likelihood is small.

Yes. Do both—do miracles and threaten to disappear. Everyone else does. This is not like school where you get rewarded for doing everything right. Your analogy to Eastern European politics is much more accurate. Miracles, threats, and promises. All part of the mix. The accomplishments are in part your collateral on the promises—you've delivered before and thus are likely to again. The threats of course should be subtle, but they keep you from being taken for granted.

If a dean/provost gets ten reports per year from support services, and one of them always is just great news and the other nine contain problems to be solved, which will get the dean/provost's attention? Which will go into a file drawer? And if your threats/promises are connected to things the admins. is thinking about anyway, so much the better. And accompanied by data— NUMBERS! Nobody is interested in anecdotal evidence or perceptions. They want hard, numerical proof.

Next meeting coming up. Yuk. Meanwhile, I can cogitate more on this.

Jeanne

- — - — - — - — - — -

Hi Jeanne:

The recent discussion on WCENTER demonstrates much of what you have been arguing about victim-hood. This "us/them" distinction, between us and faculty no less, is one that limits our success in the institution. As you have argued, we need to see ourselves as an integral part of the institution rather than some outside mutant in order to be successful. Paolo Freire argues that change can never come from outside. Change must come from within the institution. We can attempt to destroy the institution from the outside, but we can't reform it.

Further, he goes on to argue that only the oppressed can generate change. People in power refuse to give up their power. They are as trapped by it as much as empowered by it. Change must always come from those who are powerless. They are the ones who can free not only themselves but their oppressors. I must be feeling revolutionary today.

If we looked at some of my original questions in this way, and at many of your ideas, we might claim it is our responsibility to assert our part in the institution so that it changes in a way we feel is more responsive to all. I know this assumes that we are oppressed and that we may or may not be. But if we are, if we are limited in the money we can acquire, etc., we must be the stimulus to overcome this oppression.

Steve

- — - — - — - — - — -

Steve:

Exactly right. I love your term "outside mutant."

I don't know if I agree that "only" the oppressed can generate change. Certainly they are the most likely to since they have a vested interest in doing so. I suppose it depends on how one defines "oppressed." Change comes when someone is dissatisfied with the status quo. Dissatisfaction can range from the mildly disgruntled to the seriously oppressed. In any case, semantics aside, I agree with the basic idea here.

Yes, we do have a responsibility to assert our part in the institution. But. That means several things. We have a RESPONSIBILITY. We must ASSERT. We must define our PART IN THE INSTITUTION. And we must understand what the INSTITUTION IS. As well as what various parts think it aspires to be. A lot of the emphasis I've seen on WCENTER is about asserting and not so much about the other parts of the sentence and the actions implied by them. They all need to get done.

It feels to me as if we are coming to some sort of closure on this discussion, since more and more, we have agreement on ideas.

Take care,

Jeanne

- — - — - — - — - — -

Jeanne:

I'm to the point where I am interested in solutions. I have a better sense of where the center fits into the institutional structure and what I need to understand in order to be successful. Now how do we balance the issues in such a way that we accomplish our goals without sacrificing our mission?

I first thought of Freire when you commented on the fact that we can isolate ourselves from the institution and render ourselves helpless. He criticizes sectarianism as a domesticating, alienating view of the world. This view of the world simplifies the dynamic quality of thinking into, at best, binary oppositions, often an "us against them" battle. Viewed in this way, solutions are nearly impossible. Instead, we must see ourselves in solidarity with those who share our goals. We must work with these people in order to change the current situation. One other point he makes relates to your idea of miracles/disaster. We participated in producing the social reality we exist within. If it is true that writing is a lower form of life, this was not created by some outside force and imposed upon us (victim-hood). We participated in its creation, we even work to maintain this system as it currently stands (your comment that if everything is going fine without a budget, why should my dean grant me one?).

In order to deal with this situation, I must first decide upon the goals and philosophy which drives the center. This doesn't mean deciding upon trivial matters, but deciding what lies at the core of the center, what values and principles lie at the heart that I cannot compromise. Second, I should identify who I am in solidarity with. Is the administration / Eng. dept / colleagues / etc. friend or foe? In all likelihood, they are both. They agree with the overall goals of the college and compete with us for funds and other forms of assistance.

But I might look at the administration, for example, and identify who is predisposed to be sympathetic and who is not. Then I work with both groups. I strive to understand their decision-making process, present ideas to them in terms and/or contexts they can understand (budget numbers mean budget numbers, nor narratives), and raise their awareness of issues relating to writing and the center. I should never assume that administrative rejection is a rejection of my ideas, but that competing issues are more important or are argued more effectively.

Am I suddenly a lawyer?

I also don't lose battles, but some victories are deferred due to institutional needs (God, I sound so logical!). I also demonstrate that I use monies and time successfully in the best interests of the college, but that we have only begun to tap our potential. We should take what we are granted and use it to serve our students in a way consistent with the philosophies of the center and the campus.

In this way, we become more solidified with the activities and direction of the college, and have a greater impact upon the college (why we need to get beyond the Eng. dept.).

That sounds too easy. Though I know there are a million snags.

Steve

- — . — . — . — . — -

Steve:

"Often thought but ne'er so well expressed."

Seriously, you've pegged it. And what's wrong with sounding logical? It doesn't mean you abandon the passion of commitment and energy that got you into this racket in the first place. You need both.

It sounds easy? No, no, no. Nobody ever said it was easy. However, defining the problem/task is terribly important, and you've done that. Responding to it, doing the things you have stated, will be tough and endless. You won't ever definitively arrive at your goal. No properly run educational institution can stop and say "well, now we are perfect and we can quit worrying about money and mission and structure." If it does, everyone in it ought to be fired forthwith.

Anyway, I hope you feel comfortable with where the discussion has taken us. I've had some insights too, from having to put my thoughts in writing.

Jeanne
p.s. Don't let the alligators chomp too hard; keep pumping.

- — . — . — . — . — -

Beth:

If you've been reading the discussions for long, you'll be aware that your dissertation topic is at the heart of some things I've been talking about for some time.

Steve Braye and I have a separate conversation going on this very topic. He is the archivist-designate for the conversation. I'll put him in touch with you. This conversation developed directly from a question Steve asked me at the CCCC workshop, about how it is possible (or is it?) to communicate with/ cooperate with administration without "selling out" the basic idea of a writing center.

Best wishes,

> Jeanne Simpson
> Eastern Illinois University
> csjhs@ux1.cts.eiu.edu

- — · — · — · — · — -

Steve,

Been re-reading your "solutions" post.

You included a sentence or two about "I must decide the core philosophy of the center," "What principles I cannot compromise," etc.

Well, yes and no. This is at the heart of our whole discussion. The basic fact is, you (any WCENTER director) do not own the center. The institution does. You are paid to run it, etc., and your expertise is obviously relevant or you wouldn't be the director. But it is dangerous to draw philosophical lines in the dirt all by yourself. Running completely counter to the rest of an institution is a quick road to isolation, both in terms of pedagogy and of budget. However strongly you might feel about some principles, it is useful, as you state, to find those who agree with you, to develop some sort of proof that you are not usurping ownership of the center from the rest of the institution. That sounds pretty negative, and no doubt your words were not intended literally.

Even so, it is natural, human, and probably inevitable that directors begin to think in terms of "my center." The sense of ownership is strong. And probably useful insofar as it encourages commitment and energy. But a two-edged sword if ever there was one. It can lead to faulty reasoning (such as: the university doesn't value the center and what happens there; therefore, the university doesn't value me as a person). A well-developed center, one properly designed and run, should be able to function in the face of personnel turnovers. Any director who develops a system based on personal attributes and not based on institutional needs and culture is headed for disappointment and frustration.

> Jeanne

- — · — · — · — · — -

Beth:

You've mentioned our "powerlessness." Lordy, don't get me started. Oops. Too late.

We are NOT powerless. Mostly, we either choose not to exercise power or we are so naive about power that we mishandle it. No entity within a university that has a budget line devoted to it is powerless, period. Other people sign the checks and have a variety of priorities, only some of which match ours, but that is not the same as being powerless. You have value in the university economy. To be powerless is to have no value in that economy.

> Jeanne Simpson

- — · — · — · — · — -

Jeanne:

Wow—I didn't realize I was making such a power-full statement! (Just kidding. I couldn't resist—)

Actually, I used the term for convenience sake, which is not always the best reason, and I know that such buzz words can be bandied about until they're practically meaningless. So I'm glad you brought this to my attention.

As I re-read your message, I'm intrigued by several of your comments:

–"Mostly, we either choose not to exercise power or we are so naive about power that we mishandle it."

–"No entity within a university that has a budget line devoted to it is powerless, period."

I'm thinking now of Hodson's "The Active Worker: Autonomy and Compliance in the Workplace" and Huspek's "Linguistic Variability and Power: An Analysis of YOU KNOW/I THINK Variation in Working-Class Speech." Don't know if you've come across either of these, but I've been thinking a lot about the power dynamic as I revise an essay on tutor resistance (again, a gross oversimplification). Hodson calls for a dynamic view of workers, stating that the view of workers as constantly resisting is as limiting as viewing them as management's automatons—critiquing neo-Marxist theories. So what I hear you saying is that there is a dynamic at work in these power relations, which I definitely agree with. So what I'm wondering (and this is a genuine issue to explore, I think) is why any entity would *choose* not to exercise power. I agree that we are often naive about these power relationships, and the Huspek article speaks to both of these comments. His conclusion is that workers will maintain their group solidarity (by using YOU KNOW) sometimes at the expense of what the *researcher* perceives to be more effective linguistic strategies (like I THINK, which is considered "boss talk"). Are you seeing the connection I'm making here? Bear with me, please, as I'm working this out for myself as well here. If we have power, but we are not effective at using that power, then aren't we contributing to a *perception* of ourselves as relatively powerless? All of this because I think we need to increase the *perception* of ourselves as powerful within our communities. And I'm not so sure it's as simple as having a budget line. Doesn't that have the potential to make us more, not less, subject to shifting tides, so to speak?

Well, I certainly have gone on. Sorry about that, but this sort of dialogue (although it looks pretty one-sided as I look at the screen now!) is really helpful to me as I try to work through these issues. Thanks a lot! I'd like to hear the "puhlenty" you have to say.

Beth Boquet
ggxjbhc@grove.iup.edu.

- - - — - — - - - — - -

Beth:

Joan Mullin is of course exactly right about the importance of knowing the language of negotiation. Which brings me to your point about naiveté.

Negotiation is the idea that there is a two-way exchange: the writing center offers information/service, the administration offers money. TWO WAY. Something most people don't recognize is that any administration MUST spend the money somewhere. They can't just sit on it. Here, we can't save it for next year, and that is probably true everywhere. So, it isn't that administration doesn't want to give the money to anybody, it's that, because there isn't enough of it, choices must be made. You have to see that you also have something somebody wants: a good place to spend the money. So it becomes a problem in effective rhetoric.

My other comment about power is this: we DO wield it, daily, in our interactions with students. We tend, as a result, to look only in that direction and to forget that we can direct power elsewhere also. Power is not as one-way as people think. Students have power over the center: if they stay away, you're roadkill. The disappearance of a valuable support program for lack of funding makes administrations look bad, too, especially if said program addresses institutional/system priorities: thus, your power in the direction of administration.

Jeanne Simpson

- — · — · — · — · — -

Hi, Beth:

Jeanne Simpson and I have both been interested in your comments about powerlessness because we have been putting together ideas about how writing centers acquire/exert/withstand institutional power.

I wonder why we see ourselves as marginalized (which, as you note, limits our access to power). Is it because we are marginalized, somehow at odds with the mission and goals of the college? Or is it because we perceive ourselves as outside (above?) the political grime of the college? We believe we serve a specific constituency. But what power do we have when budgets are drawn, when building plans are made, when we are evaluated for what we do? Is it our fault that we have so little power in determining the mission of the college? Is it our fault that we are paid less, often on non-tenure track lines?

As Jeanne helped me to see, not having a budget line doesn't help me at all. As Foucault notes, power can be either positive or negative. But my acquisition of a budget of my own doesn't increase my exposure or make me more vulnerable. Nothing is easier than destroying an entity that, by college standards, doesn't exist. Acquiring a budget line can be positive or negative, depending upon how I use it. If I use it to pander to administration, it is negative. But if I use it to help students through the center, I am making the college more responsive to student needs. I know I am oversimplifying many issues here, but can there be any weaker state than powerlessness? If we are in this position, for whatever reason, we need to discover ways of accessing power more effectively. I can blame my dean all I want. But ultimately it must be my inability to make a case for the center that is responsible.

Wow. I almost sound like I know what I'm talking about. Don't think I'm nearly as settled in my thinking as this sounds.

Steve Braye
BRAYES@Vax 1.Elon.edu.

- — . — . — . — . — -

Steve,

I just was re-reading your note to Beth.

Statement from you: "Not having a budget line doesn't help me."

Ah, but you DO have a budget line, even if it isn't one labeled writing center. The fact that you have release time, however modest, to attend to the center means the institution is spending money on that. Part of your salary. Which is NOT going to direct instruction. That is a sign of commitment, believe it or not. Also, the center occupies space. At my institution, space is more valuable than rubies. People fight over broom closets. Devoting space to any enterprise is a signal of serious institutional commitment here. It is elsewhere, also, because said space has to be heated (and cooled, if you're lucky), furnished, cleaned, insured, etc. All that comes out of the university's budget. Your space has, I suspect, been modified in some way to meet your needs. That also requires money and, by implication, commitment.

It is too easy to identify institutional support as something obvious, like cash on the barrelhead. Nobody gets all the money they want, with no strings and no accountability. What they get is dribs and drabs, tied up with all sorts of strings. And this quantity of "hidden" support. I'm sure you'd like more released time. Wouldn't we all. But my guess is that your institution has pressures on it to keep non-instructional costs low. We have to justify every dollar that doesn't go to direct instruction, in huge horrible reports and byzantine calculations. So, if you fight for more release time, you've got to find a way to indicate a payoff for the institution. The big one is retention and graduation rates (does this sound like a broken record?) More release time = better tutor training and more contacts with students = higher retention.

I sure hope your year begins smoothly and proceeds well.

Jeanne

- — . — . — . — . — -

Jeanne and Beth:

Robert Brooke, in a 1987 CCC article, discussed underlife and writing instruction, which may have something to do with our discussion. As he defines it, "Institutional underlife is exactly such a case: actors in an institution develop behaviors which assert an identity different from the one assigned them" (*CCC*, 38 May 1987, 143).

This may help us see the struggle writing programs face within the institution. Perhaps Eng. departments have come to grips with the identity the college has assigned and its underlife activities are more contained. I'm wondering if writing centers, in their search for identity, or writing programs, in general, are more resistant of the identity the college assigns to it. Perhaps the college assigns the same identity to the writing program that it does the

English department (and we can quickly see how this would lead to mis-assigned expectations, given the different focus each may have in a scholarly and/or pedagogical sense). But since we may not have a strong sense of identity, we may be more forceful in resisting the assigned role. (Goffman says "looking at the activities through which individuals resist or reject the identity assigned to them by institutions is a way of looking at how individuals form their sense of identity" [qtd. in Brooke, "Underlife" 144].)

I know this isn't very clear, but I wonder if writing programs aren't resisting and meeting resistance as a natural part of their identity formation within the institution. Thus, our discussion of "inside/outside" should really be re-phrased in identity formation terms. Brooke suggests "writing instruction comes into greatest conflict with the existing educational system." Perhaps this is because writing has yet to establish an identity within the institution and this identity formation requires changes in both the institution and ourselves. If so, our struggles to be accepted may be a normal part of our evolution into a discipline.

Crazy? Could be. Hope both of you are well.

Steve Braye

- — - — - — - — - -

Steve and Beth:

Interesting. But "underlife" implies a hierarchical structure. It implies resistance and all that other terminology. I think that the assumption that an institution has a definition of a writing center and its mission is entirely too coherent and logical to match with the facts. It assumes somebody (who? provost? dean? president?) has sat down and articulated, clearly and completely, a definition for same. Ha. At best, there is a half-defined, hazy notion floating around. Maybe a vague "mission statement" kind of thing. Deans and provosts don't have TIME for this stuff. The only group who has a clear, coherent, salient definition is almost certainly the writing center staff. The discrepancy is not so much based on differences in kind but in differences of degree: the writing center staff knows more about writing centers and writing pedagogy than anybody else further up the line. Unless your provost was an English professor, chances are his/her last contact with this stuff was as an undergraduate. So, it is not a problem of power and control, at least not entirely. It is a problem of information and communication.

Let's use an analogy. Do you know what the dean does? Seriously? Do you have a clear definition of DEAN in your head that includes all duties and responsibilities of same? Probably not. Undoubtedly, the dean has a clearer definition than yours. But you don't have to BE the dean, either. No doubt the dean wishes, devoutly, that faculty understood what deans are and do more clearly.

I guess, Steve, that I still don't buy completely into this terminology that implies oppression/victimhood. It is important to talk about it because the whole mindset that goes with it influences our mental constructs and therefore our decisions. I continue to believe that acting like a victim can help induce real victimization. The big question is: what if this idea I have isn't true? What if the way I imagine things to be is inaccurate? Is there evidence to suggest that that might be true? Too often we spend time looking for evidence to support our assumptions. But it is more honest to look for evidence that we might be wrong.

Theodore Clevenger wrote compellingly about audience analysis long before it was fashionable. He talked about the concept of salience and completeness, that audiences seldom share our vision of what is salient, accurate, complete, etc., and that our task is to make our vision and our audience's vision match. That is a gross simplification, but it made so much sense then and still does.

Jeanne

- — - — - — - — -

Hi Steve and Jeanne!

I was intrigued by your post, Steve, yesterday. I like the Brooke quote, and it reminded me of an article by Mark Hurlbert and Michael Blitz titled "The Institution('s) Lives." This ties us into documentation, which brings us around to budgets, etc. Let me clarify. From what I can see, there is a myth and a counter-myth at work in the writing center literature: that writing centers, while at once "needing" to develop relationships with other departments in order to become central to the overall mission of the university, also "need" to remain on the margins if we are going to carry out the work we were created to do. (Sorry, Jeanne, I know you hate that "margin" metaphor. I'll try to refrain!) I guess my question is, how and why would a service/structure/entity (or whatever you could call a writing center) "choose" to remain on the margins. What can we hope to gain by that. Shouldn't we instead be fighting for inclusion, for ourselves and for the students we were (ostensibly) created to serve? By acknowledging, in fact reveling, in our marginal status, aren't we sending a dangerous message to the university at large?

I must admit, I'm playing devil's advocate here because my immediate reaction is to remain outside of what typically goes on in the English dept and in other arenas at the university. I find it ironic—just as many folks want to leave the "dirty work" of teaching writing to us comp slaves, I want no part of them and their cynical perceptions of students' intelligence (or lack thereof), writing abilities, and general worth as human beings.

Back to my original point: Neither, however, does the solution to our image problem seem to be in defining our existence in terms of other programs or in terms of the departments we serve. Here's where Hurlbert and Blitz come in. As you two have already mentioned, writing center directors have developed all kinds of ways to try to prove success. Hurlbert and Blitz write: "[D]ocuments and the literacy demands they contain teach us our place(s) within the institution, institutionalize us, (con)figure us into the autobiography of the institution, incorporate us, make us part of the institution's scene. They tell us what to do and where to do it as they describe, for us, what we 'are' doing." A pretty obvious statement, but in some ways that's the beauty of it. I guess the tension that I feel is that this emphasis on documentation places us squarely in the middle of a quantitative tradition of justification that few of us believe in. I know that this may be an economic reality, but that doesn't mean that I have to be comfortable with it. So much of what we do can't be reduced, shouldn't be reduced, to a system of circles and checks on a page, stuck in a file folder in the back of some cabinet somewhere. So we fudge a little here and a little there—as Jeanne mentions, propose something about retention, diversity, assessment—and then work it in where it needs to go. But by doing so aren't we failing to educate? Maybe so, maybe not. As Jeanne wrote, there are some people who don't want to know. Pick your battles, etc.

This idea of how to educate others about our mission brings me to the point I wanted to make about the history of our center, which you alluded to in earlier discussions. However, I won't do it now because I've gone on long enough and also because I think I must be getting carpal tunnel syndrome in my left hand. Not a good sign.

Again, I'm really enjoying this and am learning so much about administration and politics. Looking forward to hearing your comments.

Beth

- — - — - — - — -

Jeanne and Steve:

My frustration level is running high right now as I just spent 45 minutes constructing a response to you only to have a power surge that caused me to lose it all. So I'm going to try to reconstruct it as best I can in the form of several shorter messages, just in case it happens again.

It seems as though there is a movement in writing centers to re-examine the role of dialogue as it relates to practice in the writing center itself. I'm thinking here of Gillam's essay "Writing Center Ecology: A Bakhtinian Perspective" and also a proposed session at NCTE this fall, not to mention my own dissertation (part of it at least). So perhaps e-mail and electronic bulletin boards like WCENTER represent a movement toward a different conception of dialogue in our own ranks.

I'll send this now, and start a new message with the rest of my thoughts...

Beth

- — - — - — - — -

Jeanne and Steve:

Back to it...

Steve, you made a comment that I see as having the potential to unify our discussion, so I'll try to explain. Your comment was "[W]e might even claim it is our *responsibility* to assert our part in the institution so that it changes in a way we feel is more responsive to all" (my emphasis). This got me thinking about the role of cultural studies in re-articulating a history of writing centers, which you made earlier allusions to—something about bringing us back to our roots.

Here's my feeling on it, drawing from Cary Nelson's essay "Always Already Cultural Studies: Two Conferences and a Manifesto." Nelson writes, "Cultural studies has a responsibility to continue interrogating and reflecting on its own commitments" (33). In order to do so, we have to understand what those commitments are, so cultural studies examines history/ies with an eye toward the present and the future. (Nelson again: "To study the present or the past is inevitably to rearticulate it to current interests" (34). In effect, cultural studies seeks to draw the political and the historical together in an effort to produce cultural action.

In my view, we need to rearticulate the history of the writing center (even though I know there are objections to this). There's a knock at the door—I'll pick this up in a few minutes.

Beth

- — - — - — - — -

Jeanne and Steve:

Sorry about all the interruptions. Maybe this time I'll get to finish what I've been trying to say.

Alright, so the point I was trying to make is this: We often refer to the field of composition as "young," and we view writing as even younger. But as your friend pointed out, Steve, and as Gere documents in *Writing Groups* much of our "new paradigm" is not "new" at all. The fact of the matter, as we know all too well, is that in the entire history of American education, entering freshmen have never written well enough to satisfy their professors. So it is intriguing to me that the emergence of university-sanctioned writing assistance outside the context of the classroom allegedly coincides with the open admissions policies of the early 1970s when much of the literature suggests otherwise.

I guess in a roundabout way I'm trying to respond to your question— "Should centers be permanently on the 'cutting edge'? Should we be disappointed if they ever become places where you can find given, traditional knowledge? Should we always maintain our subversive roots?" I'm not so sure those roots were very subversive at all. I think many centers (and I'm broadening the conception of centers perhaps to include, as I mentioned earlier, any university-sanctioned writing assistance outside the classroom) were conceived as places to find very traditional knowledge and to teach "questionable" students their places and to further perpetuate the service mentality of composition. So maybe we've come a long way.

Here I feel I need to bring up a contradiction in the discussion about our perceptions of the goals of the writing center and how they coincide (or fail to coincide) with the goals of the university at large. Jeanne, you write, "[T]here still exists a basic shared vision: the need to help students." Later on, you note, "Most institutions have only the goal of survival as a genuine one. . . . Your goal in the center is 1) survive and 2) do the function as well as possible." Being the cynic that I am, I tend to agree with the second statement more than the first. Here is where I really see the separation between the individuals who operate within an academic institution and the actual institution itself. (A difficult split to maintain, as you both demonstrate so well in the discussion, but one I'm going to use for now.) On an individual level, most of us who choose the university life do so because we want to work with/help students, but somewhere along the line that goal becomes secondary to the much more basic goal, as you note—survival.

Look forward to hearing from you—

Beth

- — - — - — - — - -

Beth:

I can see how you might perceive the goals of survival and of helping students as contradictory.

Actually, I see helping students as a subset of the survival goal. As I said, the institution CAN'T survive unless it can prove that it performs the function society requires of it. One of those functions is to graduate students who know something. I guess my statement about the institution having the goal of survival sounds altogether negative and cynical. I don't think it is, though. It's just realistic. We all want to keep our jobs. We want to preserve a thing we've committed big chunks of our lives to. We believe it's a good thing, don't we? So survival and helping students are not, to my mind, antithetical. They are connected: survival = educating and graduating students = helping students so they can do that.

Thanks! And I really like the things you are saying. I knew you'd be a good addition to this dialogue.

Jeanne

Works Discussed

Brooke, Robert. "Underlife and Writing Instruction." *CCC* 38 (May 1987): 141-232.

____.*Writing and Sense of Self: Identity Negotiation in Writing Workshops*. Urbana: NCTE. 1991.

Brooks, Jeff. "Minimalist Tutoring: Making the Student Do All the Work." *The Writing Lab Newsletter* 15.6 (1991): 1-4.

Clevenger, Theodore. *Audience Analysist*. Indianapolis: Bobbs Merrill, 1966.

Foucault, Michel. "Power and Strategies." *Power/Knowledge: Selected Interviews and Other Writing*. New York: Pantheon, 1980. 139-41.

Freire, Paolo. *Pedagogy of the Oppressed*. New York: Continuum, 1970. 50-56.

Gere, Anne Ruggles. *Writing Groups: History, Theory, and Implications*. Carbondale: Southern Illinois UP, 1987.

Hobson, Eric. "Writing Center Politics and Prose: WAC, Administration, and Publication." Pre-convention workshop. CCCC, San Diego, California, 31 March 1993.

Hurlbert, C. Mark, and Michael Blitz. "The Institution('s) Lives!" *Marx and Rhetoric*. Special issue of *Pre/Text*. 13.1-2 (1992): 59-78.

Huspek, Michael. "Linguistic Variability and Power." *Journal of Pragmatics* 13 (1989): 661-83.

Nelson, Cary. "Always Already Cultural Studies: Two Conferences and a Manifesto." *Journal of the Midwest MLA* 24.1 (1991): 24-38.

A Defense of Dualism:
The Writing Center and the Classroom
by Dave Healy

People who work in writing centers often fall prey to professional insecurity. We feel misunderstood and unappreciated in our own departments (if we even have a department) and in the larger academy. Our marginal status makes us feel exploited by those with more institutional power and vulnerable in times of retrenchment. Our insecurity has led, as Thomas Hemmeter observes, to ongoing attempts at self-definition. Since no one else recognizes or understands us, we feel the need to continually announce and invent ourselves. And we do so, says Hemmeter, through "a discourse articulated in dualities," the fundamental one being a "contrast of writing center instruction to classroom instruction" (37). To give ourselves a distinctive identity, we oppose ourselves to something with which every one is familiar: the classroom.

Hemmeter is critical of these efforts, arguing that our self-definition is self-defeating. His way out of the logical trap writing center apologists find themselves in is to eliminate that pesky "self." Perhaps the writing center is not a thing at all, but rather an "idea . . . a linguistic phenomenon . . . a text still in the process of composition" (44). But this is sheer evasion. Whatever its phenomenology, the place where I work is a place. Until the writing center gives up its locational status altogether in favor of virtual reality (a not unimaginable prospect, but one Hemmeter doesn't imagine), the work that writing center people do, like the work that classroom teachers do, will take place somewhere, and denying or ignoring the where-ness of that work won't help us much—either in the quest for self-awareness or in the attempt to improve our services.

For I want to argue that the writing center is a place, and a place with political as well as metaphorical status. Hemmeter is helpful in unpacking the metaphors by which writing centers have defined themselves, but he is curiously silent about what Harvey Kail and John Trimbur have called "the politics of peer tutoring." If the writing center has a raison d'être, it must be politically grounded, for in the center, as in the academy at large, there is no non-political reality.

Reprinted from *The Writing Center Journal* 14.1 (1993): 16-29. Used by permission

Kail and Trimbur observe that peer tutoring[1] has been institutionalized within the academy, claiming that "[c]ollaborative learning and peer tutoring are now recognized as innovative contributions not only to the writing abilities but more broadly to the liberal education of undergraduates" (5). For them, the question "is no longer why such programs are necessary, but how tutoring can best contribute to the development of writing abilities and the intellectual life of undergraduates" (5). Central to such inquiry is the issue of where and under what conditions tutoring should take place. According to Kail and Trimbur, the exploration of that issue has profound political implications. They distinguish between two general approaches to peer tutoring: the curriculum-based model and the writing center model. In the former, "peer tutors are, as it were, written into the plan of instruction. They're part of the course" (6). In the writing center model, on the other hand, tutoring takes place outside the classroom, in a writing center.

Kail and Trimbur favor what they call the writing center approach to tutoring because they believe that by locating itself "at a remove from the normal delivery system of curriculum and instruction, in the semi-autonomous space of writing centers," (9) such tutoring, which is based on the principle of collaborative learning, "precipitates a crisis of authority" in the traditional hierarchical approach to teaching and learning. Curriculum-based approaches, on the other hand, reinforce that hierarchy by identifying the tutor with the teacher and classroom—the traditional seat of knowledge and authority in academe. Such programs "suppress the crisis of authority precipitated when students work together, domesticate it, and channel the social forces released by collaboration into the established structures of teaching and learning," while tutoring based on the writing center model "provides students with a form of social organization to negotiate the crisis successfully and reenter the official structures of authority as active agents rather than as passive objects of transmission" (11-12).

For Kail and Trimbur, authority in the academy is tied to hierarchy. Teachers have authority and power over students because teachers are higher on the academic ladder; they have accomplished more and presumably know more. This authority teachers have is intrinsically neither good nor bad, but one danger posed by teachers' authority is that it can breed student passivity. To the extent that students see themselves as acted upon rather than as agents of their own destiny, as subject to the authority of others rather than subjects of their own academic journey, they do not develop the independence and initiative necessary for intellectual growth. That independence and initiative (or power) is facilitated, say Kail and Trimbur, by forms of social organization that enable students to locate themselves within "the official structures

---

[1] I use the term "tutor" reluctantly. As Lex Runciman has argued, "tutor," whether in its British sense of aristocratic privilege or its American sense of remediation, has connotations that are hardly consonant with most current pedagogies. Nevertheless, "tutor" is still a widely-used term for which no replacement has yet been widely adopted. Also, since I make extensive use of Kail and Trimbur and since they use the term "tutor," I use it here.

of authority," not as "passive objects of transmission" but rather as "active agents."

Writing centers, as "semi-autonomous" spaces, can serve as one of those forms of social organization through which students learn to negotiate issues of authority and learn to take more responsibility for their own learning. Such an enterprise is especially important for those students who previously have not been successful at working within the educational hierarchy. Such students may have suffered at the hands of the system. Often their lack of success results in an apathy born of the conviction that school is someplace where they don't fit. If these student are going to succeed, they need to develop confidence, initiative, and persistence. While the classroom is a place where those qualities can be developed, it is also ultimately the arena where they must be displayed and where they will be evaluated. The writing center affords students the vantage point to stand apart from the arena, to get out of the game for a time, to develop the necessary critical distance before re-entering as active, intentional participants.

To be sure, most composition teachers are interested in developing purposefulness and intentionality in students, and many take concrete steps to foster such traits. For example, Dana Heller describes a "paragraph of intention" assignment which offers "the student's own account of what he or she has tried to do" in a draft. In it, the students "moves from a private engagement with the text to a public engagement with the text. The switch is aimed at encouraging awareness of intention along with a sense of authority in reference to both the internal and external life of the work" (212). But what about the student whose statement of intention boils down to, "I want to fulfill the assignment," or "I hope I'll get a good grade"? What can the person who created the assignment and who will assign a grade on it say to such a writer?

The teacher's dilemma in such instances is similar to that faced by parents interested in helping their children learn independence and initiative. As a parent, I recognize certain responsibilities to set boundaries, communicate expectations, and model mature decision making. I have some vision of the kind of person I hope my children will become, but I don't envision either passive automatons or duplicates of myself. Yet my parental power—conferred by legal, economic, and social sanctions—constantly threatens to stifle some of the very traits I want my children to develop. Abdication of that power is probably not possible, short of abandoning my children, nor is it desirable. I don't think it is egotism or power mongering to assert that my children need parental influence. But they need another kind of influence as well, one that I cannot provide. As a parent, I depend on other people and other institutions to help my children develop certain qualities, a development over which my influence is limited. Some of those limitations are physical and emotional, but others are social and political. The very fact that I'm their dad imposes constraints on our relationship and on their development, constraints that may sometimes need to be transcended by someone outside the family.

Who those someones are and what my children need from them varies. Sometimes my children need to hear what I have already told them, but they need to hear it from someone else, someone with no overt authority over them or no obvious vested interest in their development. Sometimes they need to hear alternatives to the old man's point of view. Often they need to be listened to and taken seriously by someone who doesn't "have to."

A parent's relationship with those someones is complex indeed. Even while recognizing the important developmental role other individuals or institutions play in my children's lives, I may feel threatened by the possibility that my parental authority is being challenged or undermined, or that my values are not being reinforced. Clearly, there are some people I don't want my kids hanging around with at all, and there may be others I'm simply not sure about because I don't know enough about them and because I know I won't be there to monitor my children's interactions with them.

One parental response to this kind of uncertainty is to look for extensions of parental authority—surrogate parents. Institutions—the church, the school, the day care facility—as well as individuals, are evaluated according to the extent to which they will reinforce parental values and dictates and are invested with an authority that flows from and feeds back into the parents' authority. The problem with this approach is that it can produce conformity, narrowness, and passivity. Unexposed to alternate points of view and unchallenged in their tacit acceptance of received wisdom, children do not develop the capacity for critical thought. Additionally, to the extent they sense that the other key players in their lives serve mainly as extensions of their parents, children will not experience the liberating feeling that others are interested in them—not out of a sense of duty or obligation—but simply for their own sake.

This dilemma of parenting I have been describing is one manifestation of the larger dilemma of education: how to provide both challenge and support, how to acknowledge values while promoting freedom and independence. Like the parent-child relationship, the teacher-student relationship is limited, constrained by political realities. Just as children need access to responsible nonfamily members, so too do students need access to responsible colleagues who have no direct relationship with an instructor or a course.

In the classroom, the most common alternative to the teacher as a point of access for students is the teaching assistant (TA). TAs serve a variety of functions, but fundamentally they exist to serve instructors. The TA, then, is part of what Kail and Trimbur call a curriculum-based approach. Its distinguishing characteristic is that it "operates through official channels" (6), i.e., the curriculum. The TA serves the curriculum by serving the instructor; only indirectly does the TA serve the student. This is well and good. Teachers can be more effective if they are well-supported, and more effective teachers will make for better-served students. But students also deserve direct support that is unmediated by the instructor, and that support can be better provided by a tutor than by a TA—by someone, in other words, who is not affiliated with the course. By standing apart from the classroom, tutors provide a means of interrogating academic hierarchy. They provide an audience whose relationship to a student's writing is not governed by the same kind of "oughtness" as is the instructor's. They constitute a different kind of authority, one which is less "given" and more negotiated. As such, they can facilitate the development of self-awareness and independence.

Where TAs primarily serve faculty, tutors primarily serve students. The role of tutors and the centers in which they work has been forcefully articulated by Steve North: "In short, we are not here to serve, supplement, back up, complement, reinforce, or otherwise be defined by any external curriculum" (440). The tutor, says North, "is a holist devoted to participant-observer methodology" who practices "a pedagogy of direct intervention" (438-439). In response to the teacher's question, "How can I make use of the writing center?" North says "[T]eachers, as teachers, do not need and cannot use, a writing center; only writers need it, only writers can use it" (440).

Tutors exist to serve students and they do so best when they are removed from the classroom—not only physically, but institutionally. Just as kids need to get out of the house and develop relationships "untainted" by family influence, so students need to get out of the classroom and meet fellow travelers who can support and empower them—without feeling like that relationship is going to affect their grade in the course, or that it is motivated primarily by a sense of institutional "oughtness." For in the final analysis, everything that happens in the classroom is influenced by the prospect of evaluation; and to the extent that TAs are identified with the instructor and with the course, their role and their image are imbricated in that prospect.

As a teacher, I am aware of certain limitations in my relationships with students. I think it's important that my students see me as a fellow traveler, as someone who is still on the road to understanding and enlightenment. But despite my best efforts to step out from behind the lectern, I suspect that my students usually see me as someone fundamentally different from them, and I cannot help wishing that they would find someone with whom they could more closely identify. It's a problem of distance and authority we're up against.

This problem is not unique to teaching. Other professionals also struggle to achieve the optimal relationship with the people they serve which means confronting this business of distance. Modern Christendom, to take a far-reaching example, represents an interesting range of approaches to this issue. Catholicism, for instance, emphasizes the priest's set-apart status: he is celibate; he wears a collar; he listens on the other side of the confessional screen. In short, he's not like you and me. Some Protestant denominations, on the other hand, make the minister more of a fellow pilgrim: she has a family, wears a dress to church, and meets you for lunch at a restaurant. And in certain groups—e.g., Quakers, Mennonites, Plymouth Brethren—there is no professional clergy at all; individuals minister to each other.

At its best, the academy presents a similar range of roles for the teacher. Sometimes she stands apart, behind the lectern. By virtue of her training, knowledge, and experience, she is different from her students. But sometimes the teacher sits with his students around a conference table. By virtue of his interests, his openness, and his willingness to listen, he is much like them. And sometimes the teacher withdraws completely for a time. Students work together in groups, drawing on and assisting and challenging each other—without any overt teacherly presence at all.

Writing center tutors help enlarge and enrich this range of options for teachers and students. Tutors can be present as fellow pilgrims in a way that faculty cannot. To be sure, a tutor can be and often is perceived as an authority figure. As Karen Spear, drawing on the work of William Perry notes, dualistic thinkers are especially prone to fusing notions of truth and authority; hence, tutors need to employ nondirective strategies that will help resist some writers' authority needs (71). What Reigstad and McAndrew call "student-centered" or "collaborative" conferences will, from the political perspective I am presenting here, be preferred over "teacher-centered" ones (28-33). The advantage tutors have over teachers in this enterprise is that even if students try to invest tutors with authority, tutors can resist that role, while teachers, as long as they give grades, have a harder time shedding their image as authority figures.

Let me be clear about two things. First, there is nothing wrong with authority figures. Authority, like power, is inherently neither good nor bad. But authority, power, and hierarchy do define and constrain relationships. What I am arguing here is that tutors and writing centers provide an alternative to the authority of teachers and classrooms, and that that alternative is important as a catalyst to students' developing sense of independence and their own authority. Second, it must be emphasized that writing centers do not constitute an authoritative or evaluative vacuum. There is no nonpolitical reality. Writing centers occupy institutional space. Tutors exercise authority and engage in evaluation. Once again, though, I am arguing that the nature of that authority and evaluation is different.

One practical manifestation of that difference emerges in students' responses to grades on papers. Most writing teachers have known the frustration of returning papers and seeing students flip immediately to the last page, note the grade, and largely ignore the instructor's careful and copious comments; or returning ungraded but carefully annotated drafts with the admonition to revise and being met with the question, "Yes, but what grade would this have received?" Writing center tutors hear that question too, but precisely because they have no grade-giving responsibility, tutors are in a better position to deflect the question ("Well, because assigning grades isn't part of my job, I'm not really familiar with the business of grade giving."), turn it around ("How are you feeling about this paper? What grade would you give yourself?"), or personalize it as a way of prompting further discussion ("I have the same concern about my own writing: I often end up worrying a lot about what grade I'm going to get.")

It might be assumed that the writing center's political distinctiveness is dependent on peer tutors, who would more likely be perceived as fellow travelers than would someone like one of Carol Severino's "lab teachers," who are all graduate students. The University of Iowa's Writing Lab is closer to the British tutorial/independent study model than it is to the peer tutoring/ drop-in writing center. Students work with the same teacher twice a week for an entire semester, so the experience is more like a course than is what goes on in the typical drop-in center. But as Severino's experience indicates, what happens in the lab is distinctive for reasons other than a shared student status between consultant and writer. "Working in the lab democratizes both students' and [lab] teachers' ideas of what writers are and do. They realize that writing is not just a unique or elitist talent bestowed on the fortunate few" (14). This democratization occurs, in part, because the dynamics of the lab are different from those of the classroom. Severino's lab teachers read, "not to correct and grade, but to get to know the student, her background and culture, her strengths and weaknesses. Teachers respond to their students' writing not so much in the persona of teachers as in the persona of the writers they themselves are; as writers of essays, stories, letters, and poems, they have the same goals as their students" (13).

In my own institution, a recent administrative decision resulted in the partial merging of roles that had hitherto been separate: the TA and the tutor. By creating a single pool of undergraduate teaching assistants (UGTAs) which would staff both the Reading & Writing Center (RWC) and the TA positions in the Humanities Department, the top brass hoped to improve the quality of UGTAs' work and also to streamline operations. They imagined that having one person responsible for hiring, training, supervising and placing all UGTAs—both tutors and classroom TAs—would result in greater consistency and better performance. They further assumed that the new arrangement would make more efficient use of UGTAs' time. If UGTAs were unengaged with students or paperwork from their courses, they would become available to work with walk-in students in the Center. That assumption was used to justify a 25% cut in the combined budgets of the RWC and Humanities TA support.

The experiment was generally unsuccessful. For one thing, many TAs (like faculty) use office hours to do paper work when no students come in, so the savings afforded by having idle TAs available for walk-in tutoring were minimal. More important, by having to wear two hats—tutor and TA— UGTAs experienced heightened role conflict. Who are they—extensions of the instructor with a responsibility to espouse her/his party line, or employees of the Center with an obligation to its philosophy and practices? Are they advocates of the curriculum and the instructor, or advocates for their fellow students? Furthermore, locating TAs in the Center complicates the institutional status of the space. Is it primarily an extension of the classroom, or is it an alternative to the classroom?

Positing the writing center as an alternative to the classroom is based on convictions more psychological and political than pedagogical. As I have argued, students need people and places in their academic lives that are free from the stigma of grades and from an atmosphere of obligation. While grades may continue to motivate most of a student's academic behavior—

including the decision to visit a writing center—being able to talk about and work on assignments with people who have no grade-giving power (or interest) is important in helping students develop intrinsic motivations for their studies.

But if my perspective is mostly psychological and political, many writing center spokespersons tend to see their distinctiveness as primarily pedagogical. Muriel Harris, for one, has long argued for the efficacy of individualized instruction, which she opposes to the "generic" instruction of the classroom:

> [M]ost educators think of education in group terms. Students sit in classes, move in groups, pass through the educational system in large numbers. If someone uses the word "student," there is a generic student in mind. Classroom teachers of writing can talk about "the writing process" as if it applies universally to all writers, about textbooks that work for whole levels of students (e.g., basic writers, traditional freshmen, advanced composition, and so on). Yet, what writing centers are about is the antithesis of generic, mass instruction. We are committed to individualized instruction, to taking the student out of the group and to looking at her as an individual, as a person with all her uniqueness (19).

While the point Harris is trying to make is valid—classrooms and writing centers are different—some of her word choices are unfortunate. Labeling the classroom as the site of "generic, mass instruction" is an overstatement that does not do justice to the manifest variety of pedagogies and classroom strategies to be found on any college or university campus. Also, as Hemmeter has observed, individualized instruction, with its essentially romantic conception of human nature, is at odds with a now widely accepted social constructionist theory of knowledge and an attendant belief in the efficacy of collaborative learning. Furthermore, emphasizing the differences between classroom and center should not obscure what those two realms have in common nor deny the ways that both realms are institutionally constructed and constrained. After all, both places are removed, physically and psychically, from where students live. Because neither exists outside the academy, both share some of the academy's inevitable artificiality.[2]

But although both the classroom and the center are institutional constructs, they are not equal. Although they share the same mission—to nurture better writing and to develop better writers—they fulfill that mission differently. Those differences can give rise to mistrust, defensiveness, and

---

[2] Some observers, such as Geoffrey Chase, have suggested that decentralizing writing centers and locating them closer to where students spend most of their time (e.g., in residence halls or in departments) will destigmatize the center and will enlarge and enrich the narrowly instrumental view of writing that most students bring to their academic work by helping them see that writing is connected to "the larger community in which they live" (2). Clearly, the center's geographical location can affect its atmosphere, and there are probably ways to lessen the institutional "feel" of the spaces we occupy. Nevertheless, I think we are naive if we assume that overstuffed chairs and a coffee pot in the dorm will significantly change the way students approach academic writing when they work with us.

cross-purposes—especially, as Mark Waldo notes, if the writing classroom and the writing center do not share a common theoretical perspective. But even when they do, some tensions between classroom and center—like the tensions between parents and nonparental alternatives—seem inevitable.

For example, there is the matter of time. Tutors can spend twenty to thirty minutes or more with students, a luxury writing teachers don't have. In our center, the average writing conference is about 35 minutes. While many composition instructors recognize the importance of talk in the improvement of writing and would like to confer individually with their students, the demands of regular half-hour one-to-one conferences simply cannot be accommodated within a normal teaching load.

Writing instructors may also be envious of tutors' freedom from the grading imperative. Being able to discuss a writer's work, without the anticipation of eventually grading that work, makes it much easier for a tutor to let the writer retain control over her own writing. "Student-centered" and "collaborative" conferences are more difficult for teachers to pull off because students know that eventually their "collaborator" is going to give them a grade. Grade-giving, of course, affects not only the teacher-student conference, but classroom dynamics in general. In the dialogic, collaborative, process-oriented classroom, the naked grade on the page can be a rude shock for writers who have hitherto seen the writing enterprise as founded on and fostered by a spirit of mutual inquiry among kindred spirits.

The classroom/center relationship is also threatened by attitudes regarding turf. Academic freedom means I decide what goes on in my class, and protocol dictates that my colleagues don't butt in. It is not uncommon for people who have been members of the same department for years to have little or no idea of what their colleagues' courses and classrooms are actually like. Their students know, of course, but the power of the grade serves to limit overt challenges to teachers from their own students. That someone with no stake in the course, however, might be sitting in judgment can be a threatening prospect for classroom teachers.

And that fact is that the writing center tutorial is a window into the classroom. Tutors, who see assignments and instructors' comments on papers and who hear students' complaints about particular teachers, are in a position to challenge the instructor's judgment and competence. Of course, we are supposed to refrain from enacting that challenge. In North's words, "[W]e never play student-advocates in teacher-student relationships . . . we never evaluate or second-guess any teacher's syllabus, assignments, comments, or grades" (441). But North's unequivocal pledge is undercut by an observation in the paragraph immediately preceding the statement just quoted: "[W]e do a fair amount of trade in people working on ambiguous or poorly designed assignments, and far too much work with writers whose writing has received caustic, hostile, or otherwise unconstructive commentary" (440). North's adjectives—"ambiguous," "poorly designed," "unconstructive"—are hardly nonevaluative, a fact not likely to be lost on classroom composition teachers. Our reassurances to instructors that we won't second-guess them may not entirely assuage the insecurity engendered by knowing that people outside their classes are getting glimpses (and incomplete and perhaps distorted glimpses at that) into their classrooms.

If tutors sometimes wonder what is going on in the classroom, teachers sometimes wonder what really goes on in a tutorial. Are students who have been to the center doing their own work? Irene Clark has shown that a concern with the ethics of collaboration and peer tutoring has run throughout writing center research/scholarship. Writing teachers are glad to get clean copy and no doubt happy if the writing center can help move papers closer to cleanliness/godliness, but teachers are also concerned that what students turn in reflects their own abilities and efforts.

So there is potential for envy, mistrust, and misunderstanding between residents of the classroom and the center. We can minimize these feelings and maximize the effectiveness of writing centers if we encourage tutors to take advantage of the semi-autonomous space they inhabit in the following ways:

- framing directive or evaluative comments as reflecting the responses of representative readers. Instead of saying "I really like this paragraph," try "For me, this part of the paper is especially effective." Rather than "You need to tone down this language," observe "Some readers may react strongly to your wording here."
- eliciting statements of authorial purpose. "What are you trying to do in this section?" "What do your readers need to know about this issue?" "What do you want your audience to believe?"
- encouraging autonomy. "Now that we've gone through this paragraph pretty thoroughly, why don't you work on the rest of this page for awhile? I'll check back with you in ten minutes."
- deflecting overt requests for evaluation (e.g., "What grade would you give this?"). Turn the question around: "What grade would you give yourself?" "How do you think this paper compares to other work you've done for this course?"
- playing up the value of other reader's responses. "You might want to have another tutor look at this and see what she thinks." "Has anyone else in your class read this?"
- showing an interest in the writer and her ideas. "I feel like I learned something by reading your paper." "Tell me more about ____."

In addition to taking advantage of our political distinctiveness in contacts with students, writing center directors need to be forthright in presenting and interpreting the center to classroom teachers in the following ways:

- opening up the center's windows. Let instructors know what we do and don't do, and why.
- behaving proactively regarding suspicions about what happens in the center. We must assert with Richard Behm that "collaborative learning as practiced in most writing centers is not plagiarism, that it is not only ethical but also reflective of the way people really

write" (9).

- recognizing the potential fluidity of both classroom and center. Why can't some of what a composition teacher wants to accomplish in class take place in the writing center? If students are working in pairs or small groups, they could do that work in the center with the opportunity to include a tutor in the discussion. Why can't some of what tutors do with writers take place in the composition classroom? On writing workshop days, tutors could join the instructor in circulating around the room and doing short conferences. Having tutors in the classroom can help defuse the anxiety that some teachers may feel about being judged by tutors, as well as help tutors appreciate the demands and constraints of classroom instruction. For students, seeing tutors outside the center can help destigmatize the center and make it easier to go there with their own writing.

The relationship between the writing center and the classroom is complex. Not everyone who works in writing centers would agree with Steve North that "we are not here to serve, supplement, back up, complement, reinforce, or otherwise be defined by any external curriculum," and even those who do might wonder where their clients will come from if teachers perceive the center as an independent entity. But unless the writing center provides an alternative to the classroom, unless writers experience something there that is qualitatively different from what they find elsewhere on their journey through the curriculum, then justifying the center's existence (and budget) seems problematic.

Colleges and universities have rightly rejected the in loco parentis role with which they have, at various times, felt saddled. The academy has insisted on its own independence and freedom as a prerequisite to its mission of fostering independence and freedom in its students. The writing center, as an academic institution, must also remain free to provide students a place to come, not because they have to, but because they experience there the freedom to realize themselves as writers—with their own intentions and purposes, with their own questions and insecurities, with their own strengths and vision.

From a parent's perspective, sending children off to school will always be at least a little threatening, for one never knows what they will learn there. But the most successful societies have always recognized that developing good citizens and whole persons is a corporate enterprise. As a place within the academic community, the writing center takes up its part in the communal effort to nurture creativity, critical thinking, and self-directedness.

Twenty years ago, Peter Elbow made a disquieting claim—disquieting for those of us who justify our existence and our paychecks by saying that we "teach": "It is possible to learn something and not be taught. It is possible to be a student and not have a teacher. If the student's function is to learn and the teacher's to teach, then the student can function without a teacher, but the teacher cannot function without a student" (ix). Elbow's reminder is still timely. Whether we're in the classroom or in the writing center, we should remember that we need students as much, and sometimes more, than they need us. Our task, if we believe in the collaborative nature of the educational enterprise, is to convince our students of what we believe in our hearts: that we all need each other.

Works Cited

Behm, Richard. "Ethical Issues in Peer Tutoring: A Defense of Collaborative Learning." *The Writing Center Journal* 10.1 (1989): 3-12.

Chase, Geoffrey. "Small is Beautiful: A Plan for the Decentralized Writing Center." *Writing Lab Newsletter* 9.8 (1985): 1-4.

Clark, Irene Lurkis. "Collaboration and Ethics in Writing Center Pedagogy." *The Writing Center Journal* 9.1 (1988): 3-12.

Elbow, Peter. *Writing Without Teachers*. New York: Oxford, 1973.

Harris, Muriel. "What's Up and What's In: Trends and Traditions in Writing Centers." *The Writing Center Journal* 11.1 (1990):15-25.

Heller, Dana A. "Silencing the Soundtrack: An Alternative to Marginal Comments." *College Composition and Communication* 40 (1989): 210-215.

Hemmeter, Thomas. "The 'Smack of Difference': The Language of Writing Center Discourse." *The Writing Center Journal* 11.1 (1990): 35-48.

Kail, Harvey and John Trimbur. "The Politics of Peer Tutoring." *Journal of the Council of Writing Program Administrators* 11 (1987): 5-12.

North, Stephen M. "The Idea of a Writing Center." *College English* 46 (1984): 433-446.

Olson, Gary A., ed. *Writing Centers: Theory and Administration*. Urbana: NCTE, 1984.

Reigstad, Thomas J. and Donald A. McAndrew. *Training Tutors for Writing Conferences*. Urbana: NCTE, 1984.

Runciman, Lex. "Defining Ourselves: Do We Really Want to Use the Word Tutor?" *The Writing Center Journal* 11.1 (1990): 27-34.

Severino, Carol. "Writers Writing." *Writing Lab Newsletter* 17.6 (1993): 11-14.

Spear, Karen I. "Promoting Cognitive Development in the Writing Center." *Writing Centers: Theory and Administration*. Gary Olson, ed. Urbana: NCTE, 1984. 62-76.

Waldo, Mark L. "What Should the Relationship Between the Writing Center and Writing Program Be?" *The Writing Center Journal* 11.1 (1990): 73-80.

The Writing Center's Role in the Writing Across the Curriculum Program: Theory and Practice

by Ray Wallace

Over the last quarter of a century, university professors and administrators have discovered an alarming trend on our campuses: many graduating seniors prove deficient in writing skills. As a result, many universities recently have developed proficiency, or "exit," exams in an attempt to stop the flow of writing-deficient graduates. However, this procedure used alone is akin to throwing water on a smoldering ruin; while much smoke and confusion occur, there is no change in the final state of the once-great building. It became increasingly clear that one semester of English composition is not sufficient to turn writing deficiencies into writing proficiencies. As a result, many universities have implemented writing-across-the-curriculum programs.

Like other universities throughout the country, our institution implemented a writing-across-the-curriculum program last year. This article describes how we coordinated this program through the writing center and discusses the solutions we developed to counter the strain of an added program to our center's already overburdened mission.

After approximately two years of heated intra- and inter-disciplinary argument, it was agreed that all general education courses in our university had to develop the students' writing and/or quantitative skills. It was then that the writing center faculty was asked to help ease the problems involved in the introduction of writing skills across the curriculum. With this added program, the writing center was now home for three highly diversified, but equally important programs:

1. One-to-one and small-group tutoring in writing for all English classes.
2. Computer-assisted remedial instruction in grammar and usage.
3. Specialized tutoring in writing for the writing-across-the-curriculum program.

Freisinger and Burkland (1982) list five components by which writing-across-the-curriculum programs can be implemented and improved in the

Reprinted from *The Writing Center Journal* 8.2 (1988): 43-48.

writing center. These components include the following guidelines:

1. The discipline professor can and should refer students with writing problems to the writing center; this referral can be voluntary or a course requirement.
2. The writing center tutor must understand what the discipline professor expects as an end-product from the student being tutored.
3. The writing center tutor and the discipline professor must communIcate with each other. The tutor must document how each student was tutored, what tutoring methods were used, the effectiveness of these methods, and the student's response to these methods. In turn, the professor must document how these methods helped, or did not help, when the student was finally evaluated.
4. The discipline professor should provide examples of effective papers, style sheets, documentation formats, and copies of each assignment question. These documents should be filed in the writing center.
5. The discipline professor should take an active interest in the administration of the writing center. (176-177)

Theorists disagree about who should tutor writing-across-the-curriculum students in the writing center. Arfken (1982) and Steward and Croft (1982) point to the almost exclusive use of English majors as the most effective tutoring personnel. Scanlon (1986), however, comments that selecting "tutors from several disciplines . . . can substantially strengthen the services of the writing center" (40). Scanlon's argument that "the discourse in each discipline also has its own features [so] an interdisciplinary writing center needs to be staffed by tutors who are familiar with these different features" (38) helped us decide that we could use non-English majors as tutors.

Making the Writing Center Work in Practice

Before any philosophical and/or structural changes could be made, the writing center faculty and the discipline professors had to define what they considered effective writing. Therefore, a two-day writing workshop was held in the center, and, as people gradually got to know each other's views on writing, effective and ineffective writing samples from many disciplines were discussed. From this intensive, but relaxed, workshop, both writing center faculty and discipline professors were able to agree that

1. There should be *at least* one out-of-class writing assignment of not less than 1000 words in each course.
2. The professor should set an appropriate deadline so each student could have *at least* one tutoring session in the writing center on each paper. Assignment deadlines therefore were approximately two weeks.
3. The professor should devote *at least* one class lecture to a discussion of rhetorical considerations, the writing process, documenta-

tion, and the benefits of visiting the writing center.
4. The professor should provide a copy of the assignment question to
   the tutor.

The writing center faculty turned to the discipline professors to nominate
their most responsible majors as possible tutors. These professors developed
their own criteria for the selection of tutors for the writing across the curriculum program. These criteria included the following:

- A declared major in the discipline to be tutored
- A cumulative grade-point average between 2.5 and 4.0
- Junior standing
- Two letters of recommendation from discipline professors

Even with these somewhat restrictive criteria, cross-disciplinary tutors were
readily available. Such availability was due to an effective recruiting strategy
used by the discipline professors. When these students were told that such
tutoring experience would enhance their resumes, help them gain admittance
to graduate school, or make them more marketable in terms of their interpersonal and administrative skills, the discipline professors were able to nominate
so many fine student writers that the writing center faculty could then select
those with the greatest potential.

Both the writing center faculty and the discipline professors viewed the
training of these new tutors as a very important task if writing-across-the-
curriculum were to succeed at the institution. The center's faculty had already
been holding tutor-training sessions for the general tutors (all English majors)
who were assigned to tutor the writing classes in English. However, the
faculty and the other discipline professors felt that the inclusion of the new
writing-across-the-curriculum tutors in the general tutor-training sessions
would be counterproductive in terms of time and goals. Therefore, these new
tutors had to attend their own weekly two-hour special training workshops.
The workshops were held for a total of twelve weeks. In the first hour of each
workshop, selected members of the writing center faculty discussed various
aspects of the composing process and tutoring techniques. In the second hour
of each workshop, the discipline professors met in small groups with their
discipline's tutors to explain future assignments, tutoring problems, course
materials, and pertinent goals. The following is a brief outline of the twelve-
week tutor-training course:

Week #1: Introduction of the center faculty, the discipline professors, and the course content and goals. A brief discussion
of the writing center layout and the ethics of tutoring.

Week #2: Beginning to Tutor: The initial meeting, roles, models,
and expectations. A discussion on how to evaluate writing
and how to develop a tutee profile.

Week #3: The Writing Process: More intensive discussion of pre-
writing, writing, and rewriting tutoring techniques.

Week #4: Discipline-Specific Writing Assignments: Small-group discussions of discipline-specific organizational/rhetorical writing patterns and individual tutoring techniques.

Week #5:   Role-Playing: How to work with the student who just wants the assignment proofread.

Week #6:   Tutoring/Counseling: How to motivate the student and an overview of counseling approaches.

Week #7:   Discipline-Specific Documentation Styles: Small-group discussions of discipline-specific styles, formats, and requirements.

Week #8:   Role-Playing: Tutoring the ESL learner. A discussion of the tutoring methods used to help these students with idioms, prepositions, tenses, count and non-count nouns, articles, and other common ESL problems.

Week #9:   Tutoring Mechanics: Grammar, punctuation and spelling. Guidelines on how to avoid proofreading for the tutee.

Week #10:   Role-Playing: Dealing with the paper which is too technical for its intended audience. Discussion of levels of formality, audience awareness, and other audience considerations.

Week #11:   Revision: How to tutor students to rethink and to reorganize their papers.

Week #12:   Evaluation: Both tutor and discipline professor evaluate each other.

Merging Theory and Practice

As the writing center became a place where professors and tutors could exchange ideas and techniques that proved effective, theory and practice merged. Although some professors were at first rather hesitant about submitting their documentation style sheets, they soon realized that they needed to update their style sheets for their own research. So, with tutors chastised into keeping better tutoring records and discipline professors persuaded that it was in their best interests to update their own writing standards, the center had accumulated over forty different examples of discipline-specific writing. By the end of the semester, these included lab reports, program documentation reports, abstracts, summaries, analyses, and mechanism descriptions. These examples, combined with individual documentation style sheets and extensive reports of which techniques worked and which did not, proved invaluable in training the next group of writing-across-the-curriculum tutors.

Conclusion

The writing center, both in theory and practice, can play an important role in the implementation of writing across the curriculum at any institution. Our institution's attempt to use the writing center worked well. While administration of the center remained securely anchored to the English discipline, other disciplines took an active interest in what was happening in the center. A completely new team of tutors was selected and trained. New insight into other disciplines' evaluation of writing was gained, and a new corpus of materials and tutoring handouts was developed.

In this situation, the writing center's role is to provide additional instruction for a group of discipline professors interested in improving their students' writing skills. The center is, and should always be, only a support service; writing-across-the-curriculum advocates should never expect writing and content to be separated in terms of instruction. As writing center personnel, we owe it to these new colleagues to provide the most effective support. If these professors demonstrate the important goals that effective written communication can achieve, then the writing center must be there to support these goals, to add to the instruction of students' writing skills, and to help these future biologists, geographers, economists, and educators reach these goals.

Works Cited

Arfken, D. "A Peer-Tutor Staff: Four Crucial Aspects." *Tutoring Writing*. Ed. Muriel Harris. Glenview: Scott, Foresman, 1982. 111-22.

Freisinger, Diana, and Jill Burkland. "Talking About Writing: The Role of the Writing Lab." *Language Connections: Writing and Reading Across the Curriculum*. Eds. Toby Fulwiler and Art Young. Urbana: NCTE, 1982. 167-79.

Scanlon, Leone. "Recruiting and Training Tutors for Cross Disciplinary Writing Programs." *The Writing Center Journal* 6.2 (1986): 1-8.

Steward, Joyce, and Mary Croft. *The Writing Laboratory.* Glenview: Scott, Foresman, 1982.

Writing Centers and Writing-for-Learning

by Richard Leahy

Where are writing centers going in their support of writing across the curriculum? I ask this question instead of "what are they doing?" because what they are doing is well documented in *The Writing Lab Newsletter* and *The Writing Center Journal.* The more we share such ideas with one another, the better. But in this essay I want to try for a look at the bigger picture.

On many campuses, writing centers have become intimately connected with writing across the curriculum. Often, the writing center director serves on a campus-wide committee, consults with faculty about designing writing-intensive courses, and trains faculty in the uses of writing. Some centers attach tutors to content courses to act as writing consultants. Most of the time this cooperation seems to be working well.

One matter keeps nagging at me, though. It is the danger that WAC programs can become one-sided, losing sight of the purpose of writing across the curriculum as a whole. And when a WAC program drifts off the mark, the writing center can drift with it.

To explain what I mean, let me go into some basic principles and problems involved in writing across the curriculum. This will take some time, but I think it's important for writing center personnel to be aware of these issues. They are issues the instructors must deal with. How they deal with them affects their students, who in turn affect the writing center by coming there for help.

The WAC movement, in its best form, has two distinct purposes: to enhance learning by means of writing and to improve students' writing abilities. These two purposes are roughly equivalent to two of the three main functions of writing identified by James Britton, expressive and transactional (the third being poetic).

Expressive writing, as Britton describes it, is close to informal talk, relaxed, free of demands imposed "by the reader or the nature of the task" (93). It is the kind of writing found in private journals and personal letters, and in such in-class activities as freewriting and written dialogues between students. The relaxed nature of expressive writing is conducive to thinking-on-paper. The writer can sort out her attitudes toward a subject, rehearse her under-

Reprinted from *The Writing Center Journal* 10.1 (1983): 31-37. Used by permission.

standing of it, question and speculate, without the burden of having to present the result in finished form. In expressive writing, the writer's own consciousness is as much the subject as is the nominal subject about which she is writing.

Transactional writing, by contrast, emphasizes not the writer's thinking processes but the finished product of that thinking. Britton summarizes it as "language to get things done": to inform, advise, persuade, or instruct (88). Virtually all writing done in the world of work—business letters, reports, proposals, etc.—is transactional, and so are almost all academic tasks, including term papers, research reports, and most writing done for English composition classes. In transactional writing the subject itself is paramount; the writer's personal voice is muted or absent altogether.[1]

In expressive writing, the writer looks for connections between ideas, explores them, and clarifies them. In transactional writing, the writer orders and explains ideas so that other people can understand, evaluate, and (or) act upon them. The two purposes are often given other labels: writing-for-learning vs. writing-for-evaluation, exploratory vs. explanatory, informal vs. formal.

The important point for WAC programs is that expressive and transactional writing can be used to complement each other. A well-designed content course uses both. The instructor uses informal, expressive writing throughout the term, in the form of journals, in-class freewritings, and written dialogues between students, and may also assign formal, transactional writing in the form of essays, summaries, reports or whatever genre fits the subject. The idea behind mixing the two function categories is that the informal writing is both a beginning from which the formal writing can grow and a means toward understanding a subject. By developing the *habit* of dealing with the subject in writing, students not only engage in valuable preparation for writing the formal assignments but also learn the subject better. In a balanced WAC program, expressive writing should get at least as much attention as transactional writing.

But introducing informal, expressive writing into the classroom also has implications for which the instructor may not be prepared. For it leads away from traditional prepared lectures and toward collaborative learning. To illustrate, let us say that Professor Sally James has her students freewrite for five minutes at the end of the hour, summarizing what they got out of the class. That night, skimming through the papers, she finds that several students missed the main point of the lecture. So the next class period she has to go

---

[1] Poetic writing (poems, short stories, etc.) does not figure prominently in writing-for-learning. A poetic writing is "a verbal artifact, a construct.... Attention to the forms of the language is an essential part of a reader's response" (Britton 93).

Transactional and poetic writing are really the extremes of a continuum, with expressive occupying a broad (and difficult to define) middle. Informal academic writing naturally lies toward the transactional end. It tends to move back and forth between expressive and transactional within a single piece of writing.

back and clarify the point before going on. Or if she asks the students to write at the beginning of class in order to raise questions about the assigned reading, she has to give over much of the hour, perhaps all of it, to the questions they raise. She may never get to her prepared lecture.

Sally realizes that when she asks for this kind of informal writing, something has to be done with it. It has to be read, discussed, and responded to, either by her or by other students in the class. The next thing Sally knows, she has begun to rethink her whole approach to teaching. Used to lecturing and then giving exams to see if the students can regurgitate the information correctly, she now finds herself involved in a collaborative effort. Her students are working in groups. She is monitoring their understanding and helping them along. She is also learning, for the first time, what works and doesn't work in her teaching. If she decides to commit herself fully to the concept of learning-through-writing, she ends up a different kind of teacher: moderator/coach rather than lecturer/authority figure.

This shift brings with it much that is desirable, including a new energy and enthusiasm for teaching. It also can bring unsettling side effects, including static from faculty in the instructor's department, who may complain that the instructor is not covering enough material, and lower evaluations from students, who are not used to evaluating an instructor who is not the traditional authority figure (and from some who resent being asked to write anything at all).

Most faculty who are trained in effective WAC programs manage to make the change successfully. Others do it on their own or catch the fever from their colleagues. Some never change. On my own campus, and on many of those I have visited that have WAC efforts, only a minority of the faculty are actively practicing writing-for-learning. Outside this knowledgeable cadre, there are many faculty members who think they are doing something for their students' writing skills by merely tacking a term-paper assignment onto a lecture/exam format.

Many instructors have learned that just assigning a term paper is not enough; they also have to nurture the project along. They have learned a number of ways to do this: by distributing sample papers, assigning and responding to drafts, setting up draft-response groups, and scheduling individual conferences. Still, even these instructors are missing part of what WAC is all about. If the end product of all this activity is a gradeable term paper, then all the writing done for the class is essentially pitched toward a transactional product. The instructor has employed writing as a mode of learning, but only in the narrow range of material leading to the term paper, not in the general subject-matter of the course.

If a WAC program promotes all the strategies used to teach the writing process, but does not also require abundant journal-writing, in-class freewriting, or other forms of informal, exploratory writing, it is still stressing only one purpose: improving students' skills in transactional writing. Expressive writing, writing-for-learning, is still being neglected.

The obvious cause for this neglect is that transactional writing needs so much more explaining than expressive writing. There is a great deal to know about selecting topics, revising drafts, and evaluating finished products. Expressive writing, by contrast, is fairly simple to explain. The difference can be seen in any WAC manual published on any campus: transactional writing takes up by far the greater bulk; expressive writing takes only a few pages. In some manuals it takes up less than a page. Judging by its physical presence in the manuals, expressive writing barely exists. Beyond these problems, there is the fact that the material on transactional writing shows faculty better ways to do what they already do, whereas the material on expressive writing asks many of them to do things they have never tried before.

There are a number of other powerful reasons why writing-for-learning is neglected. First, administrators may not be inclined to support it. They respond easily to the idea of improving students' transactional writing, because they like the idea of their graduates' writing better when they enter the working world, thus reflecting well upon the school. But writing-for-learning is a less product-oriented concept, harder to explain, and it promises no immediate, obvious rewards. Second, faculty may deceive themselves into believing they are doing a lot for WAC just by assigning more transactional writing. They can support the cause of improving writing, because that motive by itself requires few changes in the way they teach. Third, expressive writing suffers from a tainted image. Many educators misunderstand it as "personal" (in a bad sense), sloppy, and unable to carry the freight of important ideas. In this, as anyone involved in WAC knows, they are profoundly mistaken.

The fourth reason is more subtle but no less powerful. It is that the classroom, though ostensibly a public forum, is from the professional point of view a very private place, where instructors expect to be able to do what they want without interference. Unsolicited suggestions on how to improve their classroom methods often result in resentment and resistance. This reasoning does an injustice to the general openness and flexibility of the faculty on my campus and probably any other, but the undercurrent is still there.

Therefore, although most WAC programs are improving writing skills, forces militate against the spread of writing-for-learning. On some campuses these forces contribute to a massive inertia that prevents significant changes in teaching from taking place. This can be especially true at large universities where close intercommunication with any sizable proportion of faculty is difficult. For the shift in teaching to take hold, it has to be a grassroots movement, a change in individual teachers. Except in rare instances, it cannot be legislated from above with any hope of general success.

The writing center, at least in its usual mode of operation, does not do much for the cause of writing-for-learning. Tutors deal mostly with students trying to write papers, not trying to learn subject-matter. As a result, the writing center deals almost exclusively with transactional writing. It has little influence on how writing-for-learning is used across the campus but rather takes writing assignments as they come and does its best to help its clients deal with them.

Tutors in the writing center encounter clients from classes that are taught from every possible kind of approach. On one extreme, they see clients for whom a writing assignment is an integral part of the course, growing out of journals and other forms of writing they have been doing all semester; on the other, they see clients for whom the assignment appears to come out of nowhere and to bear little relation to anything else going on in the course. (Tutors may secretly feel that some instructors should not be allowed to use writing in their classes at all.) Students coming from these various classes are likely to feel different degrees of ownership over their writing. It is good that tutors learn to be flexible, but it bothers me that the writing center should always be responding to situations and not actively working to change them. My purpose so far has been to express some cautions about the writing center's role in WAC, and about how the writing center can become unintentionally involved in preserving a one-sided emphasis on writing-for-evaluation at the expense of writing-for-learning. Let me try to be more constructive now by proposing some what-ifs.

(1) What if the writing center offered to help students learn to write productive journal entries?

I have students in my classes who have never written journals and have no idea now to use a journal to enhance their learning. Many instructors solve this problem by devoting plenty of class time to nurturing the journals along. Many instructors do not; they leave the students to struggle on their own. Writing centers could solicit good examples of journals from faculty in various disciplines, as they do with formal papers.

(2) What if the writing center offered to coach students in freewriting, showing them how to focus it and get the most out of it? Or what if the writing center offered to help students write productive responses to textbooks and lectures—not just notes, but active responses, dialogues with the text?

Some centers, particularly those that work with study skills and those that are part of larger learning centers, already offer this kind of help. But couldn't more centers do so? Especially on campuses where writing-for-learning is widely promoted? Students—all of us—are sometimes afraid to take chances and play with ideas on paper. Getting over that fear is rather like getting over computer fear. It takes plunging in, with encouragement from the sidelines. Tutors could provide the encouragement.

(3) What if writing centers appealed directly to students in writing-for-learning courses and worked with them on the new methods of learning being used in their classes?

Some students resist writing-for-learning as much as some teachers do. They prefer the comfortable format of lectures. They see the professors as "vast storehouses of knowledge" (a quote from one of my own students) and want only to soak up the stream of information pouring forth. Some of them resent class time given over to writing and discussion, counting it only as time when information is not flowing. These students need help to conceive of learning in different, deeper ways.

Such help might get rid of the residual anxiety a student might have that "Professor James, no matter what she says, *is* secretly grading my journal, and if I look like a fool in this week's entries, she'll remember, and it will somehow be figured in my grade." If students talk with a tutor about how writing-for-learning really works, they might begin to trust it and benefit from it.

(4) What if more writing centers sponsored ongoing education of faculty in writing-for-learning?

On my campus, we started a monthly newsletter on various WAC topics, written by writing center staff. The newsletter has received an enthusiastic response from faculty. Admittedly, most of the issues are about transactional writing; that's hard to avoid. But we try to keep a balance. Writing centers on other campuses have been successful in attracting faculty to mini-seminars and workshops. Writing-center directors (at least those who are not also teaching heavy course loads) sometimes wangle invitations to department meetings around campus to demonstrate writing-for-learning and explain the writing center's services.

I admit some of my suggestions are untested, and some are not even new to all centers. It might be hard to attract a clientele of students interested in learning how to learn through writing. But more of us might try going in that direction. Preparing tutors to help with writing-for-learning should mesh easily with existing training programs.

Aggressive promotion of writing-for-learning would keep a WAC program on target. It would also make the writing center a more influential force in the program.

Works Cited

Britton, James. *The Development of Writing Abilities*. Schools Council Research Studies. London: Macmillan, 1975.

The Politics of Peer Tutoring

by Harvey Kail and John Trimbur

Over the past ten years or so, peer tutoring has worked its way up from the margins of academic life, from the realm of academic support services and soft money, to claim an integral position in many, if not most, writing programs.[1] Collaborative learning and peer tutoring are now recognized as innovative contributions not only to the writing abilities but more broadly to the liberal education of undergraduates. Exemplary peer tutoring programs such as Kenneth A. Bruffee's Brooklyn Plan and Tori Haring-Smith's Writing Fellows at Brown University have become models in the field, with an identity, a coherent rationale, and a capacity for replication.

Thus the question to be asked about peer tutoring is no longer why such programs are necessary, but how tutoring can best contribute to the development of writing abilities and the intellectual life of undergraduates. Indeed, peer tutoring has reached the point where distinct models are vying for influence to disseminate their sense of purpose and possibility. What follows is our attempt to sort peer tutoring programs under two broad headings: the writing center model such as Bruffee's Brooklyn Plan and the curriculum-based model such as Haring-Smith's Writing Fellows Program. We propose to discuss these two models of peer tutoring in terms of their administrative structures and, more significantly, to analyze their underlying educational ideologies, the political assumptions which are often hidden in educational programs by the very process of institutionalization. We want to talk, that is, about the way peer tutoring programs constitute the educational consciousness of peer tutors and tutees. We will argue that while the curriculum-based model may be administratively more efficient, the writing center model offers an educational setting in which collaboration among peers can help students reach a critical understanding and redefinition of themselves as learners.

Two Models: Writing Center and Curriculum-Based

First, let's characterize the two models as organizational strategies. The writing center model such as Bruffee's Brooklyn Plan is organized as a voluntary association where students who want to improve their writing drop

---

Reprinted from *The Writing Center Journal* 11.1-2 (1987): 5-12. Used by permission.
[1] For a description of the range of current peer tutoring programs, see *A Guide to Writing Programs, Writing Centers, Peer Tutoring, Writing Across the Curriculum.* Ed. Tori Haring-Smith. Glenview: Scott Foresman, 1984.

in or make an appointment to work with a peer tutor in a writing center (Bruffee, "The Brooklyn Plan"). Students can be at any stage in composing. Sometimes they want to talk to a tutor to clarify the assignment or to get some initial ideas down on paper. Other times students come to tutoring sessions with drafts in progress, specific questions, and specific requests for response. Or students may bring in graded papers to discuss their strengths and weaknesses and the instructor's comments. And in still other cases, students call on peer tutors to deal with nonacademic writing—job letters, graduate school applications, résumés, and so on. Most students refer themselves, while some seek peer tutoring on the recommendation of an instructor. As a rule, though, the success of the writing center model depends on publicity and word of mouth, the extent to which the benefits of peer tutoring have penetrated the informal networks of student life.

The curriculum-based model, such as Haring-Smith's Writing Fellows Program, on the other hand, seems to grow out of the premise that if peer tutoring is good for those students who seek it voluntarily, it's even better to require it, to make sure that students in composition classes or writing intensive courses in other fields hook up with peer tutors. In the curriculum-based model, tutors are typically attached to a course as much as to a writing center. Ten years ago, when peer tutoring was still viewed mainly as a remedial activity, the curriculum-based model often provided a required lab component in basic writing courses, where peer tutors administered drills and exercises. More recently, however, the curriculum-based model has expanded the scope of its activities in new and much more sophisticated directions. Sometimes peer tutors provide in-class tutoring in coordination with the course instructor. Other times, the peer tutors provide written or oral responses to early drafts of writing assignments to encourage revision before the students turn in final drafts for their instructors to grade. In any case, in the curriculum-based model, peer tutors are, as it were, written into the plan of instruction. They're part of the course.

Thus the curriculum-based model operates through official channels; student writers receive peer tutoring as a part of their classes. By building peer tutoring into the course structure, the curriculum-based model makes peer tutors an extension of the writing program, a way to deliver state-of-the-art peer responses to student writers. Building peer tutoring into the plan of instruction in such courses guarantees moreover a certain level of efficiency: tutors will have someone to tutor and program administrators will be able quite accurately to predict the number of tutoring sessions that will take place, the number of tutors necessary, the best times to schedule tutoring, and so on.

Looking at the writing center and curriculum-based models as organizational strategies, the issue that divides them seems to be how best to plug in tutors with tutees. We have, that is, two delivery systems and the meaningful question to ask appears to be which one works better, which one better delivers the knowledge it takes to learn to write well. By such operational criteria, the curriculum-based model has some real strengths compared to the writing center model: it makes sure tutors and tutees connect: it promotes communication between tutors and faculty; it simplifies administration by concentrating peer tutoring in selected courses. And it avoids some of the potential pitfalls in the writing-center model: the no-shows, the stigma of seeking help, the indifference, the parasitical behavior. For these reasons, the curriculum-based model has become increasingly widespread. Compared to the Writing Fellows Program at Brown University, the writing center model appears to be diffuse and unfocused, at best an adjunct service for those students not enrolled in courses targeted by the curriculum-based peer tutoring program.

If, however, we stop thinking solely in terms of operational efficiency for a moment and begin talking in terms of educational ideology, we can make some distinctions we couldn't make by looking at these models as administrative strategies. The differences we are going to see at this level of analysis are not operational but political; they concern not the delivery of services but the powers ascribed to and internalized by tutors and tutees—the ideology of peer tutoring.

Models and the Ideology of Generation and Transmission

According to the traditional ideology of teaching and learning, universities "generate" knowledge and then "transmit" this knowledge into the academic community and eventually to the community outside the university. One need only look in the front of a dozen college catalogues to see how habitual and commonsensical this ideology of generation and transmission has become. The metaphor is worth unpacking: knowledge is generated like heat is produced in a college's steamplant or electricity from a nuclear reactor and then transmitted through the steamlines or electrical cables to a radiator or an electric typewriter—or a student. Scholars on the "cutting edge" of their fields, on the boundary between what we know and what we don't, generate new knowledge, turning darkness into light. While the moment of ignition or transformation is so mysterious that we cannot explain it, the process of transmission can be easily traced. Slowly new knowledge works its way back from the "cutting edge," from scholar to scholar, in articles, monographs, books, to where it is assimilated by teachers who, eventually, transmit it to students. For convenience sake, we will label this cluster of ideas the "gen/tran" ideology, for generation and transmission. Where does peer tutoring fit into the gen/tran ideology? According to the gen/tran ideology of knowledge, peer tutoring is conceived as a new fixture in the transmission lines. It is a substation along the way designed to jump up the signal or change the quality of transmission. With the help of peer tutors, students who aren't receiving the signals properly can tune in better to the same message, except that now it is in a new voice, the voice of the students' peers. The key word for understanding the politics of peer tutoring within the gen/tran ideology is supplement—more power for transmission.

Peer tutors then get the authority to transmit knowledge through an act of installation: They are installed in the existing power grid. They receive knowledge from their tutor trainers, turn and pass this know-how on to their tutees. Within gen/tran, the pedagogy—that is, the relationship among students, teachers, and curriculum—remains what it always was, hierarchical. A new component has been put in place to improve the system's performance: a teacher teaches a student or group of students to then turn and teach other students. The only difference in education after the installation of peer tutors is that the transmission lines are a little longer. They can now reach a larger and perhaps more diversified audience. But the authority to generate and transmit knowledge, even though mediated by new voices and new social relationships remains where it always was—firmly in faculty hands.

In the curriculum-based model of peer tutoring, students working as peer tutors can't help but experience their own activity, and with it a sense of themselves, as part of a delivery system, a supplement to repair the short circuits, recharge the sources of power, and keep the transmission lines functioning smoothly. By attaching peer tutoring to the official structures of teaching and learning, by writing them into the plan of instruction, the curriculum-based model makes the peer tutors an extension of the faculty. In effect, peer tutoring in the curriculum-based model removes tutors from the student community by installing them a power station or two above their peers, a step away from student culture, a step closer to the faculty. Thus, the curriculum-based model keeps tutors from collaborating with tutees as peers because the tutors are already identified with the functions of the faculty and the writing program, already implicated in the lines of transmission. In the curriculum-based model, the key collaboration is designing a plan of instruction, a collaboration that takes place between faculty and student-tutors, and not among themselves.

Enter Collaborative Learning

It might be argued that the writing center model of peer tutoring, with its system of paying tutors and locating them in an officially sanctioned writing center, operates under the aegis of gen/tran as much as the curriculum-based model. And that seems to us often to be the case, that in fact many writing centers are designed to be part of a larger delivery system of writing instruction. It is the exceptions, however, such as those based on Bruffee's Brooklyn Plan, that interest us, the writing centers that emphasize collaboration between faculty and peer tutors.

Peer tutoring programs based on collaborative learning are, of course, located inside the institutions of higher education, but they are situated at a remove from the normal delivery system of curriculum and instruction, in the semi-autonomous space of writing centers. What gives such writing centers their semi-autonomous character is that although they are part of the official institutional structure, they operate primarily as voluntary associations of peers. As we have pointed out elsewhere, peer tutoring based on collaborative learning taps into the networks of mutual aid already present in student culture (Kail, Trimbur). Students have always banded together informally, in rap sessions and study groups, to deal with the intellectual demands of their experience as undergraduates. Collaborative learning, in this respect, is an effort by educators to mobilize the power of peer influence toward the intellectual activity of co-learning. By organizing tutors and tutees as co-learners, peer tutoring based on collaborative learning does not so much repair a dysfunctional system of transmissions as it offers an alternative to the dominant hierarchical model of teaching and learning, an alternative based on voluntary social interaction among students. It replaces the metaphor of the generation and transmission of knowledge with that of a conversation. To replace generation and transmission with conversation is to challenge some of the basic beliefs and practices in higher education. For one thing, it challenges the traditional reward system, with its emphasis on individual performance and competition among students for grades and faculty esteem. Collaboration among students in the form of peer tutoring may make faculty nervous because it seems to verge on plagiarism, cheating, and ghostwriting. More important, though, collaboration among students challenges the way we habitually think about the authority of knowledge.

As Kenneth A. Bruffee has pointed out, to think of knowledge as conversation among knowledgeable peers is to abandon the view that knowledge is fixed once and for all, something that once generated needs only delivery ("Collaborative Learning and the 'Conversation of Mankind'"). Nor is knowledge hierarchical in the sense that we think of the individual scholar at the "cutting edge" confronting the unknown and wrestling meaning out of the void. We get knowledge not from some higher authority but from ourselves and our activity talking to others, even when this inherently social activity of conversation is displaced into the solitude of reading and writing. We are never really alone facing the void, as tempting as such mythology may be. Knowledge, rather, is a social process, a part of and inseparable from what we call the "social fabric," authorized by the mutual consent of knowledgeable peers.

Locating the sources of knowledge in the social fabric rather than in the power lines of generation and transmission offers a way to talk about peer tutoring that goes beyond the operational model of plugging tutors into the grid. Peer tutoring, in this view, is not a supplement to the normal delivery system but an implicit critique of gen/tran ideology and the official structures of curriculum and instruction. To reorganize the relationship among students is simultaneously to probe the traditional relationships of teaching and learning.

Peer Tutoring and the Crisis of Authority

By posing an alternative to the prevailing hierarchy of generation/transmission, collaborative learning precipitates a crisis of authority. It asks students to rely on themselves, to learn on their own in the absence of faculty authority figures or their surrogates. In tutoring programs based on collaborative learning, tutors and tutees not only must learn to work together. They must also learn to free themselves from their dependence on the faculty continually measuring and certifying their learning. To do this, of course, requires that students break with some of the habitual behaviors of schooling and form new habits of thought and action. Collaborative learning in this sense begins as an exercise in unlearning. Unless tutors and tutees unlearn the ideology of gen/tran, they will inevitably reproduce competitive, individualistic, authority-dependent behaviors embedded in traditional education. The power of collaborative learning, we believe, is that it offers students a way to unlearn what the sociologist and cultural critic Richard Sennett calls "visions of a satisfying omnipotent authority," to reinterpret the power of the faculty, and to see that their own autonomous co-learning constitutes the practical source of knowledge.

This process of unlearning and reinterpretation is a complex one. At the risk of appearing overly schematic, however, we can trace its broad outlines. As Sennett points out in his book *Authority*, a crisis of authority that leads to renouncing an authority as omnipotent proceeds through three stages: detachment, reflection, and reentrance. According to Sennett, the first stage is marked by "detachment from the influence of authority," This is what can happen, we believe, in the semi-autonomous space of writing centers. By removing themselves from the lines of transmission, tutors and tutees form their own co-learning communities, establish their joint purposes, decide on a plan to work together, and evaluate the results. The point of peer tutoring, in this respect, is not the delivery of knowledge from tutor to tutee but an experience of their own power as learners that will lead peers to discover authority in each other. Peer tutoring based on collaborative learning begins, then, by organizing tutors and tutees outside the normal channels of teaching and learning so that they can constitute each other as active subjects in the social interaction of co-learning.

The process of co-learning leads to the second stage of Sennett's sequence, to the reflection "What was I like under the authority's influence?" As students detach themselves from faculty influence in order to work together collaboratively, they may also come to a mutual recognition of their shared status as undergraduates, their common position at the bottom of the academic hierarchy where they compete as individuals for personal success and faculty esteem. This mutual recognition can take students beyond an atomized perception of their own personal predicament to a social understanding of a system that frequently pits student against student in a struggle for the scarce resource of faculty approval. The experience of co-learning can help students not only to remove themselves from faculty influence. It can also help them to understand the structures of authority they have internalized.

Finally, based on the work of detachment and reflection, a further question, Sennett says, can be asked: "Is the authority legitimate?" The point of collaborative learning, in this regard, is not to reject the authority of the faculty out of hand. Such rejection, in fact, does not lead to autonomy but can lead instead to withdrawal from authority into individual isolation and cynicism. Or it may lead students to substitute idealized versions of authority for the real forms of power that dominate their lives, as sometimes occurs in peer tutoring when tutees rehabilitate the authority of the faculty by transferring it to the tutor, thus establishing a new relationship of dependence.

These sequences of events need not necessarily occur, however. Another possibility, as Sennett suggests of crises of authority in general and we see as one of the educational goals of peer tutoring, is that once students have removed themselves from the official structures, they can then reengage the forms of authority in their lives by demystifying the authority of knowledge and its institutions.

It is this reentrance that offers the most dramatic argument for peer tutoring based on the ideology of collaborative learning. It is not that writing center-based peer tutoring works better than curriculum-based programs and their implied gen/tran ideology. Our argument is that it does a different kind of work. Curriculum-based programs, in our view, suppress the crisis of authority precipitated when students work together, domesticate it, and channel the social forces released by collaboration into the established structures of teaching and learning. Peer tutoring based on collaborative learning, by contrast, provides students with a form of social organization to negotiate the crisis successfully and reenter the official structures of authority as active agents rather than as passive objects of transmission. The power of the faculty and transmitted knowledge is still there, embedded in the institutions of higher education. What students can gain is the ability to reinterpret that power by defining the authority of knowledge as a relationship among people —not a hierarchical structure of generation and transmission. When peer tutoring works (and we are the first to admit that the complex schema we have outlined frequently short circuits), it does more than help students learn. The experience of co-learning changes students and helps them to see that the power ascribed to the faculty depends on the students' own sense of powerlessness and their need for omnipotent authority.

The benefits of peer tutoring can be considerable. Once faculty lose the omnipotence ascribed to them, they become more interesting and useful to students. The faculty's struggle to generate and authorize knowledge through conversation with their peers becomes more accessible to students, divested of the mystery that surrounds the scholar on the cutting edge. And by reinterpreting the authority of the faculty, students learn to recognize their own powers as learners and to invest authority in each other. And what this leads to is not so much a better delivery system but a student culture that takes learning and intellectual activity seriously.

Works Cited

Bruffee, Kenneth A. "The Brooklyn Plan: Attaining Intellectual Growth Through Peer Group Tutoring." *Liberal Education* (1978): 447-468.

____. "Collaborative Learning and the 'Conversation of Mankind.'" *College English* 46 (1984): 635-52.

Haring-Smith, Tori. *A Guide to Writing Programs, Writing Centers, Peer Tutoring, Writing Across the Curriculum.* Glenview: Scott Foresman, 1984.

Kail, Harvey. "Collaborative Learning in Context: The Problem with Peer Tutoring." *College English* 45 (1983): 35-40.

Maxwell, Martha. *Improving Student Learning Skills.* San Francisco: Jossey-Bass, 1979.

Sennett, Richard. *Authority.* New York: Knopf, 1980.

Trimbur, John. "Collaborative Learning and Teaching Writing." *Perspectives on Research and Scholarship in Composition.* Eds. Ben W. McClelland and Timothy R. Donovan. New York: MLA, 1985. 87-109.

"Whispers of Coming and Going": Lessons From Fannie

by Anne DiPardo

As a man with cut hair, he did not identify the rhythm of three strands, the whispers of coming and going, of twisting and tying and blending, of catching and of letting go, of braiding.

—Michael Dorris, *A Yellow Raft in Blue Water*

We all negotiate among multiple identities, moving between public and private selves, living in a present shadowed by the past, encountering periods in which time and circumstance converge to realign or even restructure our images of who we are. As increasing numbers of non-Anglo students pass through the doors of our writing centers, such knowledge of our own shape-shifting can help us begin—if *only* begin—to understand the social and linguistic challenges which inform their struggles with writing. When moved to talk about the complexities of their new situation, they so often describe a more radically chameleonic process, of living in non-contiguous worlds, of navigating between competing identities, competing loyalties. "It's like I have two cultures in me," one such student remarked to me recently, "but I can't choose." Choice becomes a moot point as boundaries blur, as formerly distinct selves become organically enmeshed, indistinguishable threads in a dynamic whole (Bakhtin 275; Cintron 24; Fischer 196).

Often placed on the front lines of efforts to provide respectful, insightful attention to these students' diverse struggles with academic discourse, writing tutors likewise occupy multiple roles, remaining learners even while emerging as teachers, perennially searching for a suitable social stance (Hawkins)—a stance existing somewhere along a continuum of detached toughness and warm empathy, and, which like all things ideal, can only be approximated, never definitively located. Even the strictly linguistic dimension of their task is rendered problematic by the continuing paucity of research on the writing of non-mainstream students (see Valdés; "Identifying Priorities"; "Language Issues")—a knowledge gap which likewise complicates our own efforts to provide effective tutor training and support. Over a decade has passed since Mina Shaughnessy eloquently advised basic writing teachers to become students, to consider what Glynda Hull and Mike Rose ("Rethinking,"

Reprinted from *The Writing Center Journal* 12.2 (1992): 125-44. Used by permission.

"Wooden Shack") have more recently called the "logic and history" of literacy events that seem at first glance inscrutable and strange. In this age of burgeoning diversity, we're still trying to meet that challenge, still struggling to encourage our tutors to appreciate its rich contours, to discover its hidden rigors, to wrestle with its endless vicissitudes.

This story is drawn from a semester-long study of a basic writing tutorial program at a west-coast university—a study which attempted to locate these tutor-led small groups within the larger contexts of a writing program and campus struggling to meet the instructional needs of non-Anglo students (see DiPardo, "Passport"). It is about one tutor and one student, both ethnic minorities at this overwhelmingly white, middle-class campus, both caught up in elusive dreams and uncertain beginnings. I tell their story not because it is either unusual or typical, but because it seems so richly revealing of the larger themes I noted again and again during my months of data collection—as unresolved tensions tugged continually at a fabric of institutional good intentions, and as tutors and students struggled, with ostensible good will and inexorable frustration, to make vital connection. I tell this story because I believe it has implications for all of us trying to be worthy students of our students, to make sense of our own responses to diversity, and to offer effective support to beginning educators entrusted to our mentorship.

"It, Like, Ruins Your Mind": Fannie's Educational History

Fannie was Navajo, and her dream was to one day teach in the reservation boarding schools she'd once so despised, to offer some of the intellectual, emotional, and linguistic support so sorely lacking in her own educational history. As a kindergartner, she had been sent to a school so far from her home that she could only visit family on weekends. Navajo was the only language spoken in her house, but at school all the teachers were Anglo, and only English was allowed. Fannie recalled that students had been punished for speaking their native language—adding with a wry smile that they'd spoken Navajo anyway, when the teachers weren't around. The elementary school curriculum had emphasized domestic skills—cooking, sewing, and especially, personal hygiene. "Boarding school taught me to be a housemaid," Fannie observed in one of her essays, "I was hardly taught how to read and write." All her literacy instruction had been in English, and she'd never become literate in Navajo. Raised in a culture that valued peer collaboration (cf. Philips 391-3), Fannie had long ago grasped that Anglo classrooms were places where teachers assume center stage, where the students are expected to perform individually: "No," her grade-school teachers had said when Fannie turned to classmates for help, "I want to hear *only* from *you*."

Estranged from her family and deeply unhappy, during fifth grade Fannie had stayed for a time with an aunt and attended a nearby public school. The experience there was much better, she recalled, but there soon followed a series of personal and educational disruptions as she moved among various relatives' homes and repeatedly switched schools. By the time she began high school, Fannie was wondering if the many friends and family members who'd dropped out had perhaps made the wiser choice. By her sophomore year, her grades had sunken "from A's and B's to D's and F's," and she was "hanging out with the wrong crowd." By mid-year, the school wrote her parents a letter indicating that she had stopped coming to class. When her family drove up to get her, it was generally assumed that Fannie's educational career was over.

Against all odds, Fannie finished high school after all. At her maternal grandmother's insistence, arrangements were made for Fannie to live with an aunt who had moved to a faraway west-coast town where the educational system was said to be much stronger. Her aunt's community was almost entirely Anglo, however, and Fannie was initially self-conscious about her English: "I had an accent really bad," she recalled, "I just couldn't communicate." But gradually, although homesick and sorely underprepared, she found that she was holding her own. Eventually, lured by the efforts of affirmative action recruiters, she took the unexpected step of enrolling in the nearby university. "I never thought I would ever graduate from high school," Fannie wrote in one of her essays, adding proudly that "I'm now on my second semester in college as a freshman." Her grandmother had died before witnessing either event, but Fannie spoke often of how pleased she would have been.[1]

Fannie was one of a handful of Native Americans on the campus, and the only Navajo. As a second-semester first-year student, she was still struggling to find her way both academically and socially, still working to overcome the scars of her troubled educational history. As she explained after listening to an audiotape of a tutorial session, chief among these was a lingering reluctance to speak up in English, particularly in group settings:

> Fannie: When, when, I'm talking...I'm shy. Because I always think I always say something not right, with my English, you know. (Pauses, then speaks very softly.) It's hard, though. Like with my friends, I do that too. Because I'll be quiet— they'll say, "Fannie, you're quiet." Or if I meet someone, I, I don't do it, let them do it, I let that person do the talking.
>
> A.D.: Do you wish you were more talkative?
>
> Fannie: I wish! Well I am, when I go home. But when I come here, you know I always think, English is my second language and I don't know that much, you know.
>
> A.D.: So back home you're not a shy person?
>
> Fannie: (laughing uproariously) No! (continues laughing).

I had a chance to glimpse Fannie's more audacious side later that semester, when she served as a campus tour guide to a group of students visiting from a distant Navajo high school. She was uncharacteristically feisty and

---

[1] "Fannie" was the actual name of this student's maternal grandmother. We decided to use it as her pseudonym to honor this lasting influence.

vocal that week, a change strikingly evident on the tutorial audiotapes. Indeed, when I played back one of that week's sessions in a final interview, Fannie didn't recognize her own voice: "Who's that talking?" she asked at first. But even as she recalled her temporary elation, she described as well her gradual sense of loss:

> Sometimes I just feel so happy when someone's here, you know, I feel happy? I just get that way. And then (pauses, begins to speak very softly), and then it just wears off. And then they're leaving—I think, oh, they're leaving, you know.

While Fannie described their week together as "a great experience," she was disturbed to find that even among themselves, the Navajo students were speaking English: "That bothered me a lot," she admitted, surmising that "they're like embarrassed...to speak Navajo, because back home, speaking Navajo fluently all the time, that's like lower class." "If you don't know the language," Fannie wrote in one of her essays, "then you don't know who you are....It's your identity...the language is very important." In striking contrast to these students who refused to learn the tribal language, Fannie's grandparents had never learned to speak English: "They were really into their culture, and tradition, and all of that," she explained, "but now we're not that way anymore, hardly, and it's like we're losing it, you know." Fannie hoped to attend a program at Navajo Community College where she could learn to read and write her native language, knowledge she could then pass on to her own students.

Fannie pointed to the high drop-out rate among young Navajos as the primary reason for her people's poverty, and spoke often of the need to encourage students to finish high school and go on to college. And yet, worried as she was about the growing loss of native language and tradition, Fannie also expressed concerns about the Anglicizing effects of schooling. Education is essential, she explained, but young Navajos must also understand its dangers:

> I mean like, sometimes if you get really educated, we don't really want that. Because then, it like ruins your mind, and you use it, to like betray your people, too....That's what's happening a lot now.

By her own example, Fannie hoped to one day show her students that it is possible to be both bilingual and bicultural, that one can benefit from exposure to mainstream ways without surrendering one's own identity:

> If you know the white culture over here, and then you know your own culture, you can make a good living with that...when I go home, you know, I know Navajo, and I know English too. They say you can get a good job with that.

Back home, Fannie's extended family was watching her progress with warm pride, happily anticipating the day when she would return to the reservation to teach. When Fannie went back for a visit over spring break, she was surprised to find that they'd already built her a house: "They sure give me a lot of attention, that's for sure," she remarked with a smile. Many hadn't seen Fannie for some time, and they were struck by the change:

> Everybody still, kind of picture me, still, um, the girl from the past. The one who quit school—and they didn't think of me going to college at all. And they were surprised, they were really surprised. And they were like proud of me too... 'cause none of their family is going to college.

One delighted aunt, however, was the mother of a son who was also attending a west-coast college:

> She says, "I'm so happy! I can't wait to tell him, that you're going to college too! You stick in there, Fannie, now don't goof!" I'm like, "I'll try not to!"

"I Always Write Bad Essays": Fannie's Struggles With Writing

On the first day of class, Fannie's basic writing teacher handed out a questionnaire that probed students' perceptions of their strengths and weaknesses as writers. In response to the question, "What do you think is good about your writing?" Fannie wrote, "I still don't know what is good about my writing"; in response to "What do you think is bad about your writing?" she responded, "everything."

Fannie acknowledged that her early literacy education had been neither respectful of her heritage nor sensitive to the kinds of challenges she would face in the educational mainstream. She explained in an interview that her first instruction in essay writing had come at the eleventh hour, during her senior year of high school: "I never got the technique, I guess, of writing good essays," she explained, "I always write bad essays." While she named her "sentence structure, grammar, and punctuation" as significant weaknesses, she also adds that "I have a lot to say, but I can't put it on paper... it's like I can't find the vocabulary." Fannie described this enduring block in an in-class essay she wrote during the first week of class:

> From my experience in writing essays were not the greatest. There were times my mind would be blank on thinking what I should write about.
>
> In high school, I learned how to write an essay during my senior year. I learned a lot from my teacher but there was still something missing about my essays. I knew I was still having problems with my essay organization.
>
> Now, I'm attending a university and having the same problems in writing essays. The university put me in basic writing, which is for students who did not pass the placement test. Of course, I did not pass it. Taking basic writing has helped me a lot on writing essays. There were times I had problems on what to write about.

There was one essay I had problems in writing because I could not express my feelings on a paper. My topic was on Mixed Emotions. I knew how I felt in my mind but I could not find the words for expressing my emotions.

Writing essays from my mind on to the paper is difficult for me. From this experience, I need to learn to write what I think on to a paper and expand my essays.

"Yes," her instructor wrote at the bottom of the page, "even within this essay—which is good—you need to provide specific detail, not just general statements." But what did Fannie's teacher find "good" about this essay—or was this opening praise only intended to soften the criticism that followed? Fannie had noted in an interview that she panicked when asked to produce something within 45 minutes: "I just write anything," she'd observed, "but your mind goes blank, too." Still, while this assignment may not have been the most appropriate way to assess the ability of a student like Fannie, both she and her instructor felt it reflected her essential weakness—that is, an inability to develop her ideas in adequate detail.

At the end of the semester, her basic writing teacher confided that Fannie had just barely passed the course, and would no doubt face a considerable struggle in first-year composition. Although Fannie also worried about the next semester's challenge, she felt that her basic writing course had provided valuable opportunities. "I improved a lot," she said in a final interview, "I think I did—I know I did. 'Cause now I can know what I'm trying to say, and in an afternoon, get down to that topic." One of her later essays, entitled "Home," bears witness to Fannie's assertion:

The day is starting out a good day. The air smells fresh as if it just rained. The sky is full with clouds, forming to rain. From the triangle mountain, the land has such a great view. Below I see hills overlapping and I see six houses few feet from each other. One of them I live in. I can also see other houses miles apart.

It is so peaceful and beautiful. I can hear birds perching and dogs barking echos from long distance. I can not tell from which direction. Towards north I see eight horses grazing and towards east I hear sheep crying for their young ones. There are so many things going on at the same time.

It is beginning to get dark and breezy. It is about to rain. Small drops of rain are falling. It feels good, relieving the heat. The rain is increasing and thundering at the same time. Now I am soaked, I have the chills. The clouds is moving on and clearing the sky. It is close to late afternoon. The sun is shining and drying me off. The view of the land is more beautiful and looks greener. Like a refreshment.

Across from the mountain I am sitting is a mountain but then a plateau that stretches with no ending. From the side looks like a mountain but it is a long plateau. There are stores and more houses on top of the plateau.

My clothes are now dry and it is getting late. I hear my sister and my brother calling me that dinner is ready. It was beautiful day. I miss home.

"Good description," her instructor wrote on this essay, "I can really 'see' this scene." But meanwhile, she remained concerned about Fannie's lack of so-phistication: "Try to use longer, more complex sentences," she added, "avoid short, choppy ones." Overwhelmed by the demands of composing and lacking strategies for working on this perceived weakness, Fannie took little away from such feedback aside from the impression that her writing remained inadequate.

Although Fannie was making important strides, she needed lots of patient, insightful support if she were to overcome her lack of experience with writing and formidable block. Only beginning to feel a bit more confident in writing about personal experience, she anticipated a struggle with the expository assignments that awaited her:

She's having us write from our experience. It'll be different if it's like in English 101, you know how the teacher tells you to write like this and that, and I find that one very hard, cause I see my other friends' papers and it's hard. I don't know if I can handle that class.

Fannie was trying to forge a sense of connection to class assignments—she wrote, for instance, about her Native American heritage, her dream of becoming a teacher, and about how her cultural background had shaped her concern for the environment. But meanwhile, as her instructor assessed Fannie's progress in an end-of-term evaluation, the focus returned to lingering weaknesses: "needs to expand ideas w/examples/description/explanation," the comments read, not specifying how or why or to whom. Somehow, Fannie had to fill in the gaps in her teacher's advice—and for the more individ-ualized support she so sorely needed, she looked to the tutorials.

"Are You Learnin' Anything From Me?": The Tutorials

Morgan, Fannie's African American tutor, would soon be student teaching in a local high school, and she approached her work with basic writers as a trial run, a valuable opportunity to practice the various instructional strategies she'd heard about in workshops and seminars. Having grown up in the predominantly Anglo, middle-class community that surrounded the campus, Morgan met the criticisms of more politically involved ethnic students with dogged insistence: "I'm first and foremost a member of the *human* race," she often said, going on to describe her firm determination to work with students of all ethnicities, to help them see that success in the mainstream need not be regarded as cultural betrayal. During the term that I followed her—her second semester of tutoring and the first time she'd worked with non-Anglo stu-dents—this enthusiasm would be sorely tested, this ambition tempered by encounters with unforeseen obstacles.

Morgan's work with Fannie was a case in point. Although she had initially welcomed the challenge of drawing Fannie out, of helping this shy young woman overcome her apparent lack of self-confidence, by semester's end Morgan's initial compassion had been nearly overwhelmed by a sense of frustration. In an end-of-term interview, she confessed that one impression remained uppermost: "I just remember her sitting there," Morgan recalled, "and talking to her, and it's like, 'well I don't know, I don't know'...Fannie just has so many doubts, and she's such a hesitant person, she's so withdrawn, and mellow, and quiet....A lot of times, she'd just say, 'well I don't know what I'm supposed to write....Well I don't like this, I don't like my writing.'"

Although Fannie seldom had much to say, her words were often rich in untapped meaning. Early in the term, for instance, when Morgan asked why she was in college, Fannie searched unsuccessfully for words that would convey her strong but somewhat conflicted feelings:

Fannie: Well...(long pause)...it's hard...

Morgan: You wanna teach like, preschool? Well, as a person who wants to teach, what do you want outta your students?

Fannie: To get around in America you have to have education... (unclear).

Morgan: And what about if a student chose not to be educated— would that be ok?

Fannie: If that's what he wants...

At this point Morgan gave up and turned to the next student, missing the vital subtext—how Fannie's goal of becoming a teacher was enmeshed in her strong sense of connection to her people, how her belief that one needs an education "to get around" in the mainstream was tempered by insight into why some choose a different path. To understand Fannie's stance towards schooling, Morgan needed to grasp that she felt both this commitment *and* this ambivalence; but as was so often the case, Fannie's meager hints went unheeded.

A few weeks into the semester, Morgan labored one morning to move Fannie past her apparent block on a descriptive essay. Fannie said only that she was going to try to describe her grandmother, and Morgan began by asking a series of questions—about her grandmother's voice, her presence, her laugh, whatever came to Fannie's mind. Her questions greeted by long silences, Morgan admitted her gathering frustration: "Are you learnin' anything from me?" she asked. Morgan's voice sounded cordial and even a bit playful, but she was clearly concerned that Fannie didn't seem to be meeting her halfway. In the weeks that followed, Morgan would repeatedly adjust her approach, continually searching for a way to break through, "to spark something," as she often put it.

The first change—to a tougher, more demanding stance—was clearly signalled as the group brainstormed ideas for their next essays. Instead of waiting for Fannie to jump into the discussion, Morgan called upon her: "Ok, your turn in the hot seat," she announced. When Fannie noted that her essay would be about her home in Arizona, Morgan demanded to know "why it would be of possible interest to us." The ensuing exchange shed little light on the subject:

Fannie: Because it's my home!

Morgan: That's not good enough...that's telling me nothing.

Fannie: I was raised there.

Morgan: What's so special about it?

Fannie: (exasperated sigh) I don't know what's so special about it...

Morgan: So why do you want to write about it, then?

Morgan's final question still unanswered, she eventually gave up and moved to another student. Again, a wealth of valuable information remained tacit; Morgan wouldn't learn for several weeks that Fannie had grown up on a reservation, and she'd understood nothing at all about her profound bond with this other world.

Two months into the semester, Morgan had an opportunity to attend the Conference on College Composition and Communication (CCCC), and it was there that some of her early training crystallized into a more definite plan of action, her early doubts subsumed by a new sense of authoritative expertise. Morgan thought a great deal about her work with Fannie as she attended numerous sessions on peer tutoring and a half-day workshop on collaborative learning. She returned to campus infused with a clear sense of direction: the solution, Morgan had concluded, was to assume an even more low-profile approach, speaking only to ask open-ended questions or to paraphrase Fannie's statements, steadfastly avoiding the temptation to fill silences with her own ideas and asides. As she anticipated her next encounter with Fannie, she couldn't wait to try out this more emphatic version of what had been called—in conference sessions and her earlier training—a "collaborative" or "non-directive" stance.

Still struggling to produce an already past-due essay on "values," Fannie arrived at their first post-CCCC tutorial hour with only preliminary ideas, and nothing in writing. Remembering the advice of Conference participants, Morgan began by trying to nudge her towards a focus, repeatedly denying that she knew more than Fannie about how to approach the piece:

Morgan: What would you say your basic theme is? And sometimes if you keep that in mind, then you can always, you know, keep that as a focus for what you're writing. And the reason I say that is 'cause when you say, "well living happily wasn't..."

Fannie: (pause)...Well, America was a beautiful country, well, but it isn't beautiful anymore.

Morgan: Um hm. Not as beautiful.

Fannie: So I should just say, America was a beautiful country?

Morgan: Yeah. But I dunno—what do you think your overall theme is, that you're saying?

Fannie: (long pause)...I'm really, I'm just talking about America.

Morgan: America? So America as...?

Fannie: (pause)...Um...(pause)

Morgan: Land of free, uh, land of natural resources? As, um, a place where there's a conflict, I mean, there, if you can narrow that, "America." What is it specifically, and think about what you've written, in the rest. Know what I mean?

Fannie: (pause)...The riches of America, or the country? I don't know...

Morgan: I think you do. I'm not saying there's any right answer, but I, I'm—for me, the reason I'm saying this, is I see this emerging as, you know, (pause) where you're really having a hard time with dealing with the exploitation that you see, of America, you know, you think that. And you're using two groups to really illustrate, specifically, how two different attitudes toward, um the richness and beauty of America, two different, um, ways people have to approach this land. Does that, does this make any sense? Or am I just putting words in your mouth? I don't want to do that. I mean that's what I see emerge in your paper. But I could be way off base.

Fannie: I think I know what you're trying to say. And I can kind of relate it at times to what I'm trying to say.

Morgan: You know, I mean, this is like the theme I'm picking up...(pause) I think you know, you've got some real, you know, environmental issues here. I think you're a closet environmentalist here. Which are real true, know what I mean. (pause) And when you talk about pollution, and waste, and um, those types of things. So I mean, if you're looking at a theme of your paper, what could you pick out, of something of your underlying theme.

Fannie: (pause)...The resources, I guess?

Morgan: Well I mean, I don't want you to say, I want you to say, don't say "I guess," is that what you're talking about?

Fannie: Yeah.

Morgan: "Yeah?" I mean, it's your paper.

Fannie: I know, I want to talk about the land...

Morgan: Ok. So you want to talk about the land, and the beauty of the land...

Fannie: Um hm.

Morgan: ...and then, um, and then also your topic for your, um, to spark your paper...what values, and morals, right? That's where you based off to write about America, and the land, you know. Maybe you can write some of these things down, as we're talking, as focussing things, you know. So you want to talk about the land, and then it's like, what do you want to say about the land?

What *did* Fannie "want to say about the land"? Whatever it was, one begins to wonder if it was perhaps lost in her tutor's inadvertent appropriation of these meanings—this despite Morgan's ostensible effort to simply elicit and reflect Fannie's thoughts. While Fannie may well have been struggling to articulate meanings which eluded clear expression in English, as Morgan worked to move her towards greater specificity, it became apparent that she was assuming the paper would express commonplace environmental concerns:

Fannie: I'll say, the country was, um, (pause), more like, I can't say perfect, I mean was, the tree was green, you know, I mean, um, it was clean. (long pause.) I can't find the words for it.

Morgan: In a natural state? Um, un-, polluted, um, untouched, um, let me think, tryin' to get a...

Fannie: I mean everybody, I mean the Indians too, they didn't wear that (pointing to Morgan's clothes), they only wore buffalo clothing, you know for their clothing, they didn't wear like...these, you know, cotton, and all that, they were so...

Morgan: Naturalistic.

Fannie: Yeah. "Naturalistic," I don't know if I'm gonna use that word...I wanna say, I wanna give a picture of the way the land was, before, you know what I'm, what I'm tryin' to say?

The Navajos' connection to the land is legendary—a spiritual nexus, many would maintain, that goes far beyond mainstream notions of what it means to be concerned about the environment. However, later in this session, Morgan observed that Fannie was writing about concerns that worry lots of people—citing recent publicity about the greenhouse effect, the hole in the ozone layer, and the growing interest in recycling. She then brought the session to a close by paraphrasing what she saw as the meat of the discussion and asking, "Is that something that you were tryin' to say, too?" Fannie replied, "Probably. I mean, I can't find the words for it, but you're finding the words for me." Morgan's rejoinder had been, "I'm just sparkin', I'm just sparkin' what you already have there, what you're sayin'. I mean I'm tryin' to tell you what I hear you sayin'."

Morgan laughed as, in an end-of-term interview, she listened again to Fannie's final comment: "I didn't *want* to find the words for her," she mused; "I wanted to show her how she could find 'em for herself." Still, she admitted, the directive impulse had been hard to resist: "I wanted to just give her ideas," Morgan observed, adding that although Fannie had some good things to say, "I wanted her to be able to articulate her ideas on a little higher level." Although it was obvious to Morgan that the ideas in Fannie's paper were of "deep-seated emotional concern," she also saw her as stuck in arid generalities: "'I don't know, it's just such a beautiful country,'" Morgan echoed as she reviewed the audiotape. While Morgan emphasized that she "didn't wanna write the paper for her," she allowed that "it's difficult—it's really hard to want to take the bull by the horns and say, 'don't you see it this way?'" On the one hand, Morgan noted that she'd often asked Fannie what she was getting out of a session, "'cause sometimes I'll think I'm getting through and I'm explaining something really good, and then they won't catch it"; on the other hand, Morgan emphasized again and again that she didn't want to "give away" her own thoughts.

Although Morgan often did an almost heroic job of waiting out Fannie's lingering silences and deflecting appeals to her authority, she never really surrendered control; somehow, the message always came across that Morgan knew more than Fannie about the ideas at hand, and that if she would, she could simply turn over pre-packaged understandings. While her frustration was certainly understandable, I often had the sense that Morgan was insufficiently curious about Fannie's thoughts—insufficiently curious about how Fannie's understandings might have differed from her own, about how they had been shaped by Fannie's background and cultural orientation, or about what she stood to learn from them.

When asked about Fannie's block, a weary Morgan wrote it off to her cultural background:

> You know, I would have to say it's cultural; I'd have to say it's her you know, Native American background and growing up on a reservation...maybe...she's more sensitive to male-female roles, and the female role being quiet.

On a number of occasions Morgan had speculated that Navajo women are taught to be subservient, a perception that contrasted rather strikingly with Fannie's assertion that she wasn't at all shy or quiet back home.[2] Hoping to challenge Morgan's accustomed view of Fannie as bashful and retiring, in a final interview I played back one of their sessions from the week that a group

---

[2] Morgan's assumption is also contradicted by published accounts of life among the Navajo, which from

of Navajo students were visiting the campus. Fannie was uncharacteristically vocal and even aggressive that morning, talking in a loud voice, repeatedly seizing and holding the floor:

Fannie: You know what my essay's on? Different environments. Um, I'm talking, I'm not gonna talk about my relationship between my brothers, it's so boring, so I'm just gonna talk about both being raised, like my youngest brother being raised on the reservation, and the other being raised over here, and they both have very different, um, um, (Morgan starts to say something, but Fannie cuts her off and continues) characteristics or somethin' like that. You know, like their personalities, you know.

Morgan: Um. That's good. (Morgan starts to say something more, but Fannie keeps going.)

Fannie: It's funny, I'm cutting, I was totally mean to my brother here. (Morgan laughs.) Because, I called, I said that he's a wimp, you know, and my brother, my little brother's being raised on the reservation, is like, is like taught to be a man, he's brave and all that.

Luis (a student in the group): That's being a man?!

Fannie: And...

Luis: That's not being a man, I don't find.

Fannie: (her voice raised) I'm sorry—but that's how I wrote, Ok?! That's your opinion, I mean, and it's...

Luis: I think a man is sensitive, caring, and lov—

Fannie: (cutting him off) No, no...

Luis: ...and able to express his feelings. I don't think that if you can go kill someone, that makes you a man.

Fannie: I mean...

Luis: That's just my opinion (gets up and walks away for a moment).

Fannie: (watching Luis wander off) Dickhead.

Morgan listened with a widening smile to the rest of this session, obviously

early on have emphasized the prestige and power of female members of the tribe. Gladys Reichard, an anthropologist who lived among the Navajos in the 1920s, reported that "the Navajo woman enjoys great economic and social prestige as the head of the house and clan and as the manager of economic affairs, and she is not excluded from religious ritual or from attaining political honors" (55). Navajo women often own substantial property, and children retain the surname of the matrilineal clan; the status accorded women is further reflected in the depictions of female deities in Navajo myths (Terrell 57; 255).

pleased with Fannie's sometimes combative manner and unflagging insistence that attention be directed back to her. "Ha! Fannie's *so* much more forceful," Morgan exclaimed, "And just more in control of what she wants, and what she needs." When asked what she thought might have accounted for this temporary change, Morgan sidestepped the influence of the visiting students:

> I would love to think that I made her feel safe that way. And that I really um, showed her that she had, you know, by my interactions with her, that she really had every right to be strong-willed and force- ful and have her opinions and you know, say what she felt that she needed to say, and that she didn't have to be quiet, you know. People always tell me that I influence people that way. You know? (laughs). "You've been hangin' around with Morgan too much!"

Hungry for feedback that she'd influenced Fannie in a positive way, Morgan grasped this possible evidence with obvious pleasure. Fannie was not a student who offered many positive signals, and it was perhaps essential to Morgan's professional self-esteem that she find them wherever she could. In this credit-taking there was, however, a larger irony: if only she'd been encouraged to push a little farther in her own thinking, perhaps she would have found herself assisting more often in such moments of blossoming.

Conclusion: Students as Teachers, Teachers as Students

When Morgan returned from the CCCC with a vision of "collaboration" that cast it as a set of techniques rather than a new way to think about teach- ing and learning, the insights of panelists and workshop leaders devolved into a fossilized creed, a shield against more fundamental concerns. Morgan had somehow missed the importance of continually adjusting her approach in the light of the understandings students make available, of allowing their feed- back to shape her reflections upon her own role. At semester's end, she still didn't know that Fannie was a non-native speaker of English; she didn't know the dimensions of Fannie's inexperience with academic writing, nor did she know the reasons behind Fannie's formidable block.

Even as Morgan labored to promote "collaborative" moments—making an ostensible effort to "talk less," to "sit back more," to enact an instructional mode that would seem more culturally appropriate—Fannie remembered a lifetime of classroom misadventure, and hung back, reluctant. Morgan needed to know something about this history, but she also needed to understand that much else was fluid and alive, that a revised sense of self was emerging from the dynamic interaction of Fannie's past and present. Emboldened by a few treasured days in the company of fellow Navajos, Fannie had momentarily stepped into a new stance, one that departed markedly from her accustomed behavior on reservation and campus alike; but if her confidence recalled an earlier self, her playful combativeness was, as Fannie observed in listening to the tape, a new and still-strange manifestation of something also oddly familiar, something left over from long ago.

Rather than frequent urgings to "talk less," perhaps what Morgan most needed was advice to *listen more*—for the clues students like Fannie would provide, for those moments when she might best shed her teacherly persona and become once again a learner. More than specific instructional strategies, Morgan needed the conceptual grounding that would allow her to understand that authentically collaborative learning is predicated upon fine-grained insight into individual students—of the nature of their Vygotskian "zones of proximal development," and, by association, of the sorts of instructional "scaffolding" most appropriate to their changing needs (Bruner; Langer and Applebee). So, too, did Morgan need to be encouraged toward the yet-elusive understanding that such learning is never unilateral, inevitably entailing a reciprocal influence, reciprocal advances in understanding (Dyson). As she struggled to come to terms with her own ethnic ambivalence, to defend herself against a vociferous chorus proclaiming her "not black enough," Morgan had reason to take heart in Fannie's dramatic and rather trying process of transition. Had she thought to ask, Morgan would no doubt have been fascinated by Fannie's descriptions of this other cultural and linguistic context, with its very different perspectives on education in particular and the world in general (John; Locust). Most of all, perhaps she would have been interested to know that Fannie was learning to inhabit both arenas, and in so doing enacting a negotiation of admirable complexity—a negotiation different in degree, perhaps, but certainly not in kind, from Morgan's own.

Having tutored only one semester previously, Morgan was understandably eager to abandon her lingering doubts about her effectiveness, eager for a surefooted sense that she was providing something worthwhile. Her idealism and good intentions were everywhere apparent—in her lengthy meditations on her work, in her eager enthusiasm at the CCCC, in her persistent efforts to try out new approaches, and in the reassurance she extended to me when I confessed that I'd be writing some fairly negative things about her vexed attempts to reach Fannie. Morgan had been offered relatively little by way of preparation and support: beyond a sprinkling of workshops and an occasional alliance with more experienced tutors, she was left largely on her own—alone with the substantial challenges and opportunities that students like Fannie presented, alone to deal with her frustration and occasional feelings of failure as best she could. Like all beginning educators, Morgan needed abundant support, instruction, and modeling if she were to learn to reflect critically upon her work, to question her assumptions about students like Fannie, to allow herself, even at this fledgling stage in her career, to become a reflective and therefore vulnerable practitioner. This is not to suggest that Morgan should have pried into hidden corners of Fannie's past, insisting that she reveal information about her background before she felt ready to do so; only that Morgan be respectfully curious, ever attentive to whatever clues Fannie might have been willing to offer, ever poised to revise old understandings in light of fresh evidence.

Those of us who work with linguistic minority students—and that's fast becoming us all—must appreciate the evolving dimensions of our task, realizing that we have to reach further than ever if we're to do our jobs well. Regardless of our crowded schedules and shrinking budgets, we must also think realistically about the sorts of guidance new tutors and teachers need if they are to confront these rigors effectively, guiding them towards practical strategies informed by understandings from theory and research, and offering compelling reminders of the need to monitor one's ethnocentric biases and faulty assumptions. Most of all, we must serve as models of reflective practice—perennially inquisitive and self-critical, even as we find occasion both to bless and curse the discovery that becoming students of students means becoming students of ourselves as well.

Works Cited

Applebee, Arthur and Judith Langer. "Reading and Writing Instruction: Toward a Theory of Teaching and Learning." *Review of Research in Education*, Vol. 13. Ed. E.Z. Rothkopf. Washington, DC: American Educational Research Association, 1986.

Bakhtin, Mikhail Mikhailovich. *The Dialogic Imagination: Four Essays by M.M. Bakhtin.* Ed. Michael Holquist, trans. Caryl Emerson and Michael Holquist. Austin: U of Texas P, 1981.

Bruner, Jerome. "The Role of Dialogue in Language Acquisition." *The Child's Conception of Language.* Ed. A. Sinclair. New York: Springer-Verlag, 1978.

Cintron, Ralph. "Reading and Writing Graffitti: A Reading." *The Quarterly Newsletter of the Laboratory of Comparative Human Cognition* 13 (1991): 21-24.

DiPardo, Anne. "Acquiring 'A Kind of Passport': The Teaching and Learning of Academic Discourse in Basic Writing Tutorials." Diss. UC Berkeley, 1991.

_____. *'A Kind of Passport': A Basic Writing Adjunct Program and the Challenge of Student Diversity.* Urbana: NCTE, forthcoming.

Dorris, Michael. *A Yellow Raft in Blue Water.* New York: Holt, 1987.

Dyson, Anne. "Weaving Possibilities: Rethinking Metaphors for Early Literacy Development." *The Reading Teacher* 44 (1990): 202-213.

Fischer, Michael. "Ethnicity and the Postmodern Arts of Memory.' *Writing Culture: The Poetics and Politics of Ethnography.* Eds. J. Clifford and G.E. Marcus. Berkeley: U of California P, 1986.

Hawkins, Thom. "Intimacy and Audience; The Relationship Between Revision and the Social Dimension of Peer Tutoring." *College English* 42 (1980): 64-8.

Hull, Glynda and Mike Rose. "Rethinking Remediation: Toward a Social-Cognitive Understanding of Problematic Reading and Writing." *Written Communication* 6 (1989): 139-154.

_____. "This Wooden Shack: The Logic of an Unconventional Reading." *College Composition and Communication* 41 (1990): 287-298.

John, Vera P. "Styles of Learning—Styles of Teaching: Reflections on the Education of Navajo Children." *Functions of Language in the Classroom.* Eds. Courtney B. Cazden and Vera P. John. 1972. Prospect Heights, IL: Waveland, 1985.

Locust, Carol. "Wounding the Spirit: Discrimination and Traditional American Indian Belief Systems." *Harvard Educational Review* 58 (1988): 315-30.

Philips, Susan U. "Participant Structures and Communicative Competence: Warm Springs Children in Community and Classroom." *Functions of Language in the Classroom.* Eds. Courtney B. Cazden and Vera P. John. 1972. Prospect Heights, IL: Waveland, 1985.

Reichard, Gladys. *Social Life of the Navajo Indians.* 1928. New York: AMS P, 1969.

Shaughnessy, Mina. "Diving In: An Introduction to Basic Writing." *College Composition and Communication* 27 (1976): 234-39.

Terrell, John Upton. *The Navajo: The Past and Present of a Great People.* 1970. New York: Perennial, 1972.

Valdés, Guadalupe. *Identifying Priorities in the Study of the Writing of Hispanic Background Students.* Grant. No. OERI-G-008690004. Washington, DC: Office of Educational Research and Improvement, 1989.

_____. "Language Issues in Writing: The Problem of Compartmentalization of Interest Areas Within CCCC." Paper presented at the Conference on College Composition and Communication. 21-23 March, 1991.

Vygotsky, Lev. *Mind in Society.* Cambridge: Harvard UP, 1978.

The Politics of Tutoring:
Feminism Within the Patriarchy

by Meg Woolbright

And why don't you write? Write! Writing is for you, you are for
you.... I know why you haven't written ... Because writing is at once
too high, too great for you, it's reserved for the great—that is for
"great men"; and it's "silly" ... Write, let no one hold you back, let
nothing stop you.... (246)

Hélène Cixous

Feminist rhetoric has been described as very different from the traditional,
patriarchal discourse of the academy. And although Hélène Cixous asserts in
"The Laugh of the Medusa" that "it is impossible to define a feminine practice of writing," (253) for doing so would encode it, stifle it, in a masculinist
framework, she does admit that we can "give form to its movement" (253) as
we approximate its "near and distant byways" (253). The characteristics of
this rhetoric have been variously described as its vibrancy, its personal voice,
its sensuousness and open-endedness, set in striking contrast to the linear,
objective, abstract, tightly argued prose of the academy. In "The Female and
Male Modes of Rhetoric," Thomas J. Farrell describes the differences this
way: "The female mode seems at times to obfuscate the boundary between
the self of the author and the subject of the discourse, as well as between the
self and the audience, whereas the male mode tends to accentuate such
boundaries" (910). A dichotomy similar to that between feminist and patriarchal rhetoric can be seen in much current scholarship on feminist
pedagogy.

In a recent volume of the *NWSA Journal*, Amy Shapiro describes a model
for the feminist classroom, one based not on the traditional paradigm of
knowledge as power, but on understanding as power. With this model, the
classroom becomes not an arena of confrontation and debate focused on
winners who "know" more than losers, but a place for conversation among
equals. Students come to realize that they have authority, that they can learn
from each other, and that through their conversations they can shape the
knowledge of the discourse. Of the teacher's role in this conversation, Shapiro
says that she "becomes a model in the sense that she must be the ultimate

Reprinted from *The Writing Center Journal* 13.1 (1992): 16-30. Used by permission.

learner. Her role is to integrate and assist the students in articulating the texts to themselves and each other" (79). The goal of this pedagogy is "to liberate the tortured voice" (Juncker 428) imprisoned in what Verena Andermatt calls the "phallogocentric system of representation" (39). Our students, says Cixous, need to write themselves.

The difficulty with these simple constructs is, of course, that in being simple constructs they are, albeit tempting, by and large misleading. In constructing these categories, our aim is to blur differences, and to focus on commonalities, on what makes up the essence or foundation of feminism and the patriarchy. Attempting to use these constructs to describe a dynamic interaction is tricky stuff. Those of us who consider ourselves academic feminists—whether we are male or female—do not choose feminism *or* the patriarchy, so much as we do at all times situate our feminism *within* a deeply-seated patriarchal academy. When our feminist values of community and equality find some space within the power of the patriarchy, the result is not an Aristotelian either/or but a complex web of conflict. Nancy Sommers has recently said that "these either/or ways of seeing exclude life . . . by pushing us to safe positions, to what is known. They are safe positions that exclude each other and don't allow for any ambiguity, uncertainty" (29). She suggests that we look at the juncture of either *and* or.

For those of us who teach writing, whether in the classroom or in a writing center, the conflicts that result at the boundary between feminist rhetoric and pedagogy and the patriarchal values of the academy are manifested in our conversations with student writers. These conversations are dynamic, and as such are fraught with uncertainty and ambiguity. As Nancy Schniedewind asserts, in these conversations students learn at least as much from our practices, what she calls the "hidden curriculum" (170) as they do from our theories. In order to determine if our "hidden curriculum" suggests feminist values, Schniedewind suggests five process goals against which we can measure our interactions with students. These are the development of an atmosphere of mutual respect, trust, and community; shared leadership; a cooperative structure; the integration of cognitive and affective learning; and action. Because I recognize that the constructs of "feminist" and "patriarchal" are more points on a continuum than discrete categories, I believe these process goals can provide a useful framework for describing the multiple conflicts that result when one writing center tutor attempts to teach what she believes to be feminist pedagogy within the patriarchal system of the academy. I think these criteria are useful for two reasons: First, they are indicative of what I believe characterizes tutoring at its best. Feminist rhetoric and pedagogy and the "idea of a writing center" (North) have never been very far apart in my mind. Both feminist and writing center commentators advocate teaching methods that are non-hierarchical, cooperative, interactive ventures between students and tutors talking about issues grounded in the students' own experience. They are, above all, conversations between equals in which knowledge is constructed, not transmitted. The second—and most important—reason that I use these criteria is that they are synonymous with what this tutor thinks she is doing when teaching feminist values to her students.

The conference I am considering is one of eight conferences between the same tutor and student that I observed and audiotaped over the course of a semester. My reason for doing this, and for conducting post-conference interviews with the tutor, was not only to learn more about what it is we do when we talk to students about their writing, but also to see if what tutors think they do when they tutor bears any resemblance to my interpretation. The participants in this conference were a junior English major and a graduate student who has just passed the qualifying exams for her doctorate. The student is working on a revision of a paper on Hemingway's short story, "The Doctor and the Doctor's Wife." The student's teacher, who was also the tutor's doctoral examiner, has read and commented on the draft and is giving the student the opportunity to rewrite it. The student, the tutor, and the teacher are all women; both the tutor and the teacher identify themselves as feminists. In a post-conference interview with me, the tutor speaks of many layers of conflict in her interactions with this student. These can be identified broadly as conflicts between feminist and patriarchal pedagogy and rhetoric. On the level of rhetoric, the tutor says that a large part of what she tries to do with undergraduates involves teaching feminist values. She says that she encourages students to think and write clearly, in their own voices. She admits, however, the conflict that doing so causes her: Although she labels herself a feminist and says she believes in teaching according to feminist practice, she thinks that the student's success—which she equates with giving the teacher the traditional thesis-and-support format she wants—is her prime responsibility. For this tutor, there is a conflict between teaching feminist rhetoric and ensuring the student's academic success. Negotiating between these two is no easy task for her.

On the level of feminist pedagogy, the issue is one of power. Negotiating the uses of power is even more complex than the issue of rhetoric. bell hooks says that as feminist teachers one of the issues we need to contend with is that of using power without dominating and coercing our students (52). This is just the issue this tutor is struggling with. She says that one of her problems in teaching and tutoring in the past has been that she didn't "know how to have authority." She says, "I didn't know how to have control. I felt powerless." When she was able to convince herself that she had some authority, she says, "I felt better because then there wasn't any resistance from the students." She overcame these feelings of powerlessness not by confronting them, but by ignoring them.

These two levels of conflict are very real for this tutor: "I try to find out where the student is, and what they want. I ask, 'What do you like about it [the paper]?' I'm afraid however, that a lot of times I take over. If I see something that's disorganized or lacks connection, I want to do that for students. I pick out the problems. I guide it. The more problems I see, the more there's the danger of my taking over." The power of the patriarchy, the power of what the tutor perceives to be academic success, coupled with her tendency to subvert conflict, overwhelms her goals of feminist practice. As she tries to negotiate between the two, she chooses an uneasy alliance: In teaching the student what she considers to be the "correct" interpretation in the "correct" thesis-and-support format, her methodology is clearly that of the patriarchy; the interpretation, however, is a feminist reading of the text.

The result for the student is little more than confusion. Her situation in this patriarchal system results not in the liberation of an imprisoned voice, but in deafening silence and alienation. This student, far from learning to "write herself," learns instead just how far her self is from the discourse of the academy. Instead of seeing herself in relation to others, she is hurled headlong into the realization of her otherness. Toril Moi claims that no matter what it is we think or say we do, in our practices we find our politics (xiii). This is certainly true in this instance as the following excerpt illustrates.

Note on the text:

S: Student

T: Tutor

. . . :   Words omitted

. . . . :   More than one line of text omitted

< > :   Other person speaks but without taking a turn

S: Did you pass?

T: Yes, thank you very much.

S: Oh, congratulations!

T: You've been sending me all sorts of support during my exams. . . . So now what are you doing?

S: Ok, we read the short story "The Doctor and the Doctor's Wife." Our duty was to either describe the doctor. . . or the wife. <Uhhuh> And I chose to describe the doctor.

T: [Reads the paper and the teacher's comments.]

S: Oh, but I wish you wouldn't go by her [the teacher's] notes. I wish you'd go by your own.

T: I like this [She reads:] "Now as far as eye teeth is concerned, I don't know whether this combo really exists in American lingo or whether it was just said out of exasperation." [Both laugh] I just love that little, your kind of expressing your own exasperation. Ok . . . um, you have a real clear attitude toward this doctor, right? <Right> And where is it that you say that all together? Where have you, is there a place, any place in the paper, where you kind of summarize your feelings about the doctor?

S: I think right at the beginning. [She reads:] "He's a typical bourgeoise. The doctor seems to be conniving, selfish, a penny pincher, demanding respect from others, but facing up to no one, not even his wife."

T: Good. . . .

S: As I was reading the story, I got the sense that they are trying to uh, prove manhood . . . I'm not sure. I didn't have that problem.

T: This is interesting because you're suggesting that one of the issues in this story sounds like it's a test of manhood. . . . Oh, that's interesting. It sounds to me like you've landed on something that Hemingway's really trying to use to say something.

S: I couldn't figure out what it was though. It's like a puzzle. I don't know.

T: That sounds to me like an interesting thesis, especially given Hemingway's general themes . . . I mean, you're probably right . . . Um, ok, do you think that you have in here any place . . . uh, the fact that what goes on between . . . Henry and Dick is a test of manhood?

S: I was going to do it . . . and I didn't do it because I thought, how am I going to prove that? Maybe I can just take a lot of quotes. I don't know.

T: Um, well, you already mentioned a couple of things. Um, how the doctor turns red . . . and how Dick walks out on him . . . Since you mentioned that, I think it's important to trust that it has something to do with this issue of manhood . . . Um, anything else that leads you to think that this is a test of manhood besides the confrontation between the two men? Um, up here you say his profession gives him status and makes him arrogant. . . . All right, I want to suggest to you that this is your thesis. . . . I want to hear some more things about why you think that this story is essentially a test of manhood. . . . So, if this is the thesis . . . what would your three main points be? . . . Ok, A) He's not intimidated and B) He knows what he's worth. What's the next thing you're going to do according to your thesis here?

S: [Silence]

T: What happens when I ask you these questions?

S: I'm trying to think of an answer—really hard!

T: Yeah, you go, "Ugh. I don't know." But . . . you know this stuff.

S: Yeah.

T: Somehow when I ask you questions, it freezes you, I think. Do you think that's possible?

S: I'm trying too hard for the answer or something. I don't know.

T: I think you have given me a whole lot of information around which I could organize your paper, given this thesis, and all I'm trying to help you do is see how you could take the information you have and all you need to do is trust your information enough to give your own explanation of how this point illustrates my main thesis. That's what I want you to be able to see.

S: I don't know. I'm really afraid of being wrong.

T: I agree. So at least in here, feel like, I can risk it. Now, how does this point support this thesis?

At the beginning of the conference, the two participants exhibit signs of the sense of respect, trust, and community that Schniedewind has identified as characteristic of feminist pedagogy. The student knows that the tutor has just taken her qualifying examinations and starts the conference by asking the tutor if she has passed. When she learns that the tutor has passed, she seems genuinely happy. The tutor in turn acknowledges that the student has given her "all sorts of support" as she was taking her exams. These two have obviously shared personal information, an indication that they are operating out of a sense of mutual respect and trust. The relationship between the tutor and student is contrasted with the student's relationship with her teacher, evident when she tells the tutor not to pay any attention to the teacher's comments on her draft. She says, "I wish you wouldn't go by her notes. I wish you'd go by your own."

In the first substantive comment on the student's paper, the tutor praises her for what she sees as a particularly unique interpretation of a line from the story. She says, "I just love . . . your expressing your own exasperation there." At this, they both laugh. The first few minutes then, read like a promise of Schniedewind's first four process goals. They not only signal the sense of mutual respect, trust, and community that Schniedewind recommends, but are an explicit example of both her and Cixous' call for a new affective order, one that will "change the overly rational premises of male-dominated social relations and institutions" and will "incorporate priorities appreciative of human needs and feeling" while at the same time strengthening intellectual abilities, "so long suppressed by those same sexist norms and institutions" (Schniedewind 176). Further, the tutor's praise of the student's particular reading of the line suggests that perhaps the product of the conference will be characterized by the personal voice called for by feminist rhetoric. From the opening exchange, it seems that the leadership will be shared and the decision-making participatory in constructing a cooperative structure.

However, this does not happen. If we look at the tutor's post-conference remarks about this praise for the student, we see that it is not what it seems. When asked about the meaning of this line, the tutor says, "She [the student] didn't understand this very well. She's not using her sources well. She's using all sorts of references but not in a clear way. I wanted her to talk about the significance of the quote." The tutor goes on to say that she thought "the student was exasperated" because she didn't understand what she was saying.

"Her intelligence," the tutor said, "is embedded in confusion." For Margo Adair and Sharon Howell, people dependent on those in power cannot afford to alienate them: "They end up thinking one thing and saying another" (221). Realizing the power of the student's teacher over both of them and uncomfortable with her own power over the student, this is what happens to this tutor. When the tutor says to the student, "I just love . . . your expressing your own exasperation here" what she is thinking is "Boy, are you confused!" In thinking one thing and saying another, the tutor is subverting the conflict she feels. This initial subversion changes to confrontation in the next exchange.

According to Amy Shapiro, one of the ways that a sense of community is formed is through the types of questions that the teacher/tutor asks. Community breaks down when individuals ask "preset questions, questions that they already know the answers to, questions designed not to build trust and share understandings, but to challenge and exhibit power" (70). This is what the tutor does here. After taking a few minutes to read the paper, she asks her first substantive question about the text: "Um, you have a real clear attitude about this doctor, right? <Right> And where is it that you say all that together? Where have you, is there a place, any place in the paper where you kind of summarize your feelings about the doctor?" The tutor does not ask the student to articulate her attitude, but instead asks a simple yes/no question of where in the paper the student has this statement. Since the tutor has just finished reading the text, we can assume that it is a question she already knows the answer to.

This movement from personal conversation to subversion to confrontation is evidence of the conflict the tutor feels. It is fine to talk to students as equals, to share information and to build the sense of trust and respect called for with feminist pedagogy as long as the topic is a personal one; when the topic shifts to the work on the student's paper, the pedagogy shifts to an uneasy subversion and finally to the confrontation of the patriarchy. In this example, instead of talking as they have been and simply shifting topics, a strategy which might result in exploring the student's attitude toward the doctor, the tutor sees it as her responsibility to locate the thesis. In doing this, she is subverting the possibility of shared leadership and community, and reinforcing the patriarchal notion that meaning not only resides in the text, but is, in this instance, already there.

Although the tutor may want to create a conversation between equals, and although she may want to establish an atmosphere of trust, her keen sense of responsibility to teach students to write in the "correct" format overwhelms her feminist values. The tutor holds on to the responsibility—and the power. The conflict that doing so causes is apparent in the tutor's explanation of this line. She says, "I was trying to get her to explain, to say more about it, so I could get her to put it together in one statement. But I was trying to get her to do it indirectly. I was afraid if I asked, 'What's the thesis?' she would shut up or back off."

When the student answers the tutor's question saying, "I think right in the beginning," and then goes on to read her summary description of the doctor, the tutor says, "Good," praising her for the correct answer. The atmosphere has changed from one of mutual respect, trust and community to one of hierarchy. The tutor is saying one thing and meaning another; she is asking leading questions with the student trying to guess the answers. This exchange puts shared leadership, participatory decision-making, and cooperative structure very much in doubt.

As the conference progresses, this dynamic is intensified. A few minutes later the student mentions that in reading the story, she had the sense that it might have something to do with "proving manhood." As soon as the student mentions that she was considering this theme as a possibility, a possibility that she rejected when writing her first draft, the tutor begins trying to convince her that this is the right way to interpret the story: "This is interesting because you're suggesting that one of the issues in this story sounds like it's a test of manhood....That's interesting. It sounds to me like you've landed on something that Hemingway's really trying to use to say something...." The topic has shifted here from what the tutor believes to be the "correct" format, to what she believes to be the "correct" interpretation. The student's uncertainty and alienation from this theme are not only evident when she says, "I'm not sure. I didn't have that problem" but in her response: "I couldn't figure out what it was though. It's like puzzle. I, I don't know." To this, the tutor responds, "That sounds to me like an interesting thesis, especially given Hemingway's general themes.... Um, ok, do you think that you have in here any place, the fact that what goes on between Henry and Dick is a test of manhood?" In her determination to teach this feminist interpretation, the tutor is, for the most part, leaving the student out of the interaction. Again, the form of the question—a yes/no location one instead of a probing one—reinforces the tutor's fervency and prevents any genuine sharing of power.

Instead of helping the student to interpret the story in a way she feels comfortable with, a way that has some connection to her own life and experience, the tutor increases the student's alienation by encouraging her to read the story through this lens. In doing this, she is not only *not* strengthening the student's intellectual abilities but she is preventing any sort of intellectual tension that could lead to cognitive growth. Further, instead of recognizing the power of the affective response the student has had to this reading, the tutor ignores it, telling her essentially that both her cognitive and affective reactions are wrong. In "Style as Politics: A Feminist Approach to the Teaching of Writing," Pamela Annas argues that we need to help our students overcome their alienation from language, their texts, their subjects, and themselves, and convince them that what they have to say is important and that they have an audience who will listen (361). This tutor, no matter how well meaning, is doing just the opposite.

In the student's response there is a conflict between her unwillingness to pursue this theme and her continuing trust and desire to please the tutor. It seems reasonable to expect that thoughts of a good grade also linger. She says, "I was going to do it...and I didn't do it because I thought, how am I going to prove that? Maybe I can just take a lot of quotes. I don't know." The tutor, firm in her resolve, suggests this theme once again: "Ok, well . . . I want to hear some more things about why you think that this story is essentially a test of manhood." Interestingly, the student has never said that she thinks the story is "essentially a test of manhood." This is what the tutor thinks, not the student. "Participatory decision-making" is taking a back seat to the "hierarchical authority" of the tutor. There is no evidence of shared leadership. The tutor is writing a paper based on what she considers to be the correct reading of the text and on what she thinks will get the student a good grade. She is not operating according to feminist pedagogy. In fact, she is simply further inculcating the masculinist values of the academy.

When asked about this exchange, the tutor comes to a realization. She says, "I just wrote the paper for her. I put it together. I didn't get her to put it together. And that's where things break down. She doesn't know what I'm talking about." The conflict between the tutor wanting to teach feminist values, wanting to encourage the student's own voice, wanting shared leadership and a cooperative goal structure—and wanting the student to succeed academically—remains in the realm of the tutor's subjectivity. The conflict is silenced. Because of this, it is not until the tutor hears herself on tape that she realizes what she is doing.

As the conference progresses, the movement away from an atmosphere of mutual trust and respect and toward one of hierarchy and domination becomes more evident both in the tutor's insistence on a thesis-support format for the paper and in the conversational patterns she uses to achieve that end. The tutor says: "So, if this [proving manhood] is the thesis . . . what would your three main points be?" She is teaching the student the traditional five-paragraph theme, with an emphasis on the objective, linear values of the patriarchy. The absence of shared leadership and participatory decision-making is evident when the tutor then answers her own question with two characteristics that will prove the thesis she is suggesting: "A) He's not intimidated; and B) He knows what he's worth." The tutor ends this exchange with a leading question, "All right, what's the next thing you're going to do according to your thesis here?" Twice more in the conference the tutor uses this conversational pattern of asking and answering her own questions. She says, "Do you have any place in here the fact that what goes on between Henry and Dick is a test of manhood?" When the student responds that, although she was thinking about that theme, she rejected it when she wrote the draft, the tutor answers the question for her. "Well," she says, "you already mentioned a couple of things. Um, how the doctor turns red . . . and how Dick walks out on him. . . ." Later on she says, "Ok, well, I want to hear some more things about why you think this story is essentially a test of manhood . . . Um, just off the top of your head, what are some of the other ways in which you think this is . . . a contest about manhood? You talk about Dick chewing the tobacco and spitting." Here she asks one question, does not wait for the student's response before rephrasing it and finally answers it herself. Later, she asks, "Um, anything else that leads you to think that this is . . . a test of manhood besides the confrontation between the two men? Um, up here you say . . . his profession gives him status and makes him arrogant."

In talking about this exchange, the tutor says, "I'm trying to show her how to develop it. I'm also doing all of the writing for her. The problem is I don't think she understands. What she's capable of isn't enough. I kept feeling that I wasn't reaching her, so I gave her more." What the tutor is doing is not authorizing this student's voice, but silencing it.

Faced with the conflict of trying to teach feminist values within a patriarchal system, and given the power that the patriarchy asserts over both her and the student, this tutor aligns herself with the patriarchy, the only concession to feminist practices being the interpretation of the text. In doing this, she assumes the role of the oppressor: Her strategies do, for the most part, undermine any hope of establishing a cooperative goal structure for the conference, a structure that "an individual can complete . . . successfully if, and only if, all others with whom she is linked do otherwise" (174). In taking control of the text and the conversation, the tutor is essentially writing the paper and talking to and for herself. There is little indication that the student will be able to complete successfully what the tutor intends for her. Toward the end of the conference, the tutor says, "You have given me a whole lot of information around which *I* could organize your paper, given this thesis." Given the interaction thus far, this seems like a safe bet: The tutor could indeed write this paper. The problem is that the student cannot.

In the last minutes of the conference, the tutor finally notices that she has been engaged in a monologue for the better part of an hour. She has been so determined to write this paper according to her interpretation that she has hardly noticed the student's inactivity. When she asks the student a direct question of how a particular idea links to this thesis, the student's response is a full minute of silence. At this, the tutor moves into meta-conferencing, asking the student, "What happens when I ask you these questions?" The student responds, "I try to think of an answer—really hard." This response is not surprising given that the tutor has spent a good deal of time and energy teaching her that there is indeed a right answer—one the tutor knows and the student needs to guess. When the tutor continues, asking her why she "freezes," the student admits that she is "really afraid of being wrong." One of the things this tutor has achieved is to reinforce this fear. Perhaps the most ironic comment is when she says to the student, "I agree, but at least in here, feel like I can risk it." This, after saying to the student, "Trust your informa- tion . . . of how this point illustrates *my* main thesis." I have to believe that the tutor is genuine in her wish that the student take risks. Unfortunately, the tutor is so dependent on the power of the academy that she cannot afford to risk alienation either for herself or for the student.

The writing conference seems the ideal location for Schniedewind's assertion that when individuals have "opportunities to come to know each other as people, speak honestly, take risks, and support each other . . . feminist values of community, communication, equality, and mutual nurturance are reinforced" (171). Throughout this conference, however, this does not happen.

These two have the opportunity to come to know each other as people through a conversation about writing. But they do not. The tutor is caught between the conflict of wanting to teach feminist values but ever-mindful of the power structure in which she is working, doing so with the "correct" interpretation and in the "correct" form for the paper. In trying to persuade the student of these things, she is reinforcing the positivistic, patriarchal value that there is a "correct" reading, that she knows what that reading is, and that her job as a tutor is to teach this reading to this student. There is no evidence of "equality" between these conversants; there is no "mutual nurturance." Further, there is little evidence of participatory decision-making, shared leadership, or a cooperative goal structure. Indeed, there is little evidence that the student is considered at all. The tutor is clearly in control. She talks more than the student does and sets the agenda for what gets talked about, when, and for how long. In taking control of both the text and the conversation, she is stifling both the student's cognitive and affective capabilities. In insisting on a reading that the student has said she feels alienated from, she is reinforcing the values of hierarchy and objectivity, while teaching the student to ignore her emotional responses. This is not only not good feminist pedagogy; this is not good tutoring.

The main reason that this interaction is neither good feminist practice nor good tutoring is that it is not honest. According to Schniedewind and others who write of feminist pedagogy, our interactions with students ought to be conversations with equals, based on the students' own experience, taking place in an atmosphere of trust, respect, nurturance. It seems to me that most of us who teach writing would agree with this. But none of this is possible if the tutor is not honest about the conflicts she feels.

So where does this leave us? It seems to me that the answer lies in Schniedewind's fifth criteria—action. About this, she says, "As long as we live in a sexist society, feminism inevitably implies taking action to transform institutions and values" (178). For Nancy Sommers, this action is "encouragement." She says that with "enough encouragement," our students will be "empowered to serve the academy and accommodate it, not to write in the persona of Everystudent, but rather to write essays that will change the academy" (30). I want to suggest that our action needs to be more than encouragement. For academic feminists, our action requires that the political circumstances in which we write and talk to students be named. In naming, we create a space in which we can talk openly about the conflicts between feminism and the patriarchy. We can consider how and why different rhetorics and pedagogies come to be privileged and the implications of this privileging for how we both construct ourselves and are constructed by the institutions in which we work. With this naming, our students can be given power and the responsibility to negotiate between feminism and the patriarchy, between writing vibrantly, sensuously, in their own voices and writing the tightly argued prose of the academy.

In the conference I have considered, the student is never given the power or the responsibility to make this choice. The tutor is so dependent on the patriarchy that she cannot afford to risk this naming. And because the conflicts are not named, they remain solely within the realm of the subjective, in this case, the tutor's head. The result for both the tutor and the student is an alienation from themselves. For the tutor, the result is that she thinks one thing and says another: Her interaction with this student is directly opposite from what she perceives it to be. Far from transforming this student's values or the values of a sexist academy, in not articulating the conflicts and the power struggles at work here, this tutor is simply reinforcing institutional norms of silence and obedience. The fact that she does this through the guise of a feminist interpretation of the story makes it all the more harmful.

For the student, the result is that at the end of the conference, she is far more alienated from language and from herself than when the conference began. Ira Shor says that this alienation is the number one problem in education today, manifesting itself in our students' passivity and apathy. Whether we realize it or not, when we are silent about the conflicts we feel, we reinforce this apathy. No matter what we say, when our interactions with students are characterized by subversion and dominance, we are encouraging passivity and reinforcing alienation.

Hélène Cixous writes of the conflict between a world in which only "great men" write and a world in which all other writing is deemed "silly." Her call to "write, let no one hold you back, let nothing stop you" locates itself in the *and* between these two worlds. In negotiating between them, we need, above all, to be honest. We need to admit to ourselves and to our students the conflicts we feel when attempting to espouse feminist values within a patriarchal system, to admit the power inequities we live with, and to admit further that the dichotomization between feminist and patriarchal practices is a false one. Only if we confront these conflicts, only if we present our students with the options and the power to choose, will we be truly honest and will feminism—and good tutoring—have any chance at all.

Works Cited

Adair, Margo and Sharon Howell. "The Subjective Side of Power." *Healing the Wounds: The Promise of Ecofeminism.* Ed. Judith Plant. New Society Publishers, 1989.

Andermatt, Verena. "Hélène Cixous and the Uncovery of a Feminine Language." *Women and Literature* 7.1 (1979): 38-47.

Annas, Pamela J. "Style as Politics: A Feminist Approach to the Teaching of Writing." *College English* 47 (1985): 360-71.

Cixous, Hélène. "The Laugh of the Medusa." *New French Feminisms.* Ed. Elaine Marks and Isabelle de Courtivron. New York: Shocken Books, 1980.

Farrell, Thomas J. "The Female and Male Modes of Rhetoric." *College English* 40 (1979): 922-27.

Freire, Paulo. *Pedagogy of the Oppressed.* New York: Continuum, 1988.

hooks, bell. "Toward a Revolutionary Feminist Pedagogy." *Talking Back: Thinking Feminist, Thinking Black.* Boston: South End Press, 1989.

Juncker, Clara. "Writing (with) Cixous." *College English* 50 (1988): 424-34.

Moi, Toril. *Sexual/Textual Politics: Feminist Literary Theory.* London: Methuen, 1985.

North, Stephen M. "The Idea of a Writing Center." *College English* 46 (1984): 433-46.

Rich, Adrienne. *On Lies, Secrets, & Silences.* New York: W. W. Norton & Co., 1979.

Rorty, Richard. *Philosophy and the Mirror of Nature.* Princeton: Princeton UP, 1979.

Schniedewind, Nancy. "Feminist Values: Guidelines for Teaching Method-ology in Women's Studies." *Freire for the Classroom.* Ed. Ira Shor. Portsmouth NH: Heinemann Educational Books, Inc., 1987.

Shapiro, Amy. "Creating a Conversation: Teaching All Women in the Feminist Classroom." *NWSA Journal* 3 (Winter 1991): 70-80.

Shor, Ira. "Educating the Educators: A Freirean Approach to the Crisis in Teacher Education." *Freire for the Classroom.* Ed. Ira Shor. Portsmouth NH: Heinemann Educational Books, Inc., 1987.

Sommers, Nancy. "Between the Drafts." *College Composition and Communication* 43 (1992): 23-31.

Bibliography

Adams, Ronald, Robert Child, Muriel Harris, and Kathleen Henriott. "Training Tutors for the Writing Lab: A Multidimensional Perspective." *The Writing Center Journal* 7.2 (1987): 3-19.

Ahlschwede, Margrethe. "No Breaks, No Time-Outs, and No Place to Hide: A Writing Lab Journal." *Writing on the Edge* 3.2 (1992): 21-40.

Allen, Chad, and Greg Lichtenberg. *Harvard University Writing Center Training Manual.* Cambridge: Harvard UP, 1986.

Allen, Nancy J. "Who Owns the Truth in the Writing Lab?" *The Writing Center Journal* 6.2 (1986): 3-9.

Amato, Katya. "Pluralism and Its Discontents: Tutor Training in a Multicultural University." *Writing Lab Newsletter* 17.4 (1992): 1-5.

Amigone, Grace Ritz. "Writing Lab Tutors: Hidden Messages That Matter." *The Writing Center Journal* 2.2 (1982): 24-29.

Anspach, Marlene. "A Paradoxical Approach to Training Tutors: A Theory of Failure." *Writing Lab Newsletter* 13.2 (1988): 14-16.

Arkin, Marian. "Using the Journal and Case Study to Train Writing Peer Tutors." *Teaching English in the Two-Year College* 9 (1983): 129-34.

Ashton-Jones, Evelyn. "Asking the Right Questions: A Heuristic for Tutors." *The Writing Center Journal* 9.1 (1988): 29-36.

Baker, Jeffrey S. "An Ethical Question about On-line Tutoring in the Writing Lab." *Writing Lab Newsletter* 18.5 (1994): 6-7.

Baker, Tracey. "Critical Thinking and the Writing Center: Possibilities." *The Writing Center Journal* 8.2 (1988): 37-42.

Beck, Paula, Thom Hawkins, and Marcia Silver. "Training and Using Peer Tutors." *College English* 40 (1978): 432-49.

Behm, Richard. "Ethical Issues in Peer Tutoring: A Defense of Collaborative Learning." *The Writing Center Journal* 10.1 (1989): 3-12.

Bell, Jim. "What Are We Talking About?: A Content Analysis of the *Writing Lab Newsletter*, April 1985 to October 1988." *Writing Lab Newsletter* 13.7 (1989): 1-5.

Besser, Pam. "Bridging the Gap: The Theoretically and Pedagogically Efficient Writing Center." *Writing Lab Newsletter* 16.3 (1991): 6-8.

Birdsall, Mary Pat. "Using Response Journals for Problem-Solving in the Writing Center." *Writing Lab Newsletter* 17.8 (1993): 12-16.

Bishop, Wendy. "Bringing Writers to the Center: Some Survey Results, Surmises, and Suggestions." *The Writing Center Journal* 10.2 (1990): 31-44.

____. "We're All Basic Writers: Tutors Talking About Writing Apprehension." *The Writing Center Journal* 9.2 (1989): 31-42.

____. "The Writing Center Through Writers' Eyes." *Writing Lab Newsletter* 14.3 (1989): 3-7.

____. "Writing from the Tips of Our Tongues: Writers, Tutors, and Talk." *The Writing Center Journal* 14.1 (1993): 30-43.

Bizzaro, Patrick, and Hope Toler. "The Effects of Writing Apprehension on the Teaching Behaviors of Writing Center Tutors." *The Writing Center Journal* 7.1 (1986): 37-44.

Bosley, Deborah, and Linda Droll. "Writing Center Directors Speak." *Writing Lab Newsletter* 15.8 (1991): 15-16.

Brainard, David. "Tutoring and Learning Disabilities." *Writing Lab Newsletter* 17.9 (1993): 15-16.

Branscomb, H. Eric. "Types of Conferences and the Composing Process." *The Writing Center Journal* 7.1 (1986): 27-35.

Brannon, Lil, Stephen North, Joyce Kinkead, and Jeanette Harris. "An Interview with the Founding Editors." *The Writing Center Journal* 11.1 (1990): 3-14.

Brinkley, Ellen. "The Writing Center Model at the Heart of Writing Instruction from Kindergarten to College." *Writing Lab Newsletter* 14.9 (1990): 1-4.

Broder, Peggy. "Writing Centers and Teacher Training." *WPA: Writing Program Administration* 13.3 (1990): 37-45.

Broglie, Mary. "From Teacher to Tutor: Making the Change." *Writing Lab Newsletter* 15.4 (1990): 1-3.

Brooks, Jeff. "Minimalist Tutoring: Making the Student Do All the Work." *Writing Lab Newsletter* 15.4 (1990): 13-15.

Brown, Lady Falls. "Stable Concept/Unstable Reality: Recreating the Writing Center." *Writing Lab Newsletter* 14.8 (1990): 6-8.

Bruffee, Kenneth A. "The Brooklyn Plan: Attaining Intellectual Growth Through Peer Group Tutoring." *Liberal Education* (1978): 447-68.

____. "Collaborative Learning and the Conversation of Mankind." *College English* 46 (1984): 635-52.

____. "Peer Tutors as Agents of Change." *Proceedings of the Seventh Annual National Conference on Peer Tutoring in Writing: 1990*. Ed. Stacy Nestleroth. University Park: Pennsylvania State UP, 1990. 1-6.

Carino, Peter. "Empowering a Writing Center: The Faculty Meets the Tutors." *Writing Lab Newsletter* 16.2 (1991): 1-5.

Carpenter, Kathy. "Tutor Training: A Director's Perspective." *Proceedings of the Midwest Writing Centers Association*. Oct. 1984. 186-91.

Chapman, David. "Evaluating the Writing Conference." *Writing Lab Newsletter* 14.5 (1990): 4-8.

Chase, Geoffrey W. "Integrating the Writing Center into the Curriculum." *Writing Lab Newsletter* 8.6 (1984): 4-5.

____. "Problem Solving in the Writing Center: From Theory to Practice." *The Writing Center Journal* 7.2 (1987): 29-35.

Clark, Beverly Lyon. *Talking About Writing: A Guide for Tutor and Teacher Conferences*. Ann Arbor: U of Michigan P, 1985.

Clark, Cheryl, and Phyllis A. Sherwood. "A Tutoring Dialogue: From Workshop to Session." *The Writing Center Journal* 1.2 (1981): 26-32.

Clark, Irene Lurkis. "Collaboration and Ethics in Writing Center Pedagogy." *The Writing Center Journal* 9.1 (1988): 3-12.

____. "Dialogue in the Lab Conference: Script Writing and the Training of Writing Lab Tutors." *The Writing Center Journal* 2.1 (1982): 21-33.

____. "Leading the Horse: The Writing Center and Required Visits." *The Writing Center Journal* 5.2/6.1 (1985): 31-34.

____. "Maintaining Chaos in the Writing Center: A Critical Perspective on Writing Center Dogma." *The Writing Center Journal* 11.1 (1990): 81-93.

____. "Portfolio Evaluation, Collaboration, and Writing Centers." *College Composition and Communication* 44 (1993): 515-24.

____. "Portfolio Grading and the Writing Center." *The Writing Center Journal* 13.2 (1993): 48-62.

____. "Preparing Future Composition Teachers in the Writing Center." *College Composition and Communication* 39 (1988): 347-50.

____. *Writing in the Center: Teaching in a Writing Center Setting*. Dubuque: Kendall Hunt, 1985.

Claywell, Gina. "Nonverbal Communication and Writing Lab Tutorial." *Writing Lab Newsletter* 18.7 (1994): 13-14.

Cobb, Loretta. "Addressing Professional Concerns." *Writing Lab Newsletter* 13.7 (1989): 11-12.

____. "Practical Techniques for Training Tutors to Overcome Defensive Blocks." *The Writing Center Journal* 3.1 (1982): 32-37.

Collins, Norma Decker. "The Role of a Writing Center in a Teacher Education Program." *Writing Lab Newsletter* 18.4 (1993): 6-7.

Connolly, Paul, and Teresa Vilardi, eds. *New Methods in College Writing Programs: Theories in Practice*. New York: MLA, 1986.

Coogan, Davis. "Towards a Rhetoric of On-line Tutoring." *Writing Lab Newsletter* 19.1 (1994): 3-5.

Cooper, Marilyn. "The Ecology of Writing." *College English* 48 (1986): 364-75.

Cosgrove, Cornelius. "Explaining and Justifying Writing Centers: An Example." *Writing Lab Newsletter* 17.8 (1993): 1-4.

Covington, David, Ann E. Brown, and Gary Blank. "An Alternative Approach to Writing Across the Curriculum: The Writing Assistance Program at North Carolina State's School of Engineering." *WPA: Writing Program Administration* 8.3 (1985): 15-24.

Crump, Eric. "Online Community: Writing Centers Join the Network World." *Writing Lab Newsletter* 17.2 (1992): 1-5.

Cullen, Roxanne. "Writing Centers as Centers of Connected Learning." *Writing Lab Newsletter* 16.6 (1992): 1-4.

Davis, Kevin. "Responding to Writers: A Multi-Variate Approach to Peer Interaction." *The Writing Center Journal* 10.2 (1990): 67-73.

Davis, Kevin, Nancy Hayward, Kathleen R. Hunter, and David L. Wallace. "The Function of Talk in the Writing Conference: A Study of Tutorial Conversation." *The Writing Center Journal* 9.1 (1988): 45-52.

DeCiccio, Albert C. "Literacy and Authority as Threats to Peer Tutoring." *Writing Lab Newsletter* 13.10 (1989): 11-13.

_____. "Moving the Boundary: Putting the Idea of a Writing Center to the Test." *Writing Lab Newsletter* 17.5 (1993): 1-4.

_____. "The Writing Center and Peer Tutoring: Some Observations." *Writing Lab Newsletter* 12.5 (1988): 3-6.

Devenish, Alan. "Decentering the Writing Center." *Writing Lab Newsletter* 18.1 (1993): 4-7.

_____. "Is Gentran Taking the Peer out of Peer Tutor?" *Writing Lab Newsletter* 11.6 (1987): 1-5.

Devet, Bonnie. "National Certification for a Writing Lab." *Writing Lab Newsletter* 17.2 (1992): 12-13.

Dinitz, Susan, and Diane Howe. "Writing Centers and Writing-Across-the-Curriculum: An Evolving Partnership?" *The Writing Center Journal* 10.1 (1989): 45-51.

Dornsife, Robert. "Establishing the Role of Audience in the Writing Center Tutorial." *Writing Lab Newsletter* 18.8 (1994): 1-2.

Downs, Virginia. "What Do English Teachers Want?" *The Writing Center Journal* 2.2 (1982): 30-32.

Droll, Belinda Wood. "Teacher Expectations: A Powerful Third Force in Tutoring Sessions." *Writing Lab Newsletter* 17.9 (1993): 1-5.

Dyer, Patricia M. "Business Communication Meets in the Writing Center: A Successful Four-Week Course." *Writing Lab Newsletter* 15.7 (1991): 4-6.

Eggers, Tilly. "Things Fall Apart: The Writing Center Will Hold." *The Writing Center Journal* 1.2 (1981): 33-40.

Elliott, M. A. "Writing Center Directors: Why Faculty Status Fits." *Writing Lab Newsletter* 14.7 (1990): 1-4.

Farrell, John Thomas. "Some of the Challenges to Writing Centers Posed by Graduate Students." *Writing Lab Newsletter* 18.6 (1994): 3-5.

Farrell, Pamela B. "Guest Artists Add Reverence for Writing." *Writing Lab Newsletter* 15.7 (1991): 7-8.

_____. *The High School Writing Center: Establishing and Maintaining One.* Urbana: NCTE, 1989.

_____. "Writer, Peer Tutor, and Computer: A Unique Relationship." *The Writing Center Journal* 8.1 (1987): 29-33.

Field-Pickering, Janet. "The Burden of Proof: Demonstrating the Effectiveness of a Computer Writing Center Program." *Writing Lab Newsletter* 18.2 (1993): 1-3.

Fishman, Judith. "The Tutor as Messenger." *The Writing Center Journal* 1.2 (1981): 7-12.

Fitzgerald, Sallyanne. "Success and Failures: Facilitating Cooperation across the Curriculum." *Writing Lab Newsletter* 13.1 (1988): 13-15.

Flynn, Thomas, and Mary King, eds. *Dynamics of the Writing Center: Social and Cognitive Interaction.* Urbana: NCTE, 1993.

Franke, Thomas L. "A Case for Professional Writing Tutors." *Teaching English in the Two-Year College* 9 (1983): 149-50.

Freed, Stacey. "Subjectivity in the Tutorial Session: How Far Can We Go?" *The Writing Center Journal* 10.1 (1989): 39-43.

Fulwiler, Toby. "Provocative Revision." *The Writing Center Journal* 12.2 (1992): 190-204.

Gadbow, Kate. "Teachers as Writing Center Tutors: Release from the Red Pen." *Writing Lab Newsletter* 14.1 (1989): 13-15.

Gajewski, Geoff. "The Tutor/Faculty Partnership: It's Required." *Writing Lab Newsletter* 15.10 (1991): 13-15.

Gehrmann, S. Kay, and James Upton. "Beyond Tutoring: Expanding the Definition and Services of the High School Writing Center." *Writing Lab Newsletter* 14.8 (1990): 4-5.

George, Claire. "Response to 'Writing Center Ethics.'" *Writing Lab Newsletter* 17.8 (1993): 7-8.

George, Diana. "Talking to the Boss: A Preface." *The Writing Center Journal* 9.1 (1988): 37-44.

____. "Who Teaches the Teacher? A Note on the Craft of Teaching College Composition." *College English* 51 (1989): 418-23.

George, Diana, and Nancy Grimm. "Expanded Roles/Expanded Responsibilities: The Changing Nature of Writing Centers Today." *The Writing Center Journal* 11.1 (1990): 59-66.

Glassman, Susan. "Training Peer Tutors Using Video." *The Writing Center Journal* 5.2/6.1 (1985): 40-45.

Goldsby, Jackie. *Peer Tutoring in Basic Writing: A Tutor's Journal.* Berkeley: U of California-Berkeley and Bay Area Writing Project, 1981.

Graham, Kathryn, Beverly Hayden, and Matthew Swinehart. "Writing Without Teachers, Writing With Tutors." *Writing Lab Newsletter* 18.7 (1994): 7-8.

Grimm, Nancy. "Contesting 'The Idea of a Writing Center': The Politics of Writing Center Research." *Writing Lab Newsletter* 17.1 (1992): 5-7.

Grinder, Kim. "Process and Processing in a Middle School Writing Lab." *Writing Lab Newsletter* 14.2 (1989): 11-12.

Haas, Teri. "The Unskilled Writer and the Formula Essay: Composing by the Rules." *The Writing Center Journal* 3.2 (1983): 12-21.

Haring-Smith, Tori. *A Guide to Writing Programs: Writing Centers, Peer Tutoring Programs, and Writing-Across-the-Curriculum.* Glenview: Scott, 1985.

Harris, Jeanette. "Expanding the Writing Center Audience." *WPA: Writing Program Administration* 6.3 (1983): 41-44.

____. "The Role of the Writing Center in Basic Writing." *English in Texas* 16.1 (1984): 20-23.

Harris, Jeanette, and Joyce Kinkead. "An Interview with the Founding Editors of *The Writing Center Journal.*" *The Writing Center Journal* 11.1 (1990): 3-14.

Harris, Muriel. "Collaboration Is Not Collaboration Is Not Collaboration: Writing Center Tutorials vs. Peer-Response Groups." *College Composition and Communication* 43 (1992): 369-83.

____. "A Grab-Bag of Diagnostic Techniques." *Teaching English in the Two-Year College* 9 (1983): 111-16.

____. "Growing Pains: The Coming of Age of Writing Centers." *The Writing Center Journal* 2.1 (1982): 1-8.

____. "The Ins and Outs of Conferencing." *The Writing Instructor* 6 (1987): 87-96.

____. "Peer Tutoring: How Tutors Learn." *Teaching English in the Two-Year College* 15 (1988): 28-33.

____. *Teaching One-to-One: The Writing Conference.* Urbana: NCTE, 1986.

____. "Theory and Reality: The Ideal Writing Center(s)." *The Writing Center Journal* 5.2/6.1 (1985): 4-9.

____. *Tutoring Writing: A Sourcebook for Writing Labs.* Glenview: Scott, 1982.

____. "Writing Labs: Why Bother?" *English Quarterly* 16.2 (1983): 6-13.

Harris, Muriel, and Tracey Baker, eds. *New Directions, New Connections.* Proceedings of the Writing Centers Association Fifth Annual Conference. West Lafayette: Dept. of English, Purdue University, 1983.

Harris, Muriel, and Tony Silva. "Tutoring ESL Students: Issues and Opinions." *College Composition and Communication* 44 (1993): 525-37.

Harris, Muriel, and Kathleen Blake Yancey. "Beyond Freshman Comp: Expanded Uses of the Writing Lab." *The Writing Center Journal* 1.1 (1980): 43-49.

Hashimoto, Irvin. "Writing Laboratory 'Image' or How Not to Write to Your Dean." *The Writing Center Journal* 3.1 (1982): 1-10.

Haviland, Carol Peterson. "Writing Centers and Writing-Across-the-Curriculum: An Important Connection." The *Writing Center Journal* 5.2/6.1 (1985): 25-30.

Hawkins, Thomas A. *Group Inquiry Techniques for Teaching Writing.* Urbana: ERIC/ NCTE, 1976.

____. "Intimacy and Audience: The Relationship Between Revision and the Social Dimension of Peer Tutoring." *College English* 42 (1980): 64-69.

____. "Training Peer Tutors in the Art of Teaching." *College English* 40 (1978): 440-49.

Hawkins, Thom, and Phyllis Brooks, eds. *New Directions for College Learning Assistance, No. 3: Improving Writing Skills.* San Francisco: Jossey-Bass, 1981.

Haynes-Burton, Cynthia. "'Hanging Your Alias on Their Scene': Writing Centers, Graffiti, and Style." *The Writing Center Journal* 14.2 (1994): 112-24.

____. "'Thirty-something' Students: Concerning Transitions in the Writing Center." *Writing Lab Newsletter* 18.8 (1994): 3-4.

Hayward, Malcolm. "Assessing Attitudes toward the Writing Center." *The Writing Center Journal* 3.2 (1983): 1-10.

Healy, Dave. "Specialists vs. Generalists: Managing the Writing Center-Learning Center Connection." *Writing Lab Newsletter* 15.9 (1991): 11-16.

____. "Tutorial Role Conflict in the Writing Center." *The Writing Center Journal* 11.2 (1991): 41-50.

____. "Varieties of Apathetic Experience." *Writing Lab Newsletter* 14.2 (1989): 5-8.

Hemmeter, Thomas. "The 'Smack of Difference': The Language of Writing Center Discourse." *The Writing Center Journal* 11.1 (1990): 35-48.

____. "Spreading the Good Word: The Peer-Tutoring Report and the Public Image of the Writing Center." *WPA: Writing Program Administration* 9.1-2 (1985): 41-50.

Hemmeter, Tom, and Carolyn Mee. "The Writing Center as Ethnographic Space." *Writing Lab Newsletter* 18.3 (1993): 4-5.

Herek, Jennifer, and Mark Niquette. "Ethics in the Writing Lab: Tutoring under the Honor Code." *Writing Lab Newsletter* 14.5 (1990): 12-15.

Hey, Phil. "Line Worker, Apprentice, Correspondent: Three Roles for Student Writers and Their Implications for Writing Management." *Proceedings of the Midwest Writing Centers Association.* Oct. 1984. 75-82.

Hey, Phil, and Cindy Nahrwold. "Tutors Aren't Trained—They're Educated: The Need for Composition Theory." *Writing Lab Newsletter* 18.7 (1994): 4-5.

Hobson, Eric H. "Coming in out of the Silence." *Writing Lab Newsletter* 17.6 (1993): 7-8.

____. "Maintaining Our Balance: Walking the Tightrope of Competing Epistemologies." *The Writing Center Journal* 17.2 (1992): 65-75.

Hoffman, Randi. "Working with ESL Students." *The Writing Center Journal* 3.1 (1982): 27-28.

Holbrook, Hilary Taylor. "Issues in the Writing Lab: An ERIC/RCS Report." *English Education* 20 (1988): 116-21. Rpt. in *The Writing Center Journal* 9.2 (1989): 67-72.

Hubbuch, Susan M. "Some Thoughts on Collaboration from a Veteran Tutor." *Writing Lab Newsletter* 16.1 (1991): 1-3, 8.

____. "A Tutor Needs to Know the Subject Matter to Help a Student with a Paper: ___Agree ___Disagree ___Not Sure." *The Writing Center Journal* 8.2 (1988): 23-30.

Hughes, Bradley T. "Reaching Across the Curriculum with a Writing Center." *Illinois English Bulletin* 74.1 (1986): 24-31.

Hylton, Jamie. "Evaluating the Writing Lab: How Do We Know That We Are Helping?" *Writing Lab Newsletter* 15.3 (1990): 5-7.

Hynds, Susan. "Perspectives on Perspectives in the Writing Center Conference." *Focuses* 2.2 (1989): 77-89.

Impson, Beth, et al. "Integrating WAC and Tutoring Services: Advantages to Faculty, Students, and Writing Center Staff." *Writing Lab Newsletter* 16.2 (1991): 6-8, 11.

Jackson, Alan. "Writing Centers: A Panorama to Teaching and the Profession." *Writing Lab Newsletter* 18.6 (1994): 1-2.

Jacobs, Suzanne, and Adele Karliner. "Helping Writers to Think: The Effect of Speech Roles in Individual Conferences on the Quality of Thought." *College English* 38 (1977): 345-57.

Jacoby, Jay. "Shall We Talk to Them in 'English': The Contributions of Sociolinguistics to Training Writing Center Personnel." *The Writing Center Journal* 4.1 (1983): 1-14.

____. "Training Writing Center Personnel to Work with International Students: The Least We Need to Know." *Writing Lab Newsletter* 10.2 (1985): 1-6.

____. "What a Peer Tutor Is Not." *Writing Lab Newsletter* 7.9 (1983): 5-7.

Janangelo, Joseph. "The Polarities of Context in the Writing Center Conference." *The Writing Center Journal* 8.2 (1988): 31-36.

Johanek, Cindy. "Learning Styles: Issues, Questions, and the Roles of the Writing Center Tutor." *Writing Lab Newsletter* 16.4-5 (1991-92): 10-14.

Johnston, Anne. "The Writing Tutorial as Ecology: A Case Study." *The Writing Center Journal* 9.2 (1989): 51-56.

Joyner, Michael A. "The Writing Center Conference and the Textuality of Power." *The Writing Center Journal* 12 (1991): 80-89.

Kail, Harvey. "Collaborative Learning in Context: The Problem with Peer Tutoring." *College English* 45 (1983): 594-99.

____. "Evaluating Our Own Peer Tutoring Programs: A Few Leading Questions." *Writing Lab Newsletter* 7.10 (1983): 2-4.

Kail, Harvey, and Ronda Dubay. "Texts for Tutors and Teachers." *The Writing Center Journal* 5.1 (1984): 14-29.

Kemp, Fred. "Getting Smart with Computers: Computer-Aided Heuristics for Student Writers." *The Writing Center Journal* 8.1 (1987): 3-10.

Kennedy, Barbara L. "Non-native Speakers in First-Year Composition with Native Speakers: How Can Writing Tutors Help?" *The Writing Center Journal* 13.2 (1993): 27-38.

Kiedaisch, Jean, and Sue Dinitz. "Look Back and Say 'So What': The Limitations of the Generalist Tutor." *The Writing Center Journal* 14.1 (1993): 63-72.

Kilborn, Judith. "Cultural Diversity in the Writing Center: Defining Ourselves and Our Challenges." *Writing Lab Newsletter* 19.1 (1994): 7-10.

Kinkead, Joyce. "Computer Conversations: E-Mail and Writing Instruction." *College Composition and Communication* 38 (1987) 337-41.

____. "The Electronic Writing Tutor." *Writing Lab Newsletter* 13.4 (1988): 4-5.

____. "Outreach: The Writing Center, the Campus, and the Community." *Writing Lab Newsletter* 10.3 (1985): 5-8.

Kinkead, Joyce A., and Jeanette G. Harris. *Writing Centers in Context: Twelve Case Studies*. Urbana: NCTE, 1993.

Klaczak, Jacqueline. "Peer Tutoring: A Holistic Approach." *Writing Lab Newsletter* 18.7 (1994): 15-16.

Kleimann, Susan, and G. Douglas Meyers. "Senior Citizens and Junior Writers: A Center for Exchange." *The Writing Center Journal* 2.1 (1982): 57-60.

Kucsma, Alexander. "The Silent Tutor: Using Patterns to Teach Writing." *Writing Lab Newsletter* 17.7 (1993): 4-5.

Lang, Frederick K. "A Substitute for Experience." *The Writing Center Journal* 7.1 (1986): 19-26.

Laque, Carol F., and Phyllis A. Sherwood. *A Laboratory Approach to Writing*. Urbana: NCTE, 1977.

Lassner, Phyllis. "Conferencing: The Psychodynamics of Teaching Contraries." *The Writing Center Journal* 4.2 (1984): 22-30.

Leahy, Richard. "Of Writing Centers, Centeredness, and Centrism." *The Writing Center Journal* 13.1 (1992): 43-52.

———. "On Being There: Reflections on Visits to Other Writing Centers." *Writing Lab Newsletter* 15.8 (1991): 1-5.

———. "Using Audiotapes for Evaluation and Collaborative Training." *Writing Lab Newsletter* 18.5 (1994): 1-3.

———. "What the College Writing Center Is—and Isn't." *College Teaching* 38 (1990): 43-48.

Leahy, Rick, and Roy Fox. "Seven Myth-Understandings about the Writing Center." *Writing Lab Newsletter* 14.1 (1989): 7-8.

Leeson, LeeAnn. "All of the Answers or Some of the Questions? Teacher as Learner in the Writing Center." *The Writing Center Journal* 2.2 (1982): 18-23.

Lichtenstein, Gary. "Ethics of Peer Tutoring." *The Writing Center Journal* 4.1 (1983): 29-34.

Livingston-Webber, Joan. "Limits on the Power of Naming." *WPA: Writing Program Administration* 14.3 (1991): 7-20.

Lochman, Daniel T. "A Dialogue of One: Orality and Literacy in the Writing Center." *The Writing Center Journal* 10.1 (1989): 19-29.

———. "Play and Games: Implications for the Writing Center." *The Writing Center Journal* 7.1 (1986): 11-18.

Lotto, Edward. "The Texts and Contexts of Writing." *The Writing Center Journal* 9.1 (1988): 13-20.

———. "The Writer's Subject is Sometimes a Fiction." *The Writing Center Journal* 5.2/6.1 (1985): 15-20.

Luchte, Jeanne. "Computer Programs in the Writing Center: A Bibliographical Essay." *The Writing Center Journal* 8.1 (1987): 11-20.

Luckett, Clinton. "Adapting a Conventional Writing Lab to the Berthoff Approach." *The Writing Center Journal* 5.2/6.1 (1985): 21-24.

Lyons, Greg. "Validating Cultural Differences in the Writing Center." *The Writing Center Journal* 12.2 (1992): 145-58.

MacLennan, Tom. "Martin Buber and a Collaborative Learning Ethos." *Writing Lab Newsletter* 14.6 (1990): 6-8, 13.

Maid, Barry, Sally Crisp, and Suzanne Norton. "On Gaining Insight into Ourselves as Writers and as Tutors: Our Use of the Myers-Briggs Type Indicator." *Writing Lab Newsletter* 13.10 (1989): 1-5.

Major, James S., and Jean S. Filetti. " 'Type'-writing: Helping Students Write with the Myers-Briggs Type Inventory." *Writing Lab Newsletter* 15.4 (1990): 4-7.

Marek, Margaret-Rose. "Right Brain Processing and Learning Disabilities: Conclusions Not to Reach in the Writing Center." *Writing Lab Newsletter* 16.4-5 (1991-92): 14-18.

Martin, Francis. "Close Encounters of an Ancient Kind: Readings on the Tutorial Classroom and the Writing Conference." *The Writing Center Journal* 2.2 (1982): 7-17.

Masiello, Lea. "Collaborative Pedagogy and Perry's Stages of Cognitive Growth." *Writing Lab Newsletter* 12.8 (1988): 1-2.

____. "Qualitative and Quantitative Strategies for Assessing Writing Center Effectiveness." *Writing Lab Newsletter* 16.6 (1992): 4-6.

Masiello, Lea, and Malcolm Hayward. "The Faculty Survey: Identifying Bridges Between the Classroom and the Writing Center." *The Writing Center Journal* 11.2 (1991): 73-80.

Maxwell, Martha, ed. *When Tutor Meets Student*. 2nd ed. Ann Arbor: U of Michigan P, 1994.

Mayher, John S. "'Uncommon' Sense in the Writing Center." *Journal of Basic Writing* 11.1 (1992): 47-57.

McAndrew, Donald A. "From Writing Center to Center for Writing: A Heuristic for Development." *Writing Lab Newsletter* 9.5 (1985): 1-5.

McCall, William. "Writing Centers and the Idea of Consultancy." *The Writing Center Journal* 14.2 (1994): 163-71.

McDonald, James C. "Rethinking the Research Paper in the Writing Center." *The Writing Center Journal* 14.2 (1994): 125-35.

Melnick, James F. "The Politics of Writing Conferences: Describing Authority through Speech Act Theory." *The Writing Center Journal* 4.2 (1984): 9-21.

Meyer, Emily, and Louise Z. Smith. *The Practical Tutor*. New York: Oxford UP, 1987.

Moreland, Kim. "The Writing Center: A Center for Writing-Across-the Curriculum Activities." *Writing Lab Newsletter* 10.3 (1985): 1-4.

Morrison, Margaret. "Peer Tutors as Postmodern Readers in a Writing Center." *Freshman English News* 18.2 (1990): 12-15.

Moseley, Ann. "From Factory to Workshop: Revising the Writing Center." *The Writing Center Journal* 4.2 (1984): 31-38.

Mullin, Joan. "Empowering Ourselves: New Directions for the Nineties." *Writing Lab Newsletter* 14.10 (1990): 11-13.

Mullin, Joan, and Ray Wallace, eds. *Intersections: Theory-Practice in the Writing Center*. Urbana: NCTE, 1994.

Murphy, Christina. "Freud in the Writing Center: The Psychoanalytics of Tutoring Well." *The Writing Center Journal* 10.1 (1989): 13-18.

Murphy, Christina, and Steve Sherwood. *The St. Martin's Sourcebook for Writing Tutors*. New York: St. Martin's, 1994.

Murray, Donald M. "The Listening Eye: Reflections on the Writing Conference." *College English* 41 (1979): 13-18.

Nash, Thomas. "Hamlet, Polonius, and the Writing Center." *The Writing Center Journal* 1.1 (1980): 36-42.

Neil, Lynn Riley. "Individual Student-Teacher Conferences: Guiding Content Revision with Sixth Graders." *The Writing Center Journal* 7.2 (1987): 37-44.

Neuleib, Janice. "Evaluating Writing Centers: A Survey Report." *Writing Lab Newsletter* 11.4 (1986): 1-5.

____. "The Friendly Stranger: Twenty-Five Years as 'Other.'" *College Composition and Communication* 43 (1992): 231-43.

____. "Research in the Writing Center: What to Do and Where to Go to Become Research Oriented." *Writing Lab Newsletter* 9.4 (1984): 10-13.

Noonan, Brendan. "Tutoring and Intuition." *The Writing Center Journal* 3.1 (1982): 29-31.

North, Stephen M. "Designing a Case Study Method for Tutorials: A Prelude to Research." *Rhetoric Review* 4 (1985): 88-97.

Nugent, Susan Monroe. "One Woman's Ways of Knowing." *The Writing Center Journal* 10.2 (1990): 17-29.

Okawa, Gail, Thomas Fox, Lucy J. Y. Chang, Shana R. Windsor, Fran Bella Chavez, Jr., and LaGuan Hayes. "Multi-Cultural Voices: Peer Tutoring and Critical Reflection in the Writing Center." *The Writing Center Journal* 12.1 (1991): 11-33.

Olson, Gary A. "Averting Negative Attitudes in Students Referred to the Writing Center." *Teaching English in the Two-Year College* 9 (1983): 105-10.

____, ed. *Writing Centers: Theory and Administration.* Urbana: NCTE, 1984.

Olson, Gary A., and John Alton. "Heuristics: Out of the Pulpit and into the Writing Center." *The Writing Center Journal* 2.1 (1982): 48-56.

Onore, Cynthia. "In Their Own 'Write': A Portrait of the Peer Tutor as a Young Professional." *The Writing Center Journal* 3.1 (1982): 20-22.

Parbst, John R. "Off-topic Conversation and the Tutoring Session." *Writing Lab Newsletter* 19.1 (1994): 1-2, 5.

Pederson, Elray L. "Writing Labs Are More than Remediation Centers." *Writing Lab Newsletter* 10.7 (1986): 3-5.

Pemberton, Michael. "The Prison, the Hospital, and the Madhouse: Redefining Metaphors for the Writing Center." *Writing Lab Newsletter* 17.1 (1992): 11-16.

____. "Writing Center Ethics." *Writing Lab Newsletter* 17.7 (1993): 6-7.

____. "Writing Center Ethics." *Writing Lab Newsletter* 17.8 (1993): 6-7.

____. "Writing Center Ethics." *Writing Lab Newsletter* 17.9 (1993): 6-7.

____. "Writing Center Ethics." *Writing Lab Newsletter* 17.10 (1993): 15-16.

____. "Writing Center Ethics: Telling Stories In and Out of School." *Writing Lab Newsletter* 18.2 (1993): 4.

____. "Writing Center Ethics." *Writing Lab Newsletter* 18.4 (1993): 10-12.

____. "Writing Center Ethics: 'The Ethics of Intervention: Part II.'" *Writing Lab Newsletter* 18.5 (1994): 8-9.

____. "Writing Center Ethics." *Writing Lab Newsletter* 18.6 (1994): 10.

____. "Writing Center Ethics: 'Confronting Controversy and Practicing Politics.'" *Writing Lab Newsletter* 18.7 (1994): 6-7.

Posey, Evelyn. "An Ongoing Tutor-Training Program." *The Writing Center Journal* 6.2 (1986): 29-36.

Powers, Judith K. "Rethinking Writing Center Conference Strategies for the ESL Writer." *The Writing Center Journal* 13.2 (1993): 39-47.

Pratt, Daniel D. "Tutoring Adults: Toward a Definition of Tutorial Role and Function in Adult Basic Education." *Adult Literacy and Basic Education* 7 (1983): 138-52.

Purdue, Virginia. "Writing-Center Faculty in Academia: Another Look at Our Status." *WPA: Writing Program Administration* 15.1-2 (1991): 13-23.

Rabianski, Nancyanne. "Accommodating the IQ and Learning Style of a Student Writer." *The Writing Center Journal* 1.2 (1981): 13-25.

Raines, Helen Howell. "Tutoring and Teaching: Continuum, Dichotomy, or Dialectic?" *The Writing Center Journal* 14.2 (1994): 150-62.

Reigstad, Thomas J. "The Writing Conference: An Ethnographic Model for Discovering Patterns of Student-Teacher Interaction." *The Writing Center Journal* 2.1 (1982): 9-20.

Reigstad, Thomas J., and Donald McAndrew. *Training Tutors for Writing Conferences.* Urbana: ERIC and NCTE, 1984.

Roberts, David H. "A Study of Writing Center Effectiveness." *The Writing Center Journal* 9.1 (1988): 53-60.

Roberts, David H., and William C. Wolff, eds. *Selected Papers of the Southeastern Writing Center Association.* Hattiesburg: U of Southern Mississippi P, 1986.

Roberts, Ian. "Writing Centers as Centers of Controlled Learning, Too." *Writing Lab Newsletter* 17.4 (1992): 12-13.

Robertson, Elizabeth. "Moving from Expressive Writing to Academic Discourse." *The Writing Center Journal* 9.1 (1988): 21-28.

Rodis, Karen. "Mending the Damaged Path: How to Avoid Conflict of Expectations When Setting Up a Writing Center." *The Writing Center Journal* 10.2 (1990): 45-57.

Runciman, Lex. "Defining Ourselves: Do We Really Want to Use the Word *Tutor*?" *The Writing Center Journal* 11.1 (1990): 27-34.

Ryan, Leigh. *The Bedford Guide for Writing Tutors.* Boston: Bedford-St. Martin's, 1994.

Scanlon, Leone C. "Learning Disabled Students at the Writing Center." *Writing Lab Newsletter* 9.5 (1985): 9-11.

____. "Recruiting and Training Tutors for Cross-Disciplinary Writing Programs." *The Writing Center Journal* 6.2 (1986): 37-42.

Schwartz, Helen J. "Planning and Running a Computer Lab for Writing: A Survival Manual." *ADE Bulletin* 86 (1987): 43-47.

Selfe, Cynthia. *Creating a Computer-Support Writing Facility: A Blueprint for Action.* Houghton: *Computers and Composition*, 1989.

Seligman, Joyce, ed. *Moving to the Center: Organization, Management, and Methods.* Proceedings of the New England Writing Centers Association 1986 Conference. Lewiston: Bates College, 1986.

Severino, Carol. "The 'Doodles' in Context: Qualifying Claims about Contrastive Rhetoric." *The Writing Center Journal* 14.1 (1993): 44-62.

____. "Rhetorically Analyzing Collaboration(s)." *The Writing Center Journal* 13.1 (1993): 63-70.

Sherwood, Steve. "Fear and Loathing in the Writing Center: How to Deal Fairly with Problem Students." *Writing Lab Newsletter* 16.8 (1992): 12-15.

____. "Humor and the Serious Tutor." *The Writing Center Journal* 13.2 (1993): 3-12.

____. "White Lies in the Writing Center: The Fragile Balance Between Praise and Criticism." *Writing Lab Newsletter* 18.4 (1993): 1-4.

Shurbutt, S. Bailey. "Integration of Classroom Computer Use and the Peer Evaluation Process: Increasing the Level of Composition Proficiency Through Student Revision." *The Writing Center Journal* 8.1 (1987): 35-42.

Simpson, Jeanne. "The Challenge of Innovation: Putting New Approaches into Practice." *Writing Lab Newsletter* 18.1 (1993): 1-3.

____. "Defining the Status of Writing Center Tutors." *Writing Lab Newsletter* 9.6 (1985): 4-6.

Singley, Carol J., and Holly W. Boucher. "Dialogue in Tutor Training: Creating the Essential Space for Learning." *The Writing Center Journal* 8.2 (1988): 11-22.

Smith, Louise Z. "Family Systems Theory and the Form of Conference Dialogue." *The Writing Center Journal* 11.2 (1991): 61-72.

____. "Independence and Collaboration: Why We Should Decentralize Writing Centers." *The Writing Center Journal* 7.1 (1986): 3-10.

Smith, Louise Z., and Emily Meyer. *The Practical Tutor*. New York: Oxford, 1987.

Smith, William L. "Using a College Writing Workshop in Training Future English Teachers." *English Education* 16 (1984): 76-82.

Smoot, Joyce. "Public Relations and the Writing Center Director: Making the Center Visible On and Off Campus." ERIC, 1985. ED 257 106.

Smulyan, Lisa, and Kristin Bolton. "Classroom and Writing Center Collaborations: Peers as Authorities." *The Writing Center Journal* 9.2 (1989): 43-50.

Sollisch, James. "From Fellow Writer to Reading Coach: The Peer Tutor's Role in Collaboration." *The Writing Center Journal* 5.2/6.1 (1985): 10-14.

Spear, Karen. "Toward a Comprehensive Language Curriculum." *The Writing Center Journal* 2.1 (1982): 34-47.

Stay, Byron. "When Re-Writing Succeeds: An Analysis of Student Revisions." *The Writing Center Journal* 4.1 (1983): 15-28.

____. "Writing Centers on the Margins: Conversing from the Edge." *Writing Lab Newsletter* 17.1 (1992): 1-3.

Steward, Joyce, and Mary Croft. *The Writing Laboratory: Organization, Management, and Methods*. Glenview: Scott, 1982.

Sullivan, Sally. "From Thought to Word: Learning to Trust Images." *The Writing Center Journal* 3.1 (1982): 11-19.

Tackach, James. "Theory Z Management and the College Writing Center." *The Writing Center Journal* 4.2 (1984): 1-8.

Taylor, David. "Peer Tutoring's Hidden World: The Emotional and Social Issues." *Writing Lab Newsletter* 13.5 (1989): 1-5.

Terry, Patricia. "Things Your Mentor Never Told You: Discovering Writing Lab Identity in the Institutional Environment." *Writing Lab Newsletter* 18.7 (1994): 1-3, 5.

Thaiss, Chris. "Of Havens, Nodes, and No-Center Centers." *Focuses* 6.1 (1993): 16-26.

Thaiss, Christopher J., and Carolyn Kurylo. "Working with the ESL Student: Learning Patience, Making Progress." *The Writing Center Journal* 1.2 (1981): 41-46.

Thompson, Thomas C. "Personality Preferences, Tutoring Styles, and Implications for Tutor Training." *The Writing Center Journal* 14.2 (1994): 136-49.

Trimbur, John. "Literacy Networks: Toward Cultural Studies of Writing and Tutoring." *The Writing Center Journal* 12.2 (1992): 174-79.

____. "Peer Tutoring: A Contradiction in Terms?" *The Writing Center Journal* 7.2 (1987): 21-28.

____. "Peer Tutors and the Benefits of Collaborative Learning." *Writing Lab Newsletter* 8.2 (1983): 1-5.

Troester, Rosalie. "Evaluating the Long-Term Effects of a Writing Program." *Proceedings of the Midwest Writing Centers Association*. Apr. 1983. 59-72.

Upton, James. "The High School Writing Center: The Once and Future Services." *The Writing Center Journal* 11.1 (1990): 67-71.

Waldo, Mark L. "What Should the Relation Between the Writing Center and Writing Program Be?" *The Writing Center Journal* 11.1 (1990): 73-80.

Walker, Carolyn. "Communications with the Faculty: Vital Links for the Success of Writing Centers." *Writing Lab Newsletter* 16.3 (1991): 11-16.

Walker, Carolyn P., and David Elias. "Writing Conference Talk: Factors Associated with High– and Low–Rated Writing Conferences." *Research in the Teaching of English* 21 (1987): 266-85.

Wallace, Ray, and Jeanne Simpson, eds. *The Writing Center: New Directions*. New York: Garland, 1991.

Wang, Xia. "Tutoring Across Cultures." *Writing Lab Newsletter* 19.1 (1994): 12-15.

Welch, Nancy. "From Silence to Noise: The Writing Center as Critical Noise." *The Writing Center Journal* 14.1 (1993): 3-15.

White, Edward M. *Developing Successful College Writing Programs*. San Francisco: Jossey-Bass, 1981.

Wiener, Harvey S. *The Writing Room*. New York: Oxford UP, 1981.

Williams, Sharon. "Body Language: The Non-verbal Path to Success in the Writing Center." *Writing Lab Newsletter* 16.4-5 (1991-92): 6-7.

Wilson, Lucy, and Olivia LaBouff. "Going Beyond Remedial: The Writing Center and the Literature Class." *The Writing Center Journal* 6.2 (1986): 19-28.

Winnard, Karin E. "Codependency: Teaching Tutors Not to Rescue." *Journal of College Reading and Learning* 24.1 (1991): 32-39.

Wolcott, Willa. "Establishing Writer Center Workshops." *The Writing Center Journal* 7.2 (1987): 45-50.

____. "Talking It Over: A Qualitative Study of Writing Center Conferencing." *The Writing Center Journal* 9.2 (1989): 15-29.

Wood, David, J. S. Bruner, and Gail Ross. "The Role of Tutoring in Problem Solving." *Journal of Child Psychology and Psychiatry* 17 (1976): 89-100.

Woolbright, Meg. "A Response to 'Contesting "The Idea of a Writing Center": The Politics of Writing Center Research.'" *Writing Lab Newsletter* 17.5 (1993): 11-13.

Wright, Anne. "Establishing a High School Writing Center." *Writing Lab Newsletter* 17.5 (1993): 4-6.

____. "Terminal Writing in the Writing Lab." *The Writing Center Journal* 8.1 (1987): 21-28.

Yahner, William, and William Murdick. "The Evolution of a Writing Center." *The Writing Center Journal* 11.2 (1991): 13-28.

Young, Art. "College Culture and the Challenge of Collaboration." *The Writing Center Journal* 13.1 (1992): 3-15.

Index

W

Z